American Heart
Association

Quick &
Easy Meals

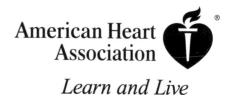

American Heart
Association

Learn and Live

Quick & Easy Meals

More Than 200 Healthy Recipes
plus Time-Saving Tips for Shopping, Planning,
and Eating Well

A revised and updated edition of the book formerly titled
American Heart Association Meals in Minutes

Clarkson Potter / Publishers
New York

Copyright ©2000, 2010 by American Heart Association

Published in the United States by Clarkson Potter/Publishers, an imprint of
the Crown Publishing Group, a division of Random House, Inc., New York.
www.crownpublishing.com
www.clarksonpotter.com

Clarkson Potter is a trademark and Potter with colophon is a registered
trademark of Random House, Inc.

A previous edition of this work was published in the United States as
American Heart Association Meals in Minutes
by Clarkson Potter/Publishers, an imprint of the Crown Publishing Group,
a division of Random House, Inc., New York, in 2000.

Your contribution to the American Heart Association supports research that
helps make publications like this possible. For more information, call
1-800-AHA-USA1 (1-800-242-8721) or contact us online at
www.americanheart.org.

Library of Congress Cataloging-in-Publication Data
American Heart Association meals in minutes cookbook : more than 200 easy,
healthy recipes and time-saving tips for shopping, planning, and eating well.
—2nd ed.
p. cm.
Includes index.
1. Low-fat diet—Recipes. 2. Quick and easy cookery. I. American Heart
Association. II. Title: Meals in minutes cookbook.
RM237.7.A45 2010
641.5'638—dc22   2009036986

ISBN 978-0-307-40758-0

Printed in the United States of America

Design by TOMATO

1 3 5 7 9 10 8 6 4 2

Second Edition

preface

MEDICAL RESEARCH CONTINUES TO SHOW THAT WHAT PEOPLE EAT directly affects their heart health. Despite the fact that Americans are increasingly aware of the important role diet plays in their health, many find it difficult to make good choices on a regular basis.

In today's world, almost everyone feels the pressure to accomplish more in less time; as a result, many people are trading nutrition for convenience by frequently eating out or opting for packaged meals. However, a diet of convenience can come at a high price since such a diet can easily be high in the nutritional villains that most sabotage good health: saturated fat, trans fat, dietary cholesterol, and sodium. If you're thinking, "Who has the time to cook?" remember that healthy eating does not have to be difficult or take much more time than you spend to pick up fast food!

With so many health concerns, such as obesity and diabetes, on the rise in the United States, it's imperative for Americans to rethink their eating habits to include more unprocessed, nutrient-rich foods that they can prepare at home. *American Heart Association Quick & Easy Meals* helps you put together a healthy home-cooked meal in almost no time. With so many appealing recipes to choose from, such as Crispy Chicken with Creamy Gravy (page 129) and Taco-Rubbed Flank Steak (page 184), you can make tasty meals in minutes and enjoy the health benefits that come with good nutrition.

We encourage you to take advantage of the more than 200 time-saving and good-for-you recipes that this cookbook has to offer because we know that the long-term health consequences of an unhealthy eating pattern are huge. For example, atherosclerosis—the buildup of plaque on the arterial lining—is strongly influenced by diet. This dangerous buildup starts as early as childhood and greatly increases the risk for cardiovascular disease, including heart attack and stroke. We also know that healthy lifestyle choices are some of the best ways to significantly improve heart health. Choosing an overall healthy diet and staying physically active can help slow—or even stop—the progression of atherosclerosis, as well as reduce blood pressure and prevent obesity and other risk factors for heart disease and stroke.

The ongoing mission of the American Heart Association is to build healthier lives, free of cardiovascular disease and stroke. We encourage you to join us in our efforts by making your own commitment to live a healthy lifestyle. Let this cookbook be your guide to eating well in your own kitchen, and let every delicious bite bring you closer to a lifetime of good health.

Rose Marie Robertson, M.D.
Chief Science Officer
American Heart Association/American Stroke Association

acknowledgments

AMERICAN HEART ASSOCIATION CONSUMER PUBLICATIONS

DIRECTOR: Linda S. Ball

MANAGING EDITOR: Deborah A. Renza

SENIOR EDITOR: Janice Roth Moss

SCIENCE EDITOR/WRITER: Jacqueline F. Haigney

ASSISTANT EDITOR: Roberta Westcott Sullivan

RECIPE DEVELOPERS

Claire Criscuolo

Frank Criscuolo

Sarah Fritschner

Nancy S. Hughes

Annie King

Kathryn Moore

Carol Ritchie

Julie Shapero, R.D., L.D.

DeeDee Stovel

Roxanne Wyss

NUTRITION ANALYST

Tammi Hancock, R.D.

contents

introduction

IF YOU ARE LOOKING FOR HEALTHIER ALTERNATIVES TO PACKAGED foods and fast-food stops, you're not alone. Life can get pretty complicated, but you still have to eat and to feed your family every day. The daily search for quick and easy meals can lead you right to a steady diet of foods chosen more for convenience than for nutrition. In these times of over-scheduling and multitasking, it may seem there isn't any time left to squeeze in a healthy meal. Well, that just isn't true. Let *American Heart Association Quick & Easy Meals* show you that it *is* possible to prepare both healthy *and* speedy dishes in about the same time as it takes for a pizza to be delivered to your home.

In this cookbook, you'll find flavor-packed recipes, easy-cooking tech-niques, *and* time-management strategies to help you be efficient in the kitchen while creating delicious and nutritious meals. Enjoy classics such as Tuna Casserole with Broccoli and Water Chestnuts (page 118) as well as fabulous new favorites such as Lemongrass Chicken with Snow Peas and Jasmine Rice (page 156)—all without the need for lots of prep time. In fact, we've made sure that each dish—from appetizers to desserts—takes only 20 minutes from the moment you open the pantry to when the cooking starts, and many recipes—including more than 60 entrées—are table-ready in 25 minutes from start to finish. You'll also find information on what makes a meal heart healthy, how to organize your kitchen, and how to shop strategically to expedite meal planning—and benefit from time-saving tips from our cooking experts. In addition to being able to serve home-cooked meals throughout the week in just minutes, you'll have the satisfaction of knowing that the foods you prepare are as good for your heart as they are tasty to eat.

Research shows that our food choices do affect our overall well-being, so it's vitally important to be able to satisfy hunger without compromising health. In fact, ongoing studies have consistently established a strong link between the risk of heart disease and a diet loaded with saturated fat, trans fat, cholesterol, and sodium—which are commonly found in many packaged and fast foods. Although the variety of food choices available in supermarkets and restaurants seems to grow every day, many of these easy-access foods provide more calories than nutrients.

Today's home cooks are looking for recipes that deliver on three fronts: taste, nutrition, and speedy preparation. With an emphasis on wholesome ingredients combined with flavorful seasonings and quick-cooking techniques, *American Heart Association Quick & Easy Meals* gives you all three.

Cooking at home can be just as quick as relying on the marketplace's convenience foods, neighborhood eateries, and local take-out. Most important for your health, *you* are in control of the ingredients, preparation method, and portion size. You can rely on the American Heart Association to provide delicious and heart-healthy recipes, as well as time-saving techniques to create meals in minutes!

eating well: the basics of a heart-healthy diet

IT'S NOT COMPLICATED OR DIFFICULT TO EAT WELL; YOU JUST NEED TO follow some basic principles and make good choices most of the time. When eating well becomes a part of your daily routine, you'll enjoy lasting benefits with real health payback. This section contains basic information, as well as some specific strategies in "Shopping Smart" on page 18, on how to make the right choices for a balanced diet.

Eat a Variety of Nutritious Foods from All the Food Groups

When choosing foods, look for quality before quantity most often, and vary your choices so you'll get the full spectrum of nutrients from different kinds of foods. Eating only to satisfy your hunger won't necessarily nourish your body over time. You need nutrient-rich foods that provide vitamins, minerals, and fiber, as well as other essentials. These foods are also usually lower in calories than nutrient-poor foods. To keep your body healthy, choose foods such as vegetables, fruits, fat-free or low-fat dairy products, whole-grain and high-fiber foods, fish rich in omega-3 fatty acids, lean meats and poultry, legumes and nuts, and heart-healthy unsaturated oils and fats. If you splurge on a cheeseburger or dessert once in a while, don't fret—it's the *overall pattern* of your choices that counts the most.

Focus most on including the following foods in your diet. (The suggested numbers of servings are based on a 2,000-calorie daily diet.)

- **Vegetables and fruits** are a good source of vitamins, minerals, and fiber; and because they're also low in calories, they can help you manage your weight. Eating a variety of fruits and vegetables also helps control your blood pressure. Aim for about five servings of vegetables and four servings of fruit a day.

- **Fat-free and low-fat dairy products** provide calcium and protein without the saturated fat found in whole milk and whole-milk products. Try to include two to three servings of fat-free or low-fat (1%) dairy foods each day.

- Unrefined **whole-grain foods** contain fiber, both soluble and insoluble, that can help lower your blood cholesterol and help you feel full, which may aid you in managing your weight. At least half your grain servings should be whole grain. Examples include whole-grain breads, whole-grain pastas, whole-grain cereals, and brown rice.

- **Fish** is an important part of a heart-healthy diet. That's especially true for fish such as salmon, tuna, trout, and other fish high in omega-3 fatty acids, which have been shown to reduce the risk of heart disease. Each week, eat at least two servings of fish (a serving is 3 ounces cooked weight).

- **Lean and extra-lean meats and poultry** are excellent sources of protein, but your body probably doesn't need as much of that nutrient as you might think. In fact, Americans tend to eat too much protein. Aim for no more than about 6 ounces of cooked lean, low-saturated-fat poultry or meat (8 ounces before cooking) each day. For a well-balanced approach, visualize a plate divided into fourths, with two sections for vegetables and fruits, one for grains or starches, and one for a protein source.

- For meatless protein and fiber, look to **legumes, nuts, and seeds**. Legumes, such as dried beans (not green beans, which are vegetables), peas, peanuts (and peanut butter), and lentils, are great additions to a balanced diet. Most nuts, such as almonds and walnuts, are rich in heart-healthy unsaturated oils. When eaten in moderation and without added salt, nuts are a good source of energy without empty calories.

- **Unsaturated oils and fats** are found in vegetable oil products such as canola, corn, and olive oils and in most nuts and seeds. These foods provide a combination of monounsaturated and polyunsaturated fats, both of which have heart-health benefits. Replace unhealthy saturated fat found in products such as butter with unsaturated fats as often as possible. Because all fats are high in calories, use them in moderation.

Eat Less of the Nutrient-Poor Foods, and Limit Foods That Contain Saturated Fat, Trans Fat, Cholesterol, and Sodium

Knowing how to limit foods and beverages that are high in calories but low in nutrients is an important part of maximizing the benefit you get from the foods you eat. You also want to limit foods that are high in saturated fat, trans fat, and cholesterol. Eating a diet that includes many foods high in these fats has been shown to increase your body's production of "bad" LDL cholesterol and decrease levels of "good" HDL cholesterol. Over time, these changes contribute to the buildup of plaque in your arteries, which in turn can lead to heart disease, heart attack, and stroke. Cutting back on these foods can reduce your risk for heart disease by helping lower levels of harmful LDL cholesterol in your blood. Saturated fat and cholesterol are usually found in meat and dairy foods and, along with trans fat, in products that are commercially baked or fried. Many processed foods are also high in sodium, which can increase blood pressure. High blood pressure also increases your risk of heart disease and stroke. You will make better food choices if you read package labels carefully—the nutrition facts panel will tell you how much of those nutrients each food or beverage contains (see page 20 for more information on how to use the nutrition facts panel).

To achieve a good balance of nutrient-rich and nutrient-poor foods, follow these general recommendations.

- **Choose the leanest cuts of meat and skinless poultry, and prepare them without added saturated and trans fats.** To reduce the saturated fat found in meats and poultry, remove and discard all visible fat *before* cooking. Grilling and broiling are heart-healthy cooking methods because they allow fat to drip away while the food cooks. In most cases, these techniques don't require added fat. Choose white meat most often when eating poultry because dark meat is higher in cholesterol. Cut back on processed meats that are high in saturated fat and sodium.

- **Replace whole-fat dairy products with fat-free and low-fat alternatives.** To cut out a lot of saturated fat and cholesterol, try to minimize your intake of whole-fat dairy products as often as you can, and look for lower-fat options if you don't find fat-free options. If you drink whole or 2% milk, for example, gradually switch to 1% and then fat-free milk.

- **Cut back on foods containing partially hydrogenated oils.** Trans fats, also called "partially hydrogenated oils," are created in the process that adds hydrogen to liquid vegetable oils to make them more solid. Eating too much trans fat raises levels of harmful LDL cholesterol, lowers levels of helpful HDL cholesterol, and has been associated with a higher risk of type 2 diabetes. You can avoid these risks by using liquid vegetable oils and soft tub margarine to replace stick margarine or shortening and by limiting products made with partially hydrogenated or saturated fats.

- **Cut back on foods high in dietary cholesterol.** A cholesterol-rich diet can contribute to your risk for heart disease, so try to eat less than 300 mg of cholesterol each day. If you eat a food that is relatively high in cholesterol at one meal, choose lower-cholesterol foods the rest of the day to balance your intake. Be aware that dietary cholesterol comes primarily from foods made from animal products. Foods that are extra high in cholesterol, for example, include egg yolks, shellfish, organ meats such as liver, and whole milk.

- **Avoid beverages and foods with added sugars.** Many beverages and snack foods with added sugars are low in vitamins and minerals but high in calories. These calories can add up quickly but don't provide nutritional value and can contribute to weight gain. Try to limit calories from added sugars to about half of your discretionary calories. For most women, this means no more than 100 calories (about 6 teaspoons or 25 grams of added sugars), and for most men, no more than 150 calories (about 9 teaspoons or 38 grams) per day. Keep in mind that a 12-ounce can of soda contains about 8 teaspoons of added sugar. When reading the ingredients lists on soft drinks, energy drinks, and snacks, choose products that don't have added sugars (for example, sucrose, fructose, and dextrose) in their first four listed ingredients.

- **Choose foods with little or no added sodium, and use less salt in cooking and at the table.** If you don't have high blood pressure, eating less salt can lower your risk of developing it. If you are at risk for or already have high blood pressure, reducing your sodium intake will help you control or lower your blood pressure. Ideally, most people should limit their intake of sodium to less than 1,500 mg each day for significant health benefits. To transition to lower levels of sodium in your diet, begin by aiming to eat less than 2,300 mg of sodium per day. Most of the sodium in the food supply today comes from processed foods. To help you control your sodium intake, compare the nutrition facts panels of similar products (for example, different brands of tomato sauce) and choose the products with less sodium and foods that are labeled "no-salt-added" or "reduced-sodium."

As you adopt healthy eating habits, it's also important to make good choices about other aspects of your lifestyle. In addition to maintaining the basics of a heart-healthy diet, follow these recommendations to help protect your heart and overall health.

- **When you eat out, watch portion sizes and be heart-smart.** You can follow the same recommendations for healthy eating when dining out as when preparing meals at home. Most restaurants serve larger portions than recommended, so plan to take the extra home or split an entrée or dessert. You can also choose dishes that are grilled, steamed, or baked instead of fried or sautéed. Ask for dressings and sauces on the side to control the fats, sodium, and calories you eat.

- **If you drink alcohol, drink in moderation.** That means one drink per day if you're a woman and two drinks per day if you're a man. One drink equals about 12 ounces of beer, 4 ounces of wine, or 1.5 ounces of hard liquor. If you don't drink now, don't start.

- **Use up at least as many calories as you take in.** Start by knowing how many calories you need to maintain your weight, and balance the amount and intensity of your physical activity with the number of calories you take in. (The right number of calories to eat each day varies based on your age and physical activity level and whether you're trying to gain, lose, or maintain your weight. For information on what is right for you, visit www.americanheart.org.) Keeping the calories you eat in line with the calories you burn is the easiest way to fight creeping weight gain. In fact, being physically active offers so many health benefits that the American Heart Association recommends at least 150 minutes (2 hours and 30 minutes) of moderate-intensity, or 75 minutes (1 hour and 15 minutes) of vigorous-intensity, aerobic physical activity each week. (Moderate intensity means that you are able to talk during exercise but not sing. Vigorous activities should significantly increase your heart rate, and you should not be able to say more than a few words without catching your breath when exercising at this level.) You can accumulate aerobic activity in episodes lasting at least 10 minutes, preferably spread out through the week. You can also combine moderate and vigorous activities to suit your schedule and preferences to reach an equivalent total. Regular exercise can help you attain physical and cardiovascular fitness, reach and maintain a healthy weight, and improve your sense of well-being.

Enjoying delicious meals while living a healthy lifestyle doesn't have to take a lot of time or effort; it just takes a commitment to do a few things differently. What you and your family eat every day really does make a difference in your long-term health, so it pays to make the right choices. Once you read the following pages and see how easy it is to plan and cook efficiently at home, you'll be comfortable devising your own shortcuts and creating foods that satisfy your taste buds, protect your heart, and leave you plenty of time to enjoy your life—in and out of the kitchen.

planning ahead:
meal organization strategies

WHEN YOU NEED TO FEED YOURSELF AND YOUR FAMILY IN LESS TIME, being organized is critical. To figure out which meal strategies work best with your family's lifestyle, think about your personal preferences, the needs of your family, and the types of scheduling issues you face. Those factors will dictate how you approach your planning and shopping. Try these ideas:

- **Make a weekly meal plan.** It can save you time in the long run by helping you shop and cook more efficiently. Build into your weekly plan at least one meal that provides enough extra to use in another recipe later in the week. (For a list of Planned-Overs, see page 325.)

- **Keep your pantry and refrigerator stocked with staples** (see the list on page 11) and your freezer full of prepped ingredients (see the list on page 14). If your schedule changes suddenly, you'll be able to cook without having to shop first. (For a list of No Shopping Required recipes, see page 325.)

- **Take advantage of shortcuts** such as buying precut produce and benefit from time-saving strategies such as buying in bulk. (See page 17 for some helpful tips.)

Plan a Week's Worth of Meals

Planning keeps you from having to frequently rethink the same question: What's for dinner tonight? It allows you to maximize your time and effort by getting most if not all of your shopping completed in only one trip each week. You can also take advantage of seasonal produce, tap into store specials to save money, and balance the nutritional content of your week's meals.

To get started on creating a meal plan for the week, pick a few family favorites and then leaf through the more than 200 recipes in this book to find some new dishes or ingredients to keep things from getting boring. Start with main courses and add side dishes, or improvise around something that you are curious about or that is on special at the grocery store. Include a variety of options from different food groups to ensure a well-balanced eating plan.

Make Lists and Keep Staples on Hand

Whether you prefer to follow a weekly menu plan or make last-minute decisions about what to prepare, you'll have to grocery shop. We have some suggestions to ensure that your shopping trips will be faster and easier.

If you wait until the last minute to decide what to cook and you don't keep a well-stocked pantry, refrigerator, and freezer, you may be tempted to eat out or heat a packaged main dish because it seems quicker to turn to these conveniences. As you'll see from the recipes in this cookbook, however, you can cook at home just as quickly, *and* you will maintain control over the nutritional value of what you eat.

To stay ahead of the game, keep lists so you will always have essential ingredients ready and waiting. We suggest that you create an electronic list of the foods on pages 11–14 and others you consider basics, make a place on the list to jot down additional items you find you need, and print it out each week. Put your list in a central location so you can note items as soon as they come to mind, such as when you use almost the last of something or when you check your shelves for what is missing. Use the following sample list as a starting point, but be sure to make it your own. For example, do you love a certain hot sauce and use it frequently but don't see it listed? Add it. Know you don't like the flavor of toasted sesame oil and would never use it? Zap it. The more you personalize the list, the more useful it will be to you.

PANTRY GOODS

RICES
- ☐ instant and/or regular brown rice
- ☐ instant and/or white rice

BEANS
- ☐ no-salt-added canned kidney beans
- ☐ no-salt-added canned white beans
- ☐ no-salt-added canned black beans
- ☐ no-salt-added canned chick-peas
- ☐ dried beans, peas, and lentils

PASTAS AND GRAINS
- ☐ assorted whole-wheat and enriched pastas, such as spaghetti, linguine, elbow macaroni, rotini, penne, and noodles
- ☐ oats and oatmeal
- ☐ couscous
- ☐ barley
- ☐ bulgur

TOMATO PRODUCTS
- ☐ no-salt-added tomato sauce
- ☐ no-salt-added diced, stewed, and whole tomatoes
- ☐ tomato paste
- ☐ spaghetti sauces (lowest sodium available)

DRY GOODS
- ☐ flour—all-purpose and wheat
- ☐ sugar—granulated, brown, and confectioners'
- ☐ baking soda
- ☐ baking powder
- ☐ cornstarch
- ☐ cornmeal
- ☐ plain dry bread crumbs or panko (Japanese bread crumbs)

CANNED AND BOTTLED PRODUCTS
- [ ] fat-free, low-sodium broths
- [ ] low-sodium soups
- [ ] salmon and very-low-sodium tuna in water
- [ ] no-salt-added vegetables
- [ ] fruits canned in their own juice or water
- [ ] 100% fruit juices
- [ ] fat-free condensed milk
- [ ] artichoke hearts packed in water
- [ ] roasted red bell peppers
- [ ] olives
- [ ] green chiles
- [ ] garlic
- [ ] ginger

DRIED FRUITS AND VEGETABLES
- [ ] sun-dried tomatoes (dry-packed preferred)
- [ ] fruits, such as raisins and cranberries

COOKING OILS
- [ ] cooking spray
- [ ] canola or corn oil
- [ ] olive oil
- [ ] toasted sesame oil

MISCELLANEOUS
- [ ] peanut butter
- [ ] all-fruit spreads
- [ ] honey
- [ ] maple syrup
- [ ] almonds
- [ ] walnuts
- [ ] pecans

CONDIMENTS (choose lowest sodium available)

- [ ] vinegars
- [ ] mustards
- [ ] no-salt-added ketchup
- [ ] hoisin sauce
- [ ] red hot-pepper sauce
- [ ] salsa
- [ ] soy sauce
- [ ] teriyaki sauce
- [ ] Worcestershire sauce
- [ ] barbecue sauce

SPICES AND SEASONINGS

- [ ] dried herbs, such as oregano, basil, thyme, rosemary, dillweed
- [ ] garlic powder
- [ ] onion powder
- [ ] chili powder
- [ ] crushed red pepper flakes
- [ ] black pepper
- [ ] cayenne
- [ ] salt-free seasoning blends, such as Italian and all-purpose
- [ ] ground spices, such as cinnamon, ginger, nutmeg, cumin, paprika
- [ ] salt
- [ ] vanilla extract
- [ ] almond extract

FRESH FOODS

- [ ] onions
- [ ] garlic
- [ ] gingerroot
- [ ] lemons
- [ ] limes

REFRIGERATED FOODS

- ☐ shredded Parmesan cheese
- ☐ fat-free and low-fat Cheddar and Monterey Jack cheese
- ☐ low-fat mozzarella cheese
- ☐ eggs
- ☐ egg substitute
- ☐ light mayonnaise
- ☐ fat-free milk
- ☐ fat-free plain, vanilla, and fruit-flavored yogurt

Rely on Freezer Basics

In addition to your pantry and refrigerator, your freezer is a ready resource for storing the building blocks for many recipes. Use it to keep staples preserved for freshness and so they will always be on hand. If you haven't done so already, designate a specific area of the freezer for basic items such as chopped onions and tomato paste. Knowing where to find those items will save time. Most fish, poultry, and meats freeze well, as do staples such as broth and chopped green bell peppers. Wrap foods airtight in heavy-duty aluminum foil or freezer paper, or use plastic freezer bags or airtight containers.

For quick meals from ingredients you can grab at any time, keep these foods in your freezer:

- **Broth:** Freeze large amounts of fat-free, low-sodium chicken, beef, and vegetable broth in airtight plastic containers. For small amounts, first measure by the tablespoonful into the compartments of an ice cube tray, then freeze and transfer the cubes to airtight freezer bags.

- **Juice:** Measure lemon, lime, and orange juice by the tablespoonful into the compartments of an ice cube tray. Freeze the cubes and transfer to airtight freezer bags.

- **Tomato paste:** Freeze tablespoon-size dollops on a baking sheet or small tray, then transfer to airtight freezer bags.

- **Fish, poultry, and meat:** Stack fish fillets, chicken breasts or tenders, and steaks and chops in layers, separated by sheets of wax paper. After you shop and before you freeze your purchases, remove the fat from all the poultry (remove the skin), beef, and pork. You'll have to wash the knives and cutting boards only once.

- **Cheeses:** Grate cheeses before freezing.

- **Onions and bell peppers:** Chop or slice extra when you have time, then store in the freezer. You don't even have to defrost them before using them. If you prefer, you can buy frozen chopped onions, chopped or sliced bell peppers, and stir-fry mixes (several colors of sliced bell pepper combined).

- **Cooked pasta:** Toss cooked pasta with a small amount of oil before freezing to keep the pasta from sticking. To reheat, drop the pasta into boiling water and let it cook for about 2 minutes.

- **Boxed or packaged vegetables:** Buy prepared frozen vegetables that don't have added butter or sauce, such as corn, spinach, peas, broccoli florets, and various mixed vegetables.

- **Seasonal berries:** Freeze berries, separated, on a baking sheet or small tray and transfer to airtight freezer bags. Use frozen berries in smoothies, desserts, breads, oatmeal, and salads.

Use Shortcuts and Time-Saving Strategies

When you've had a long day, give yourself a break. Try the following ideas to turn meal prep from tense to tranquil.

- Use packages of prewashed lettuces and spinach to speed up salad prep.
- Keep packages of sliced or shredded carrots and shredded slaw mix on hand to make quick side dishes easy.
- Choose prepared veggies from the supermarket salad bar to cut down on washing, slicing, and dicing.
- Stock up on packaged grated fat-free and low-fat cheeses.
- Rely on bottled garlic that is already peeled and minced.
- Buy staples such as fruits and vegetables in bulk and freeze what you can or share with a neighbor. By doing so, you can save money and also avoid having to add these items to your shopping list so frequently.

shopping smart:
grocery shopping strategies

TO FOCUS ON NUTRIENT-RICH FOOD, IT'S A GOOD IDEA TO START SHOPping in the produce section and fill your basket with the vegetables and fruits you need. Choose your dairy, fish, poultry, and meats next, and finish with the items left on your list.

Supermarket Savvy

Use these guidelines as you shop to be sure you get the most nutritional payback from your choices.

Vegetables and fruits: Look for a variety of produce, especially deeply colored choices such as blueberries; spinach, broccoli, and lettuces; carrots, sweet potatoes, cantaloupe, and oranges; and tomatoes, red bell peppers, and red berries. Experiment with vegetables and fruits you haven't tried before to find new flavors and textures you like. Make use of the prepped vegetables in your supermarket, including the ones in the salad bars. The produce is fresh, trimmed, and sliced or chopped, and you can buy exactly the mix and quantity you need.

Fat-free and low-fat dairy: An important source of calcium, fat-free and low-fat dairy products offer many alternatives to whole-milk products. The difference in saturated fat, cholesterol, and calories is significant, so it's well worth trying the fat-free and lower-fat (preferably 1%) versions of your favorites: milk, cheeses, cream cheese, sour cream, ice cream, yogurt— even creamy-tasting fat-free half-and-half.

Whole grains and high-fiber foods: Make at least half your grain selections whole-grain because these provide more nutrients than do processed grains. Choose products carefully, since front-of-package labeling can be confusing. It's a good idea to choose breads, flours, cereals, and pastas that list whole grains, such as whole wheat, first in the ingredient list. White rices count as grains, but not as whole grains. Brown rice, though, is a whole grain and has more nutritional value. Less-common choices that are rich in fiber and nutrients include bulgur, barley, and quinoa.

Fish and shellfish: To be sure you get at least two servings of fish (4 ounces raw, 3 ounces cooked per serving) each week, look for your favorite catch in either the seafood department or the frozen food section. Most fish is low in saturated fat; salmon, trout, tuna, herring, and other fatty fish offer the health benefits of omega-3 fatty acids as well. Shellfish, such as shrimp, are high in cholesterol; you can still enjoy them as part of a healthy diet, however, as long as you don't go overboard.

Meats and poultry: Focus on lean varieties, and keep portion size to about 4 ounces raw (3 ounces cooked). Some cuts of beef and pork are as lean as chicken breast. Lean cuts of beef include sirloin, round steak, and flank steak; good pork choices include tenderloin and loin chops. When choosing poultry, keep in mind that the white meat is leaner than the dark. Be sure you don't eat the skin. Before cooking beef, pork, or poultry, be sure to trim away all the fat you see. Remember to take advantage of services your butcher may offer, such as chopping or otherwise preparing meats to your specifications.

Convenience foods: Many convenience foods, such as prepared meals or entrées, are high in sodium, saturated fat, cholesterol, and calories. Read the nutrition facts panel carefully when you shop, since products vary widely in how well they adhere to heart-healthy guidelines. Don't rely exclusively on front-of-package labeling; the wording of many claims can be misleading. For example, a product labeled "low-fat" may be high in sodium.

Snacks and beverages: Most snack foods are highly processed, which usually means they are high in one or more of the nutritional "villains"—saturated fat, trans fat, cholesterol, and sodium. Also, watch out for sugary beverages;

they are often devoid of nutrition and contain empty calories. Limit these foods and beverages as much as possible, and try to find healthier alternatives to substitute. For example, keep fruit such as apples, grapes, and bananas on hand, and buy unsalted nuts for a quick and healthy alternative to chips or candy.

Nutrition Labels and Food Icons

To determine how a particular manufactured food fits into your eating plan, check the package for the helpful information there. The U.S. Department of Agriculture (USDA) regulates the nutrition facts panel, found on all food manufactured in the United States, to help you compare products and understand what you are buying. Other organizations use their own icon systems to help you make decisions, and some grocery stores have introduced on-shelf labeling programs. When you see a health claim or an icon that signals a health claim on the front of food packaging, consider the source of the information before you make your selections.

How to Read the Nutrition Facts Panel

Start at the *Serving Size* and determine how many servings you will really be consuming. If you intend to eat double the servings, you must also double the calories and nutrients. Think about how eating the food will affect your calorie balance, keeping in mind that for a 2,000-calorie diet, 40 calories per serving is considered low, 100 calories per serving is considered moderate, and 400 calories or more per serving is considered high.

The *% Daily Value* column tells you the percentage of each nutrient in a single serving, in terms of the daily recommended amount. As a guide, if you want to consume less of a nutrient, such as saturated fat, cholesterol, or sodium, choose foods with a lower % Daily Value (5% or less is considered low). If you want to consume more of a nutrient, such as fiber, look for foods with a higher % Daily Value (20% or more is considered high).

Nutrition Facts

Start here ●

Serving Size 1 slice (47g)
Servings Per Container 6

Amount Per Serving

Check the
total calories
per serving ●

Calories 160   Calories from Fat 90

	% Daily Value*
Total Fat 10g	15%
Saturated Fat 2.5g	11%
Trans Fat 2g	
Cholesterol 0mg	0%
Sodium 300mg	12%
Total Carb 15g	5%
Dietary Fiber less than 1g	3%
Sugars 1g	
Protein 3g	

Limit these
nutrients ●

Get enough of
these nutrients ●

Vitamin A 0%	Vitamin C 4%
Calcium 45%	Iron 6%
Thiamin 8%	Riboflavin 6%
Niacin 6%	

Quick Guide to
% Daily Value:
5% or less
is low
20% or more
is high ●

*Percent Daily Values are based on a 2,000 calorie diet. Your daily values may be higher or lower depending on your calorie needs.

What to Watch for When Shopping

Compare products by reading the ingredients lists as well as the nutrition facts panels. Keep in mind the following information about potential problem foods.

HIGH IN BOTH SATURATED FAT AND CHOLESTEROL

- Animal fats found in meats and poultry
- Whole-milk products, such as cheese, butter, and cream
- Egg yolks

HIGH IN SATURATED FAT

- Palm kernel oil and palm oil
- Coconut and coconut oil
- Vegetable oil made from coconut, palm, or palm kernel oil
- Cocoa butter

HIGH IN TRANS FAT

- Partially hydrogenated vegetable oil
- Vegetable shortening

HIGH IN SODIUM

(Some of these items are also available without added salt or in a lower-sodium form. It pays to check and compare labels.)

- Processed or cured meats, such as bacon, bologna, hot dogs, ham, canned meat, pastrami, pepperoni, salami, and sausage
- Brined products, such as anchovies, capers, olives, and pickles
- Seasonings such as celery salt, garlic salt, and onion salt
- Condiments such as barbecue sauce, ketchup, mustard, soy sauce, steak sauce, and Worcestershire sauce
- Canned soups and bouillon cubes or granules
- Breads and bread products
- Cheeses
- Crackers and chips
- Frozen entrées including pizza and frozen vegetables with sauces
- Canned vegetables
- Salted nuts

American Heart Association Food Certification Program

Our heart-check mark helps you quickly find heart-healthy foods in the grocery store. When you see the heart-check mark on food packaging, you can be confident that the food has been certified by the association to meet our criteria for saturated fat and cholesterol. Visit www.heartcheck mark.org to learn how to use the heart-check mark when you shop.

Low in Saturated Fat & Cholesterol

CERTIFIED by
American Heart Association
heartcheckmark.org

getting organized:
kitchen essentials

TAKE A GOOD LOOK AROUND YOUR KITCHEN. IS IT SET UP SO YOU CAN enjoy cooking? If not, find out what's not working and what you can do to make the minutes you spend preparing meals as productive and stress-free as possible. Investing some time up front to organize your kitchen environment and tools will improve your efficiency and will save you time and hassle in the long run. Try the following strategies to get your kitchen organized:

- Tidy up and reduce clutter in your kitchen workspace.
- Equip your kitchen with the basic kitchen tools (see page 24 for a list).
- Before you start cooking, review the recipe and organize your ingredients and tools.

Organize Your Cooking Space

Your goal is to stage your kitchen so the different steps of cooking will flow smoothly, without your having to wrestle pots and pans or search for necessary equipment. When you stand at your stove and countertop, is everything you need within easy reach? Cooking will go faster if the essentials are nearby—potholders hanging near the stove and the microwave, and knives organized on a magnetic rack or in a block near the cutting area.

To get started, clear clutter such as mail, keys, and homework from countertops and other work surfaces. Next, simplify your kitchen drawers. Start by giving away equipment and utensils you no longer use. (As a rule of thumb, if you haven't used something in two years, you'll probably never miss it.) Maybe something as simple as putting dividers in your utensil drawers would make them more user-friendly. If you have long-handled spoons that take up too much space, try using large jars to hold them upright on the counter. Of course, having easy access to your most-used skillets and saucepans is very important. You might find that hanging them on hooks would be helpful. If you need more space, try putting drawers or turntables in lower cabinets.

Equip Your Kitchen with the Right Tools

Here are the basic tools of the trade most well-prepped cooks consider essential:

- Several well-sharpened, high-quality knives
- A medium and a large skillet, each with a tight-fitting lid
- A covered pan you can use both on the stovetop and in the oven
- A few nonstick pots and pans
- A Dutch oven
- A variety of covered casserole dishes
- Two dishwasher-safe chopping boards
- A slow cooker
- A food processor or blender
- A nest of mixing bowls
- A whisk, at least one big spoon, a slotted spoon, kitchen scissors, tongs, and spatulas
- At least one set of measuring spoons and measuring cups (for both liquid and dry ingredients)
- A vegetable peeler
- A can opener
- A colander
- A set of baking pans (including 8- or 9-inch square, 11 x 8 x 2-inch or 13 x 9 x 2-inch, and loaf) and baking sheets
- Potholders, trivets, and cooling racks
- A grater and a zester (or microplane)
- Aluminum foil, wax paper, plastic wrap, and cooking parchment
- A variety of plastic storage containers with airtight lids

Make Efficiency as Easy as 1-2-3

Once you've organized your kitchen, consider ways you can make your cooking habits more efficient. Unless you've prepared a dish many times, your first step should be to read the recipe thoroughly—at least once. Second, it helps to plan a timing strategy if you're cooking more than one dish. Most cooks agree that you should pull out all the necessary ingredients and line them up on the counter. This is called *mise en place* (French for "everything in its place"), and it helps curb mid-preparation panic when you suddenly realize you have no baking powder for the cake you've already begun. It also helps keep you from forgetting to use an ingredient. Third, assemble the utensils you'll need. Now you're ready to get cooking!

cooking healthy:
heart-smart techniques

THE TECHNIQUE YOU CHOOSE TO COOK CERTAIN FOODS WILL AFFECT both the time needed to prepare a recipe and the health benefits the foods provide, so the recipes in this cookbook use a combination of cooking methods that keep saturated fat, sodium, and prep time to a minimum. Some methods, such as slow cooking or roasting, require a little planning ahead and longer cooking, but the actual time you need to spend in preparation is usually very little.

Grilling and Broiling

Both grilling (cooking over direct heat) and broiling (cooking under direct heat) usually provide a crisp, browned crust and a moist, tender interior while allowing excess fat to drip away into the grill or the broiler pan. Trim and discard all visible fat from poultry and meats before grilling or broiling; this will both cut down on saturated fat and help prevent flare-ups. Marinades, rubs, and glazes provide extra flavor as well as variety. Remember that if a broiling recipe specifies a distance from the heat, it means the number of inches from the heat element to the top of the food you are broiling, not to the top of the broiling rack. While you have the grill or broiler going for the entrée, try grilling or broiling some vegetables and fruit, too.

Stir-Frying

A favorite preparation technique for fast meals, stir-frying simply involves quickly cooking food in a minimum of hot oil while stirring constantly. This technique seals in the natural juices of meats and seafood and preserves the texture and color of vegetables. Although traditionally done in a wok, stir-frying can also be done in a large skillet. Because of the high temperature and the constant movement, food will not stick and burn. You will need to move fast once you start stir-frying, so prepare sauces and slice or dice each ingredient into uniform pieces (for more even cooking) before you begin.

Steaming

Steaming, or cooking food in a basket over simmering liquid (water, broth, wine, and fruit juice are common ones), is appropriate for almost any food that can be boiled or simmered, such as chicken breasts and vegetables. Since it doesn't make direct contact with the liquid, steamed food retains flavor, color, and nutrients. (Be sure the liquid does not touch the bottom of the basket.) Add herbs to the steaming liquid for extra flavor.

Microwave Cooking

Fast and easy, microwave cooking uses moist heat, making it an especially healthy way to cook vegetables, fruits, and fish. That's because very little liquid is needed, so nutrients are retained. Foods don't stick, so you don't need much if any added fat, and cleanup is easy. To adapt a recipe for the microwave oven, find a similar microwave recipe to use as a guide, then cut the cooking time of the original recipe to one-fourth or one-third. If the food isn't done when you check it, gradually increase the cooking time until it is. Also, reduce the amount of liquid used in most foods by about one-third because less liquid evaporates during microwave cooking.

Roasting or Baking

Both roasting and baking use the dry heat of an oven to cook foods. Typically, preparation time is limited, so although the food may be in the oven a while, you won't need to spend much hands-on time. The line between the two methods is blurry, but roasting is usually done without a cover and at higher heat, whereas baking may or may not use a cover and usually is at somewhat lower heat. Some sources consider meats and poultry (especially large cuts and whole birds) to be roasted and breads, desserts, and casseroles to be baked. You can use either method for firm fruits and vegetables. When roasting meat, discard the visible fat and place the meat on a rack in a roasting pan to prevent the meat from sitting in its fat drippings. If needed, baste with fat-free liquids, such as wine, fruit juice, or fat-free, low-sodium broth. Plan on removing the meat from the oven 15 to 20 minutes before serving. Letting the meat "rest" makes it easier to carve. For whole birds, discard as much fat as you can before roasting, but leave the skin on until the poultry is cooked. Discard the skin before serving the poultry. Roasting also works well for a number of fruits, such as peaches and bananas, and for vegetables from asparagus to zucchini, but not for green, leafy vegetables.

Braising or Stewing

Braising (for a pot roast with vegetables, for example) and stewing (for stews and chilis) are similar slow-cooking methods that are great ways to tenderize tougher cuts of meat. Lightly spray a pan with cooking spray or use a small amount of oil, then brown the food on all sides. (This step intensifies the flavor and adds color to the meat or chicken, but you can leave it out if you wish.) Pour off any fat. Simmer the food in a tightly covered pot on the stovetop or in the oven, using a small amount of flavorful liquid if braising and enough to cover the food if stewing. Because braising or stewing meat or poultry cooks the fat out into the sauce, begin a day ahead if possible. Prepare the dish, then refrigerate it overnight. The extra time lets the flavors blend and causes the chilled fat to rise to the top and harden, making it easy to remove. Braising is also a good method for cooking firm vegetables. Stewing is good for some fresh fruits, such as plums and cherries, and for dried fruits. Braising and stewing are not recommended for tender cuts of meat.

Poaching

Poaching is an excellent way to prepare delicate foods, such as seafood, chicken, and fruit. To poach food, immerse it in a pan of almost-simmering well-seasoned liquid (the bubbles should not break the surface of the liquid), and cook it without a cover. Although you can use water as the liquid, some more-flavorful choices are fruit juice, wine, or fat-free, low-sodium broth. After the food is cooked, remove it from the pan and reduce the remaining liquid (decrease the volume by boiling the liquid rapidly) to make a delicious sauce.

Slow Cooking

Although the actual cooking process in a slow cooker almost always takes hours, this useful piece of kitchen equipment saves time by allowing you to simply fill and cover the cooker, turn it on, and leave it alone. (You may want to brown meats first to add color and deepen flavor.) When you use a slow cooker, don't fill it more than one-half to two-thirds full. Since slow cookers work by keeping heat and moisture in, in general it's not necessary—or recommended—to lift the lid and stir the ingredients as they cook. Be sure to layer ingredients according to the recipe, because foods placed at the bottom of the cooker will cook faster than those at the top. Once your meat and vegetables are cooked and you've removed them from the slow cooker, you can thicken the remaining liquid into a delicious sauce by reducing it in the cooker, uncovered on high, or in a saucepan.

time-saving tips:
from our cooking experts

NO ONE KNOWS HOW TO SAVE TIME IN THE KITCHEN BETTER THAN the people who work there all day. Here are some favorite tricks of the trade that our experts use to keep time spent on meal preparation and cleanup to a minimum.

EASY EFFICIENCY
- Store your utensils near where you're most likely to use them. For instance, it's convenient to keep your spoons, whisks, and soup ladle near the stove.
- Keep knives handy and sharpened to make prep work quick and easy.
- Keep your dried herbs and spices in alphabetical order so you don't have to search for the right jar. This works especially well if you have lots of them and/or you can't see all of them at a glance.
- If you prefer using fresh garlic instead of that in a jar, use a garlic peeler (a rubber cylinder that rubs off the papery peel) to speed up the task. If you have a rubber jar opener, you can use it to do the same thing.
- When you use a cutting board, lay a damp paper towel under it to keep it from sliding as you work.
- Use kitchen scissors to snip small amounts of parsley, cilantro, and other herbs.

GO-TO INGREDIENTS
- Add flavor in no time with high-intensity ingredients such as mint, pine nuts, currants, or just a few olives, any of which can make a simple dish outstanding.
- Remember that some pastas cook more quickly than others. When

you're pressed for time, use angel hair or vermicelli (choose whole-grain pasta for added nutrients) for the speediest result.

- Be flexible and swap out ingredients to save prep time or prevent a last-minute dash to the store for the "right" ingredient. (The exception is when baking foods such as cakes and yeast breads, for which precision is the key to success.) For example, if a recipe calls for oregano but all you have is basil, chances are that the results will be fine if you make the switch.

TIMELY TECHNIQUES

- Look for ways to cut down on time in the recipe order when you can take care of prep work for other steps. For example, you can start the water boiling for pasta while waiting for the onions to cook down for a sauce.
- To bring water to a boil faster, start with hot tap water and cover the pot. If you're using a lot of water, divide it between two pots until it starts boiling.
- Use wide skillets and higher temperatures to speed up cooking time. A wide skillet allows more liquid to evaporate, so food cooks more quickly.
- Cover saucepans and skillets to both speed up cooking and keep foods moist.
- Remove fat fast from hot broth by dropping in an ice cube and moving it through the accumulating fat. Quickly take out the cube before it melts—and take the fat with it.
- Rinse frozen vegetables in a colander under cold running water (not hot, which would cook them slightly) for 15 to 20 seconds. This refreshes them and makes them cook faster.
- Microwave lemons and limes for about 10 seconds on high to make them easier and faster to juice.

QUICK CLEANUP

- To have a place for messy spoons and spatulas, set a single sheet of wax paper with the curved side down on your work surface. (Lightly wiping the counter first with a moist paper towel helps keep the wax paper in place.) You can then just throw away one piece of wax paper, rather than having to scrub a whole counter.
- Make cleanup easier by filling the sink or a large pan or bowl with

hot, soapy water before you start cooking. Drop in dirty utensils (not knives or other sharp items) as you go so they'll be easy to clean, especially if you will need them again as you cook.

- When you're grating cheese or lemon peel, put your measuring cup or spoon on a sheet of wax paper. Aim for the measuring cup or spoon as you grate, then spoon the "misses" into the implement. This also works well for measuring flour and confectioners' sugar.

- Measure dry ingredients before wet ones so you can reuse measuring spoons and cups without having to wash them between steps.

FREEZER TRICKS

- Plan to keep emergency meals in the freezer for those nights when you're just too short on time or energy to cook.

- Even if you won't need them right away, roast vegetables such as bell peppers and onions while you roast or bake other things; then freeze the veggies for later use.

- Freeze lemon wedges or slices for quick access when you're in a hurry.

- Remove the visible fat from boneless, skinless chicken breasts before freezing them. The chicken will be ready when you need it, and you'll need to wash the cutting board and knife only once instead of each time you need some chicken.

Because you can count on the recipes in this book to be nutritious, delicious, and speedy to prepare, you can spend less time in the kitchen and serve homemade meals more often. If you cook dishes that you enjoy, from ingredients you love, in a place you find comfortable, you'll look forward to making meals in minutes for yourself and your family.

using this book:
about the recipes

Super-Saver Entrée Recipes

To help you manage your mealtime, we've developed entrée recipes for each of four categories: No Shopping Required, Planned-Overs, All-in-One, and Express—each offering a different time-saving slant. Read about these categories—and note the icons that let you identify them quickly—below. We've also listed the recipes with page numbers for each category in the Entrée Recipe Icon Index, starting on page 325.

No Shopping Required. These are your go-to recipes when you have no time to shop but want to put a tasty dish on the table right away. Every ingredient called for is a staple that you are likely to keep on hand, ready at a moment's notice. (For a list of suggested items, see pages 11–14.) With your pantry, fridge, and freezer well stocked, you'll be able to put together, for example, Grilled Chicken with Green Chiles and Cheese (page 137) or Five-Flavor Fish (page 101) in about 15 minutes—without a trip to the supermarket.

Planned-Overs. When you make soups, stews, or casseroles, you probably prepare extra for leftovers. But it's easy to get tired of eating the same thing several times in a row. That's why we created Planned-Overs—recipes that feature tonight's leftovers as a part of another night's main dish. For example, when you prepare Apricot-Barbecue Chicken Chunks (page 141), you'll have enough chicken already cooked to make Asian Chicken and Wild Rice Salad (page 87) for another meal. Likewise, the Tuscan Braised Beef (page 172) leaves just what you need for Thai Beef Salad (page 91) later in the week.

All-in-One. These one-dish meals save time by combining meat or a meat substitute, at least one serving of a vegetable or fruit, and at least one serving of carbohydrate, usually a whole grain—and often they require only one pot or pan. Serve these recipes with simple sides, such as whole-wheat rolls, fresh fruit, or a salad or dessert you make while the dish is cooking.

Express. The quickest of the quick, these entrées are ready in 25 minutes or less. That's 25 minutes max for all the preparation *and* all the cooking, if there is any. Many are ready in even less time. For example, Citrus Pesto Tuna (page 83) takes a total of only 10 minutes, start to finish, and Honey-Mustard Salmon (page 106) takes only 11.

How to Use the Nutrition Analyses

To help you plan meals and determine how a recipe fits into your overall eating plan, we have provided a nutrition analysis for each recipe in the book. The following guidelines give some details on how the analyses were calculated.

- Each analysis is for a single serving; garnishes or optional ingredients are not included.
- When ingredient options are listed, the first one is analyzed. When a range of ingredients is given, the average is analyzed.
- We use the lowest-sodium products that are widely available for analysis, and we encourage you to shop for low-sodium products whenever possible. To keep the level of sodium in our recipes low, we call for unprocessed foods or no-salt-added and low-sodium products and add table salt sparingly for flavor. For instance, a recipe using a

can of no-salt-added tomatoes and a quarter-teaspoon of salt will be lower in sodium than one using regular canned tomatoes and no salt.

- Because product labeling in the marketplace can vary and change quickly, we use the generic terms "fat-free" and "low-fat" throughout to avoid confusion.
- Nutrient values except for fats are rounded to the nearest whole number. Fats are rounded to the nearest half gram; because of the rounding, the amounts for saturated, trans, monounsaturated, and polyunsaturated fats may not add up to the amount of total fat.
- We specify canola, corn, and olive oils in these recipes, but you can also use other heart-healthy unsaturated oils, such as safflower, soybean, and sunflower.
- When meat, poultry, or seafood is marinated and the marinade is discarded, we calculate only the amount of marinade absorbed.
- Analyses of meat are based on cooked lean meat with all visible fat discarded.
- We use 95 percent fat-free ground beef for analysis.
- When alcohol is used in a cooked dish, we estimate that most of the calories from alcohol evaporate during cooking.
- We use the abbreviations "g" for gram and "mg" for milligram.

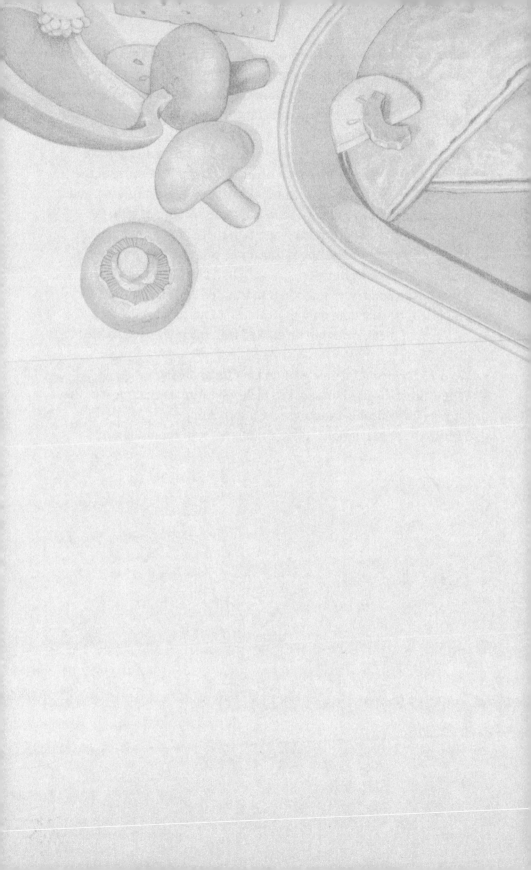

Freezing at a consistent temperature of 0°F keeps food safe indefinitely, but freezing can affect the quality of the food over time. When freezing foods, date your containers and wrapped packages and refer to this chart as a guide for best results.

Ground beef	3 to 4 months
Stew meat	3 to 4 months
Steaks and roasts	6 to 12 months
Chops	4 to 6 months
Chicken or turkey, whole	1 year
Chicken or turkey, breasts and pieces	9 months
Ground turkey	3 to 4 months
Fatty fish (salmon, tuna)	2 to 3 months
Lean fish (tilapia, sole, flounder, cod)	6 months
Shellfish (shrimp, scallops, clams)	3 to 6 months
Broths and soups	2 to 3 months
Juices	8 to 12 months
Cheeses	6 months
Vegetables (such as onions, peas, and broccoli)	8 months
Berries	4 to 6 months

For safe defrosting, thaw foods in the refrigerator, in cold water, or in the microwave, not on the counter at room temperature.

appetizers, snacks, and beverages

dill and sour cream dip

SERVES 7 · 2 tablespoons per serving
PREPARATION TIME · 5 minutes

The subtle, fresh taste of dill is at its best when teamed with cucumbers. Cut some into spears, rounds, or wedges and try them with this super-simple dip.

3/4 cup low-fat sour cream

1 1/2 tablespoons snipped fresh dillweed or 1 1/2 teaspoons dried dillweed, crumbled

1 tablespoon lemon juice

1 tablespoon olive oil (extra-virgin preferred)

1/4 teaspoon salt

In a small bowl, whisk together all the ingredients. Serve or cover and refrigerate until serving time.

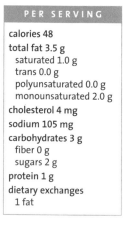

PER SERVING

calories 48
total fat 3.5 g
  saturated 1.0 g
  trans 0.0 g
  polyunsaturated 0.0 g
  monounsaturated 2.0 g
cholesterol 4 mg
sodium 105 mg
carbohydrates 3 g
  fiber 0 g
  sugars 2 g
protein 1 g
dietary exchanges
  1 fat

mexican bean dip

SERVES 6 · ¼ cup per serving
PREPARATION TIME · 10 minutes

You can enjoy this protein- and fiber-packed, easy-to-prepare dip on baked tortilla chips or in Vegetarian Taco Salad (page 94).

1 15-ounce can no-salt-added black beans, rinsed and drained

½ cup chopped green bell pepper

¼ cup coarsely chopped fresh cilantro or parsley (optional)

2 tablespoons salsa (lowest sodium available)

2 tablespoons lime juice

1 teaspoon bottled minced garlic or 2 medium garlic cloves, coarsely chopped

1 teaspoon chili powder

½ teaspoon ground cumin

In a food processor or blender, process all the ingredients for 45 seconds, or until fairly smooth. Serve or cover and refrigerate for up to four days.

PER SERVING

calories 72
total fat 0.0 g
  saturated 0.0 g
  trans 0.0 g
  polyunsaturated 0.0 g
  monounsaturated 0.0 g
cholesterol 0 mg
sodium 24 mg
carbohydrates 14 g
  fiber 3 g
  sugars 3 g
protein 4 g
dietary exchanges
  1 starch

COOK'S TIP ON CANNED BEANS

To give canned beans a clean taste, pour them into a colander and rinse with cool running water until all the bubbles have disappeared. If salt was added to the beans during processing, rinsing will remove some of the sodium. When buying canned beans, choose the no-salt-added variety if available.

mini vegetable cheese balls

SERVES 6 · 2 cheese balls per serving
PREPARATION TIME · 20 minutes

Don't let the small size of these cheese balls fool you. They're loaded with flavor and crunch!

½ cup bell pepper (any color), diced or minced

1 medium rib of celery, diced or minced

2 medium green onions, thinly sliced

2 ounces light tub cream cheese

2 tablespoons soft goat cheese

¼ teaspoon garlic powder

½ cup finely snipped fresh parsley

In a medium bowl, stir together all the ingredients except the parsley.

Put the parsley on a plate. Using a round tablespoon measure, scoop up 1 scant tablespoon cheese mixture. Roll into a ball. Roll in the parsley, turning to coat. Shake off any excess parsley. Repeat with the remaining cheese mixture. Serve or cover and refrigerate for up to 1½ hours (the mixture weeps if refrigerated longer).

TIME-SAVER Make a tasty cheese spread instead of the balls. Stir the ingredients as directed, then transfer to a serving dish. Reduce the amount of parsley to ¼ cup and sprinkle over the spread.

PER SERVING
calories 43
total fat 2.5 g
saturated 1.5 g
trans 0.0 g
polyunsaturated 0.0 g
monounsaturated 0.5 g
cholesterol 8 mg
sodium 70 mg
carbohydrates 3 g
fiber 1 g
sugars 2 g
protein 2 g
dietary exchanges
½ fat

cheese-filled bell pepper boats

SERVES 8 · 3 pieces per serving
PREPARATION TIME · 15 minutes

When the colorful allure of the many bell pepper varieties draws you in at the supermarket's produce section, try this recipe for an unusual vegetable tray. The cream cheese mixture is also wonderful on celery, on cucumber rounds, or in hollowed-out cherry tomato halves.

½ cup light tub cream cheese (about 4 ounces)

2 tablespoons shredded or grated Parmesan cheese

1 teaspoon lime juice

1 1-inch-thick slice of English, or hothouse, cucumber or thin regular cucumber (cut crosswise)

2 medium bell peppers (any colors)

½ teaspoon chili powder

In a small bowl, stir together the cream cheese, Parmesan, and lime juice. Spoon into a piping bag fitted with a wide star or round tip or a sturdy plastic bag with a bottom corner snipped off.

Cut the cucumber slice crosswise into 12 rounds, then cut each in half (you'll have 24 thin half-circles). Set aside.

Cut the bell peppers in half lengthwise, discarding the stems, ribs, and seeds. Cut each half into 6 squares. Lay the pieces with the skin side down on a serving platter.

Pipe about 1 teaspoon cream cheese mixture onto each square. Sprinkle with the chili powder. Stand a cucumber half-circle in the cream cheese mixture on each square.

PER SERVING
calories 44
total fat 2.5 g
saturated 1.5 g
trans 0.0 g
polyunsaturated 0.0 g
monounsaturated 1.0 g
cholesterol 10 mg
sodium 88 mg
carbohydrates 3 g
fiber 1 g
sugars 2 g
protein 2 g
dietary exchanges
½ fat

COOK'S TIP

Substitute small, feathery pieces of fresh dillweed for the chili powder and cucumber.

roasted vegetable spread

SERVES 4 · ¼ cup per serving
PREPARATION TIME · 15 minutes
COOKING TIME · 20 to 25 minutes

With their slightly caramelized flavor, roasted vegetables make a wonderful spread. Serve with pieces of toasted whole-grain pita rounds or baked tortilla chips.

Olive oil spray

1 medium zucchini, halved lengthwise

1 medium yellow summer squash, halved lengthwise

1 medium carrot, cut crosswise into ¼-inch slices

1 medium onion, quartered

2 ounces asparagus, trimmed

2 medium Italian plum (Roma) tomatoes, halved

2 medium garlic cloves

2 tablespoons balsamic vinegar

1 teaspoon dried Italian seasoning, crumbled

⅛ teaspoon pepper

1½ tablespoons shredded or grated Parmesan cheese

Preheat the oven to 400°F.

Lightly spray a large baking sheet with olive oil spray. Arrange the zucchini, squash, carrot, onion, asparagus, tomatoes (with the cut side up), and garlic in a single layer. Lightly spray the tops with olive oil spray.

Bake without stirring for 20 to 25 minutes, or until tender.

Put half the vegetables in a food processor or blender. Process for 1 to 1½ minutes, or until the mixture is the desired consistency (almost smooth but with some texture is recommended). Transfer to a medium bowl. Repeat with the remaining vegetables.

Stir in the vinegar, Italian seasoning, and pepper. Sprinkle with the Parmesan.

PER SERVING
calories 60
total fat 1.0 g
saturated 0.5 g
trans 0.0 g
polyunsaturated 0.0 g
monounsaturated 0.0 g
cholesterol 1 mg
sodium 55 mg
carbohydrates 12 g
fiber 3 g
sugars 8 g
protein 3 g
dietary exchanges
2 vegetable

COOK'S TIP

You can serve the leftover vegetable spread chilled or reheated. To reheat, put in a microwaveable dish and microwave, uncovered, on 100 percent power (high) until warm.

curried chicken salad
in mini phyllo shells

SERVES 10 · 2 mini phyllo shells per serving
PREPARATION TIME · 16 minutes
COOKING TIME · 8 to 9 minutes

Your guests will be amazed at the flavor packed into these phyllo shells.
You'll love how easy they are to make.

$1/2$ cup fat-free plain yogurt

2 tablespoons all-fruit orange
    spread or orange marmalade

$3/4$ teaspoon curry powder

$1/4$ teaspoon salt

$1/4$ teaspoon pepper

1 medium rib of celery, finely
    chopped

1 medium green onion (green and
    white parts), finely chopped

$1/2$ medium red bell pepper, finely
    diced

9 to 10 ounces canned white
    chicken chunks in water, drained
    and flaked

20 frozen mini phyllo shells

20 green grapes, halved

Preheat the oven to 350°F.

In a medium bowl, stir together the yogurt, orange spread, curry powder, salt, and pepper.

Stir in the celery, green onion, bell pepper, and chicken.

Put the phyllo shells on a nonstick baking sheet. Spoon about 1 heaping tablespoon filling into each.

Bake for 8 to 9 minutes, or until heated through. Transfer to a serving platter.

Place 2 grape halves diagonally on each filled shell.

PER SERVING
calories 90
total fat 2.5 g
saturated 0.5 g
trans 0.0 g
polyunsaturated 0.0 g
monounsaturated 0.0 g
cholesterol 12 mg
sodium 205 mg
carbohydrates 10 g
fiber 0 g
sugars 5 g
protein 6 g
dietary exchanges
$1/2$ carbohydrate
1 lean meat

COOK'S TIP

Prepare the filling, cover it with plastic wrap, and refrigerate it for up to 6 hours before filling the shells if you wish.

stacked mushroom nachos

SERVES 8 · 2 nachos per serving
PREPARATION TIME · 15 minutes
COOKING TIME · 10 minutes

These nachos use mushrooms instead of high-fat fried chips as their base. Plan on having plenty around—they disappear quickly!

16 large fresh button mushrooms, stems discarded

Olive oil spray

1/4 teaspoon chili powder

1/3 cup fat-free refried beans

4 cherry tomatoes, quartered

1/3 cup shredded low-fat Cheddar cheese (about 1 1/2 ounces)

16 black olive slices

Preheat the oven to 350°F.

Put the mushrooms with the rounded sides up on a large nonstick baking sheet. Lightly spray the tops with olive oil spray. Sprinkle with the chili powder. Turn the mushrooms over.

Spread 1 teaspoon beans over the cavity of each mushroom. Place a cherry tomato quarter with the cut side up on the beans. Slightly press the tomato into the beans to secure it. Sprinkle with the Cheddar. Top with the olive slices.

Bake for 10 minutes, or until warm.

PER SERVING
calories 31
total fat 1.0 g
saturated 0.5 g
trans 0.0 g
polyunsaturated 0.0 g
monounsaturated 0.5 g
cholesterol 1 mg
sodium 102 mg
carbohydrates 4 g
fiber 1 g
sugars 1 g
protein 3 g
dietary exchanges
1/2 very lean meat

sweet ginger crunch

SERVES 5 · 1/2 cup per serving
PREPARATION TIME · 3 minutes
COOKING TIME · 4 minutes

This trail mix, updated with crystallized ginger, is ready in a flash. It's great to have on hand when you need a grab-and-go snack.

1/4 cup slivered almonds (about 1 ounce)

1 cup high-fiber cereal (clusters preferred) (about 2 ounces)

1 cup multigrain cereal squares (about 2 ounces)

1/4 cup sweetened dried cranberries

2 tablespoons crystallized ginger, finely chopped

1/8 teaspoon salt

1/2 teaspoon grated orange zest

In a small skillet, dry-roast the almonds over medium heat for about 4 minutes, or until just fragrant, stirring frequently. Pour into a medium bowl.

Stir in the remaining ingredients except the orange zest. Sprinkle the zest evenly over the mixture. Toss until well blended. Store in an airtight container for up to two weeks.

COOK'S TIP
Adding the orange zest separately helps distribute it more evenly.

PER SERVING
calories 146
total fat 3.5 g
saturated 0.5 g
trans 0.0 g
polyunsaturated 1.0 g
monounsaturated 2.0 g
cholesterol 0 mg
sodium 167 mg
carbohydrates 28 g
fiber 4 g
sugars 12 g
protein 4 g
dietary exchanges
1 starch
1 carbohydrate
1 fat

strawberry mint spritzers

SERVES 6 · 1 cup per serving
PREPARATION TIME · 5 minutes

This sparkling drink is ideal as a refreshing spritzer for brunch or on a hot summer day.

1 pound strawberries, stemmed
    and halved
½ cup sugar
6 fresh mint leaves, finely chopped
Grated zest from 1 medium lime
    (about 1 teaspoon)

2 tablespoons lime juice
4 cups club soda or sparkling water
6 lime wedges (optional)
6 mint sprigs (optional)

In a food processor or blender, process the strawberries until smooth.

Add the sugar, mint leaves, lime zest, and lime juice. Process until blended.

To serve, pour ⅓ cup strawberry mixture and ⅔ cup club soda into each glass. Add ice and stir. Garnish with the lime wedges and mint sprigs.

PER SERVING
calories 91
total fat 0.0 g
saturated 0.0 g
trans 0.0 g
polyunsaturated 0.0 g
monounsaturated 0.0 g
cholesterol 0 mg
sodium 34 mg
carbohydrates 23 g
fiber 2 g
sugars 21 g
protein 1 g
dietary exchanges
½ fruit
1 carbohydrate

Strawberry Mint Smoothies

SERVES 4 · 1 cup per serving

For a smoothie-like drink, reduce the club soda or sparkling water to 1 cup, well chilled. Process the strawberry mixture as directed above. Pour ½ cup strawberry mixture and ¼ cup club soda or sparkling water into each glass.

PER SERVING
calories 136
total fat 0.5 g
saturated 0.0 g
trans 0.0 g
polyunsaturated 0.0 g
monounsaturated 0.0 g
cholesterol 0 mg
sodium 14 mg
carbohydrates 35 g
fiber 2 g
sugars 31 g
protein 1 g
dietary exchanges
½ fruit
2 carbohydrate

soups

Tomato-Basil Soup

Sweet Curried Pumpkin Bisque

Creamy Mushroom Barley Soup

Chilled Strawberry-Orange Soup

Chinese-Style Chicken Soup with
Fresh Ginger

Corn and Chicken Chowder
Corn and Cheddar Chowder

Turkey Tortilla Soup

Pizza Soup
Spaghetti Soup

Broccoli and Cannellini Bean Soup

White Bean and Pasta Soup

tomato-basil soup

SERVES 4 · ³/₄ cup per serving
PREPARATION TIME · 5 minutes
COOKING TIME · 18 minutes

Fresh herbs add a lively taste to this refreshing, light soup.

1 14.5-ounce can no-salt-added diced tomatoes, undrained

1 14.5-ounce can fat-free, low-sodium chicken broth

2 tablespoons fresh basil, thinly sliced, or 2 teaspoons dried basil, crumbled

1 teaspoon sugar

¹/₄ teaspoon Worcestershire sauce (lowest sodium available)

¹/₈ teaspoon crushed red pepper flakes (optional)

¹/₄ to ¹/₂ cup snipped fresh cilantro or parsley

2 teaspoons olive oil (extra-virgin preferred)

¹/₄ teaspoon salt

In a medium saucepan, stir together the tomatoes with liquid, broth, basil, sugar, Worcestershire sauce, and red pepper flakes. Bring to a boil over high heat. Reduce the heat and simmer, uncovered, for 15 minutes, stirring occasionally. Remove from the heat.

Stir in the cilantro, olive oil, and salt.

> **COOK'S TIP**
> If you prepare this soup in advance, stir in the cilantro, olive oil, and salt after reheating.

PER SERVING
calories 49
total fat 2.5 g
saturated 0.5 g
trans 0.0 g
polyunsaturated 0.0 g
monounsaturated 1.5 g
cholesterol 0 mg
sodium 213 mg
carbohydrates 6 g
fiber 2 g
sugars 4 g
protein 2 g
dietary exchanges
1 vegetable
¹/₂ fat

sweet curried pumpkin bisque

SERVES 5 · ³/₄ cup per serving
PREPARATION TIME · 6 minutes
COOKING TIME · 8 minutes

Probably one of the easiest soups you will ever make, this smooth, creamy delight is perfect whether you're entertaining or curling up in front of the fire.

½ 15-ounce can solid-pack pumpkin (not pie filling)

1 cup fat-free, low-sodium chicken broth

3 tablespoons sugar

1 teaspoon curry powder

¾ teaspoon ground cinnamon

¼ teaspoon ground cumin

⅛ teaspoon cayenne (optional)

2 cups fat-free half-and-half

¼ teaspoon salt

¼ cup snipped fresh cilantro (optional)

In a medium saucepan, whisk together the pumpkin and broth until smooth. Whisk in the sugar, curry powder, cinnamon, cumin, and cayenne. Bring to a boil over high heat, about 3 minutes, whisking occasionally. Reduce the heat and simmer, covered, for 3 minutes.

Whisk in the half-and-half and salt. Increase the heat to medium low and cook, covered, for 2 minutes, stirring frequently. Serve topped with the cilantro.

COOK'S TIP

The cayenne helps heighten the flavors in this soup. The level of heat intensifies as it sits, though, so if you aren't serving the soup right away, stir in the cayenne at serving time.

PER SERVING

calories 112
total fat 0.5 g
  saturated 0.0 g
  trans 0.0 g
  polyunsaturated 0.0 g
  monounsaturated 0.0 g
cholesterol 0 mg
sodium 224 mg
carbohydrates 24 g
  fiber 2 g
  sugars 15 g
protein 8 g
dietary exchanges
  1 fat-free milk
  ½ carbohydrate

creamy mushroom barley soup

SERVES 8 · scant 1 cup per serving
PREPARATION TIME · 12 minutes
COOKING TIME · 30 minutes

Using presliced fresh mushrooms and frozen chopped onions will hurry things along in this recipe.

³/₈ cup very hot tap water
¹/₂ ounce dried porcini mushrooms
1 teaspoon canola or corn oil
¹/₂ cup chopped onion
1 large carrot, finely chopped
8 to 10 ounces presliced fresh
 button mushrooms
³/₄ teaspoon dried thyme, crumbled
1¹/₂ cups water

2 cups fat-free, low-sodium chicken
 broth
¹/₂ cup uncooked quick-cooking
 barley
¹/₄ teaspoon pepper
¹/₄ teaspoon salt
³/₈ cup fat-free milk
1¹/₂ teaspoons all-purpose flour
1 tablespoon dry sherry (optional)

In a small shallow bowl, stir together the hot water and dried mushrooms. Set aside.

In a stockpot or large saucepan, heat the oil over medium heat, swirling to coat the bottom. Cook the onion and carrot for about 5 minutes, or until beginning to soften, stirring occasionally.

Stir in the fresh mushrooms and thyme. Cook for 5 minutes.

Increase the heat to high. Stir in the water, broth, barley, and pepper. Bring to a boil, about 2 minutes. Reduce the heat and simmer, covered, for 12 minutes, or until the barley is tender.

Just before the barley is ready, put the dried mushrooms in a sieve. Rinse thoroughly and drain. Chop the mushrooms. Stir the mushrooms and salt into the pot.

In a small bowl, whisk together the milk and flour until the flour is dissolved. Stir into the soup. Increase the heat to medium high and bring to a boil, 1 to 2 minutes. Reduce the heat and simmer for at least 2 minutes. Stir in the sherry.

PER SERVING
calories 66
total fat 1.0 g
saturated 0.0 g
trans 0.0 g
polyunsaturated 0.5 g
monounsaturated 0.5 g
cholesterol 0 mg
sodium 104 mg
carbohydrates 12 g
fiber 2 g
sugars 2 g
protein 4 g
dietary exchanges
¹/₂ starch
1 vegetable

chilled strawberry-orange soup

SERVES 6 · $^2/_3$ cup per serving

PREPARATION TIME · 5 minutes

CHILLING TIME · 1 hour, if using fresh strawberries

Serve this chilled fruit soup as a light summer appetizer or with your favorite sandwich or salad.

1 pound fresh or frozen
    unsweetened strawberries,
    slightly thawed

1$^1/_2$ cups orange juice

$^1/_4$ cup sugar

1 teaspoon grated peeled
    gingerroot

2 tablespoons lime juice (optional)

In a food processor or blender, process all the ingredients until smooth.

If using fresh strawberries, cover and refrigerate for 1 hour to chill thoroughly. If using frozen strawberries, serve or cover and refrigerate until needed.

COOK'S TIP
Serve this soup within 24 hours for peak flavor.

PER SERVING
calories 85
total fat 0.5 g
saturated 0.0 g
trans 0.0 g
polyunsaturated 0.0 g
monounsaturated 0.0 g
cholesterol 0 mg
sodium 1 mg
carbohydrates 21 g
fiber 2 g
sugars 17 g
protein 1 g
dietary exchanges
1 fruit
$^1/_2$ carbohydrate

chinese-style chicken soup with fresh ginger

SERVES 4 · 1¼ cups per serving
PREPARATION TIME · 8 minutes
COOKING TIME · 4 minutes
STANDING TIME · 5 minutes

This light, garden-fresh soup is double-quick to fix. Just bring it to a boil, remove it from the heat, and let it stand for a few minutes!

2 14.5-ounce cans fat-free, low-sodium chicken broth

1½ cups diced skinless cooked chicken breast, cooked without salt

3 ounces fresh or frozen snow peas, thawed, halved diagonally

½ medium red bell pepper, thinly sliced lengthwise, then cut in 2-inch pieces

½ cup finely chopped green onions (green and white parts)

¼ to ½ cup snipped fresh cilantro

1 tablespoon grated peeled gingerroot

½ teaspoon salt

¼ teaspoon crushed red pepper flakes

1 medium lime, quartered

In a large saucepan, stir together the broth, chicken, snow peas, and bell pepper. Bring to a boil over high heat, about 4 minutes. Remove the saucepan from the heat.

Stir in the remaining ingredients except the lime. Cover and let stand for 5 minutes to absorb flavors. Serve with the lime to squeeze over the soup.

PER SERVING
calories 122
total fat 2.5 g
saturated 0.5 g
trans 0.0 g
polyunsaturated 0.5 g
monounsaturated 1.0 g
cholesterol 45 mg
sodium 388 mg
carbohydrates 5 g
fiber 2 g
sugars 2 g
protein 19 g
dietary exchanges
1 vegetable
2½ very lean meat

corn and chicken chowder

SERVES 6 · 1¼ cups per serving
PREPARATION TIME · 5 minutes
COOKING TIME · 11 to 12 minutes

express

Simple to prepare, this chowder has a rich flavor and an interesting texture that make it enormously satisfying. For a delectable light dinner, serve it with a crisp salad and follow with fruit for dessert.

2 14-ounce cans no-salt-added cream-style corn

2 cups frozen whole-kernel corn

2 cups fat-free milk

2 4.5- to 5-ounce cans white chicken chunks in water, drained

¼ cup minced red or green bell pepper

½ teaspoon dried thyme, crumbled

½ teaspoon salt

¼ teaspoon pepper (white preferred)

In a medium saucepan, stir together the corns, milk, and chicken. Heat over low heat for 5 minutes, stirring occasionally.

Stir in the remaining ingredients. Increase the heat to medium low and cook for 3 to 4 minutes, or until the soup just begins to simmer. Simmer for 3 minutes, or until hot.

PER SERVING

calories 226
total fat 2.0 g
 saturated 0.0 g
 trans 0.0 g
 polyunsaturated 1.0 g
 monounsaturated 0.5 g
cholesterol 22 mg
sodium 263 mg
carbohydrates 41 g
 fiber 3 g
 sugars 11 g
protein 17 g
dietary exchanges
 2½ starch
 2 very lean meat

Corn and Cheddar Chowder

Reduce the cream-style corn to 1 can. Increase the whole-kernel corn to 3 cups. Substitute 1 to 1½ cups grated low-fat Cheddar cheese for the chicken.

PER SERVING

calories 199
total fat 2.5 g
 saturated 1.0 g
 trans 0.0 g
 polyunsaturated 0.5 g
 monounsaturated 1.0 g
cholesterol 7 mg
sodium 380 mg
carbohydrates 36 g
 fiber 3 g
 sugars 10 g
protein 12 g
dietary exchanges
 2½ starch
 1½ very lean meat

turkey tortilla soup

SERVES 4 · 1½ cups per serving
PREPARATION TIME · 10 minutes
COOKING TIME · 17 minutes

Use leftover turkey from the holidays for this festive soup, or for a grilled turkey version, use leftover turkey from the Grilled Turkey Cutlets with Pineapple—without the pineapple (page 162).

TORTILLAS

2 6-inch corn tortillas, halved

Cooking spray

¼ teaspoon chili powder

SOUP

1 tablespoon light tub margarine

½ cup chopped onion

½ cup chopped carrot

1 Anaheim pepper, seeded and chopped

2 cups fat-free, low-sodium chicken broth

2 cups water

1 14.5-ounce can no-salt-added stewed tomatoes, undrained

1 8-ounce can no-salt-added tomato sauce

1 cup diced cooked skinless turkey breast, cooked without salt (about 6 ounces)

1 tablespoon ground cumin

1 teaspoon chili powder

¼ cup shredded fat-free Cheddar cheese (about 1 ounce)

Preheat the oven to 350°F.

Lightly spray one side of the tortillas with cooking spray. Sprinkle with ¼ teaspoon chili powder. Pour a small amount of water into 8 cups of a 12-cup muffin tin (to keep them from burning or warping). Hold one tortilla half with the cut side down and wrap it in one of the remaining muffin cups, curving the tortilla slightly to fit and frame a "bottomless" cup. Repeat with the remaining tortilla halves.

Bake for 5 minutes, or until crisp. Remove the muffin pan from the oven, leaving the tortillas in the muffin cups. Set aside.

PER SERVING
calories 167
total fat 2.5 g
saturated 0.0 g
trans 0.0 g
polyunsaturated 0.5 g
monounsaturated 1.0 g
cholesterol 31 mg
sodium 200 mg
carbohydrates 19 g
fiber 4 g
sugars 9 g
protein 17 g
dietary exchanges
½ starch
2 vegetable
2 very lean meat

Meanwhile, in a large stockpot, melt the margarine over medium-high heat, swirling to coat the bottom. Stir in the onion, carrot, and pepper. Cook for about 3 minutes, or until tender, stirring occasionally.

Stir in the remaining ingredients except the Cheddar. Increase the heat to high and bring to a boil. Reduce the heat and simmer for 10 minutes, stirring occasionally.

Ladle the soup into bowls. Stand a tortilla half in each bowl. Sprinkle the soup with the Cheddar.

pizza soup

SERVES 4 · 1¾ cups per serving
PREPARATION TIME · 5 minutes
COOKING TIME · 14 minutes

You can make this robust soup in less time than it takes to have a pizza delivered. The soup is a lot more nutritious—and costs less, too.

3 ounces Italian turkey sausage, casing discarded

1 teaspoon bottled minced garlic or 2 medium garlic cloves, minced

¾ cup chopped green bell pepper

½ cup chopped onion

8 ounces presliced fresh button mushrooms

3 cups fat-free, low-sodium chicken broth

1 15-ounce can no-salt-added chick-peas, rinsed and drained

1 14.5-ounce can no-salt-added diced tomatoes, undrained

1 teaspoon dried basil, crumbled

½ teaspoon dried oregano, crumbled

½ teaspoon crushed red pepper flakes

¼ teaspoon salt

In a 4-quart stockpot, cook the sausage and garlic over medium heat for 5 minutes, breaking the sausage into small pieces with a spoon as it cooks.

Stir in the bell pepper, onion, and mushrooms. Increase the heat to high. Cook until the vegetables have softened, about 6 minutes, stirring occasionally.

Stir in the remaining ingredients. Bring to a boil, covered, about 3 minutes.

PER SERVING
calories 214
total fat 3.0 g
saturated 0.5 g
trans 0.0 g
polyunsaturated 1.0 g
monounsaturated 1.0 g
cholesterol 18 mg
sodium 391 mg
carbohydrates 31 g
fiber 7 g
sugars 7 g
protein 14 g
dietary exchanges
1½ starch
2 vegetable
1 very lean meat

Spaghetti Soup

SERVES 5 · 1¹/₃ cups per serving

Break 2 to 3 ounces dried vermicelli into small pieces. Prepare using the package directions, omitting the salt and oil. Drain and add to the soup. Lots of pasta makes a very thick, stewy soup; less just adds a nice "chew."

broccoli and cannellini bean soup

SERVES 5 · 1½ cups per serving
PREPARATION TIME · 8 minutes
COOKING TIME · 17 to 20 minutes

all-in-one

Soup's on! This colorful and creamy soup is a delicious way to eat your veggies.

1 teaspoon olive oil

1 cup chopped onion

1 teaspoon bottled minced garlic or 2 medium garlic cloves, minced

4 cups fat-free, low-sodium chicken broth

12 ounces fresh broccoli florets

2 15-ounce cans no-salt-added cannellini beans, rinsed and drained, divided use

¼ teaspoon salt

¼ teaspoon pepper

1 teaspoon red hot-pepper sauce (plus more as needed)

½ cup fat-free half-and-half

⅓ cup shredded or grated Parmesan cheese

In a large saucepan or Dutch oven, heat the oil over medium-high heat, swirling to coat the bottom. Cook the onion for 3 minutes, or until soft, stirring frequently.

Stir in the garlic. Cook for 30 seconds, stirring frequently.

Pour in the broth. Cook, still over medium-high heat, for 5 to 6 minutes, or until the mixture comes to a boil, stirring occasionally.

Stir in the broccoli. Cook, covered, for 7 to 8 minutes, or until tender, stirring occasionally.

Stir in 1 can of beans, the salt, pepper, and 1 teaspoon hot-pepper sauce.

PER SERVING
calories 223
total fat 4.0 g
saturated 1.0 g
trans 0.0 g
polyunsaturated 1.0 g
monounsaturated 1.5 g
cholesterol 4 mg
sodium 363 mg
carbohydrates 33 g
fiber 9 g
sugars 5 g
protein 15 g
dietary exchanges
2 starch
1 vegetable
1 lean meat

In a food processor or blender, process the soup in batches until smooth. Carefully return the soup to the saucepan. Stir in the half-and-half, Parmesan cheese, and remaining 1 can beans. Cook over medium heat for 1 to 2 minutes, or until heated through, stirring constantly. Serve with additional hot-pepper sauce if desired.

COOK'S TIP ON PUREEING SOUPS

Making creamy soups right in the saucepan is a breeze when you use a hand blender, also known as an immersion blender. This wand-shaped gadget with a blender blade at the bottom has become a staple in many kitchens. It's easy to use and less messy than transferring the soup between the saucepan and a blender or food processor.

white bean and pasta soup

SERVES 4 · 1 cup per serving

· PREPARATION TIME · 5 minutes

COOKING TIME · 10 minutes

For a taste of Italy in minutes, prepare this simple vegetarian soup. Serve with a hearty whole-grain bread.

3 cups low-sodium vegetable broth

1 15-ounce can no-salt-added Great Northern beans, rinsed and drained

1 cup no-salt-added canned diced tomatoes, drained

½ teaspoon dried oregano, crumbled

½ cup dried whole-grain medium pasta shells

1 tablespoon plus 1 teaspoon shredded or grated Parmesan cheese

In a large saucepan, stir together the broth, beans, tomatoes, and oregano. Bring to a boil over medium heat.

Stir in the pasta. Cook, partially covered, for 7 minutes, or until the pasta is just cooked through. Serve sprinkled with the Parmesan.

PER SERVING
calories 158
total fat 1.5 g
saturated 0.5 g
trans 0.0 g
polyunsaturated 0.0 g
monounsaturated 0.0 g
cholesterol 1 mg
sodium 131 mg
carbohydrates 28 g
fiber 8 g
sugars 3 g
protein 9 g
dietary exchanges
1½ starch
1 vegetable
½ very lean meat

COOK'S TIP

If you expect to have leftovers, you may want to save the liquid you drain from the tomatoes. When the soup is refrigerated, the pasta will tend to absorb the liquid. The tomato liquid is good for returning the leftovers to the proper soupy consistency. You can also use water or more broth.

COOK'S TIP

Substitute a can of no-salt-added mixed beans, rinsed and drained, for the Great Northern beans, and add 1 cup frozen green beans to the mix. You'll have enough soup for five one-cup servings.

salads

Mixed Salad Greens and Fruit with
   Fresh Strawberry Vinaigrette

Red and Greens Salad

Warm Napa Slaw
   Warm Napa Slaw with Chicken

Sweet and Spicy Slaw

Italian Asparagus Salad

Marinated Vegetable Salad
   with Poppy Seed Dressing

Marinated Roasted Beets

Pear and Goat Cheese Salad

Mixed Fruit Salad
   with Raspberry Vinaigrette

Peach Fans on Blackberry-Lime
   Sauce
   Pear Fans on Raspberry Sauce

Orange-Pineapple Gelatin Salad
   Lime-Pineapple Gelatin Salad

Strawberry-Mango Salsa
   Peach-Berry Salsa

Barley and Vegetable Salad

Bulgur Salad with Avocado
   and Tomatoes

Herbed Brown Rice Salad

German Potato Salad

Mexican Potato Salad

Edamame, Salmon, and Pasta Salad

Citrus Pesto Tuna

Italian Bean and Tuna Salad

Island Shrimp Salad

Chicken and Grapefruit Salad

Asian Chicken and Wild Rice Salad

Southwestern Chicken Salad

Salad Greens with Chicken,
   Mandarin Oranges, and Asian
   Vinaigrette

Thai Beef Salad

Beef Salad with Vinaigrette Dressing
   *Beef Salad with Horseradish
   Dressing*

Vegetarian Taco Salad

Fresh Herb Couscous Salad

Orzo Salad with Green Peas
   and Artichokes

mixed salad greens and fruit with fresh strawberry vinaigrette

SERVES 4 · 2¼ cups per serving
PREPARATION TIME · 10 minutes
COOKING TIME · 4 minutes

Serve this brilliantly colored salad of mixed salad greens, blueberries, mandarin oranges, and pears with Grilled Sirloin with Honey-Mustard Marinade (page 176).

STRAWBERRY VINAIGRETTE

2 cups strawberries, stemmed
¼ cup sugar
¼ cup raspberry vinegar

SALAD

3 tablespoons sliced almonds
8 ounces mixed salad greens
1 11-ounce can mandarin oranges in water or juice, well drained
1 large pear, thinly sliced
1 cup blueberries or quartered strawberries
½ cup thinly sliced red onion

In a food processor or blender, process the vinaigrette ingredients until smooth.

In a small skillet, dry-roast the almonds over medium heat for about 4 minutes, or until just fragrant, stirring frequently. Remove from the skillet so they don't burn.

Just before serving, arrange the salad greens on plates. Drizzle with the vinaigrette. Top with the remaining ingredients.

PER SERVING

calories 200
total fat 2.5 g
  saturated 0.0 g
  trans 0.0 g
  polyunsaturated 1.0 g
  monounsaturated 1.5 g
cholesterol 0 mg
sodium 21 mg
carbohydrates 45 g
  fiber 7 g
  sugars 34 g
protein 3 g
dietary exchanges
  2 fruit
  1 carbohydrate
  ½ fat

red and greens salad

SERVES 4 · 1³/₄ cups per serving
PREPARATION TIME · 8 to 10 minutes
COOKING TIME · 4 minutes

With its sweet and sour crunch, this salad is sure to be a winner at your table.

2 tablespoons chopped walnuts
6 cups torn romaine
1 cup frozen green peas, thawed
¼ cup chopped red onion
¼ cup dried sweetened cranberries
2 tablespoons lemon juice

1 tablespoon whole-grain mustard
½ teaspoon bottled minced garlic
   or 1 medium garlic clove, minced
2 teaspoons olive oil (extra-virgin preferred)
2 teaspoons honey

In a small skillet, dry-roast the walnuts over medium heat for about 4 minutes, or until just fragrant, stirring frequently. Remove from the skillet so they don't burn.

In a salad bowl, gently toss together the romaine, peas, onion, and cranberries.

In a small bowl, whisk together the lemon juice, mustard, garlic, oil, and honey. Drizzle over the salad. Toss gently.

Sprinkle with the walnuts.

PER SERVING
calories 131
total fat 5.0 g
saturated 0.5 g
trans 0.0 g
polyunsaturated 2.0 g
monounsaturated 2.0 g
cholesterol 0 mg
sodium 137 mg
carbohydrates 19 g
fiber 4 g
sugars 12 g
protein 4 g
dietary exchanges
1½ carbohydrate
1 fat

COOK'S TIP
You can substitute 3 or 4 thinly sliced strawberries for the dried cranberries if you prefer.

warm napa slaw

SERVES 6 · 1 cup per serving
PREPARATION TIME · 15 minutes
COOKING TIME · 7 minutes

This versatile Asian-flavored slaw can be as mild or as spicy as you like. Use it as a salad, or add chicken and serve over rice for a main dish (recipe on page 65).

6 cups slivered cabbage (napa preferred)

1 tablespoon canola or corn oil

2 tablespoons sesame seeds

6 medium green onions, sliced

1 teaspoon bottled minced garlic or 2 medium garlic cloves, minced

1/4 cup fat-free, low-sodium chicken broth or water

2 tablespoons vinegar (plain rice vinegar preferred)

1 to 1 1/2 teaspoons soy sauce (lowest sodium available)

1/8 teaspoon crushed red pepper flakes, or to taste (optional)

1 teaspoon red hot-pepper sauce, or to taste (optional)

Put the cabbage in a large serving bowl. Set aside.

In a medium skillet, heat the oil over medium-high heat. Cook the sesame seeds for 1 minute, or until they begin to brown, stirring constantly with a long-handled spoon (be careful—sesame seeds will "spit").

Stir in the green onions and garlic. Cook for 1 minute, or until aromatic, stirring frequently.

Stir in the broth, vinegar, soy sauce, and red pepper flakes. Boil for 1 to 2 minutes, or until the liquid is reduced to about 3 tablespoons. Pour over the cabbage. Toss to blend. Drizzle with the hot-pepper sauce.

PER SERVING
calories 67
total fat 4.0 g
saturated 0.5 g
trans 0.0 g
polyunsaturated 1.5 g
monounsaturated 2.0 g
cholesterol 0 mg
sodium 46 mg
carbohydrates 5 g
fiber 2 g
sugars 2 g
protein 2 g
dietary exchanges
1 vegetable
1 fat

Warm Napa Slaw with Chicken

SERVES 5 · 1½ cups per serving

Prepare ⅔ cup uncooked brown rice using the package directions, omitting the salt and margarine. Meanwhile, cut 2 boneless, skinless chicken breast halves (about 4 ounces each) into slivers. Add them to the skillet after browning the sesame seeds and cooking the green onions and garlic as directed on page 64. Cook for 2 minutes, stirring constantly. Stir in the broth, vinegar, soy sauce, and red pepper flakes and simmer for 2 to 3 minutes, or until the chicken is no longer pink in the center, stirring occasionally. Pour over the cabbage and toss. Serve over the rice.

page 64

PER SERVING

calories 212
total fat 5.5 g
 saturated 0.5 g
 trans 0.0 g
 polyunsaturated 2.0 g
 monounsaturated 3.0 g
cholesterol 26 mg
sodium 85 mg
carbohydrates 24 g
 fiber 3 g
 sugars 2 g
protein 14 g
dietary exchanges
 1½ starch
 1 vegetable
 1½ very lean meat
 1 fat

COOK'S TIP ON CHINESE CABBAGE

There are many kinds of Chinese cabbage, and they seem to have multiple names. Don't worry. You can use Chinese cabbages interchangeably. They are usually milder than hard-headed green cabbage, but even that, and savoy cabbage, can be used in this recipe.

Napa cabbage has pale, crinkly green leaves. It's easy to prepare: Stack the leaves and thinly slice, starting at the tip end and working back toward the root end. The closer you get to that end, the narrower you should cut the cabbage. Then you won't have large bites of tough stem.

sweet and spicy slaw

SERVES 6 · ²/₃ cup per serving
PREPARATION TIME · 4 minutes

This sweet-hot slaw gets its "attitude" from a combination of several highly flavored ingredients.

3 cups packaged shredded cabbage
   and carrot slaw
½ cup packaged matchstick carrots
⅓ cup dried sweetened cranberries
1 medium fresh jalapeño, cut into
   thin rounds

2 tablespoons sugar
2 tablespoons cider vinegar
2 teaspoons canola or corn oil
1 teaspoon grated orange zest

In a medium bowl, stir together all the ingredients. Serve immediately for peak flavor.

COOK'S TIP
For a milder slaw, cut the jalapeño in half lengthwise, discard the ribs and seeds, then chop the pepper.

PER SERVING

calories 67
total fat 1.5 g
   saturated 0.0 g
   trans 0.0 g
   polyunsaturated 0.5 g
   monounsaturated 1.0 g
cholesterol 0 mg
sodium 15 mg
carbohydrates 13 g
   fiber 1 g
   sugars 11 g
protein 1 g
dietary exchanges
   1 carbohydrate
   ½ fat

italian asparagus salad

SERVES 6 · $\frac{1}{2}$ cup per serving
PREPARATION TIME · 7 to 8 minutes
COOKING TIME · 10 to 12 minutes

This colorful and crisp medley of fresh vegetables is easy enough to prepare for everyday meals, yet elegant enough for guests.

1 pound asparagus spears (about 24), trimmed
$\frac{1}{2}$ cup chopped red onion
$\frac{1}{2}$ cup chopped red bell pepper
$\frac{1}{4}$ cup chopped fresh basil (about $\frac{2}{3}$ ounce before removing stems)

$\frac{1}{4}$ cup light balsamic vinaigrette
2 tablespoons shredded or grated Parmesan cheese
2 tablespoons pine nuts, dry-roasted if desired

In a skillet large enough to hold the asparagus in a single layer, bring 1 inch of water to a boil over high heat. Spread the asparagus evenly in the skillet. Cook for 2 minutes. Using tongs, carefully transfer the asparagus to a colander. Run under cold water for 1 to 2 minutes, or until cool. Dry the asparagus well on paper towels. Cut the asparagus into 1-inch pieces. Transfer to a medium bowl.

Stir in the onion, bell pepper, and basil.

Just before serving, add the vinaigrette, tossing to coat. Top with the Parmesan and pine nuts. Serve immediately for peak flavor.

PER SERVING
calories 52
total fat 2.0 g
saturated 0.5 g
trans 0.0 g
polyunsaturated 0.5 g
monounsaturated 0.5 g
cholesterol 1 mg
sodium 126 mg
carbohydrates 7 g
fiber 2 g
sugars 4 g
protein 3 g
dietary exchanges
1 vegetable
$\frac{1}{2}$ fat

marinated vegetable salad with poppy seed dressing

SERVES 6 · $\frac{1}{2}$ cup per serving

PREPARATION TIME · 12 to 15 minutes

CHILLING TIME · 30 to 60 minutes

Unlike many other poppy seed dressings, the one used in this fresh vegetable salad is sweet and sour.

SALAD

1 small unpeeled zucchini (about 4 ounces), cut crosswise into $\frac{1}{8}$-inch slices

$\frac{1}{2}$ medium red, yellow, or orange bell pepper, chopped

$\frac{1}{2}$ cup preshredded carrots

$\frac{1}{2}$ cup grape tomatoes, halved

$\frac{1}{2}$ cup frozen corn, thawed

$\frac{1}{4}$ medium red onion, sliced into rings and quartered (about $\frac{1}{2}$ cup)

DRESSING

2 tablespoons sugar

2 tablespoons plain rice vinegar

2 tablespoons water

2 teaspoons olive oil (extra-virgin preferred)

1 teaspoon poppy seeds

In a medium bowl, toss together all the salad ingredients.

In a small bowl, whisk together the dressing ingredients. Pour over the salad. Stir gently to coat. Cover and refrigerate for 30 minutes to 1 hour, stirring occasionally.

PER SERVING
calories 61
total fat 2.0 g
saturated 0.5 g
trans 0.0 g
polyunsaturated 0.5 g
monounsaturated 1.0 g
cholesterol 0 mg
sodium 12 mg
carbohydrates 11 g
fiber 1 g
sugars 7 g
protein 1 g
dietary exchanges
$\frac{1}{2}$ starch
1 vegetable
$\frac{1}{2}$ fat

marinated roasted beets

SERVES 4 · ½ cup per serving
PREPARATION TIME · 6 to 8 minutes
COOKING TIME · 26 to 32 minutes
COOLING TIME · 10 minutes
CHILLING TIME · 2 to 24 hours

Zesty, tangy, and naturally sweet—this salad is all those rolled into one.

4 medium beets with greens

1 teaspoon olive oil

⅓ cup cider vinegar

⅓ cup red wine vinegar

⅓ cup chopped onion

¼ teaspoon ground cloves

¼ teaspoon ground cinnamon

¼ teaspoon pepper (coarsely ground preferred)

Preheat the oven to 425°F.

Cut off all but 1 to 2 inches of the beet stems, and don't cut off the root ends. (This helps retain flavor and keep the color from bleeding.) Put the beets on a rimmed baking sheet. Drizzle with the oil.

Roast for 25 to 30 minutes, or until the beets are tender when tested with the tip of a knife. Let cool on the baking sheet for 10 minutes. Discard the root ends. Peel the beets, discarding the skins. Cut the beets crosswise into ⅛- to ¼-inch slices. Place the beets in a single layer in a shallow glass dish, such as 12 x 8 x 2 inches.

In a small saucepan, stir together the remaining ingredients. Heat over medium-high heat until the mixture comes to a boil, 1 to 2 minutes. Pour over the beets, making sure all the beets are coated. Cover and refrigerate for 2 to 24 hours, stirring once or twice if all the beets are not covered in liquid. Drain and discard the marinade before serving the beets.

COOK'S TIP ON FRESH BEETS

Red beets can stain, so you might want to wear an apron and plastic gloves when peeling and cutting the cooked beets. If you don't use gloves, you can sprinkle your hands with salt and rub them vigorously, then wash them with soap and water to eliminate stains.

PER SERVING

calories 56
total fat 1.5 g
  saturated 0.0 g
  trans 0.0 g
  polyunsaturated 0.0 g
  monounsaturated 1.0 g
cholesterol 0 mg
sodium 66 mg
carbohydrates 10 g
  fiber 3 g
  sugars 7 g
protein 2 g
dietary exchanges
  2 vegetable

pear and goat cheese salad

Crunchy pecans and a mildly tart dressing enhance juicy, sweet pears topped with tangy goat cheese.

¼ cup pecans (about 1 ounce)

4 Bartlett or Anjou pears

2 ounces soft goat cheese, cut into 8 pieces

4 cups chopped or torn salad greens

2 tablespoons balsamic vinegar

1 teaspoon sugar (optional)

1 tablespoon olive oil (extra-virgin preferred)

In a small skillet, dry-roast the pecans over medium heat for about 4 minutes, or until just fragrant, stirring frequently. Remove from the skillet so they don't burn.

Meanwhile, cut the pears in half lengthwise and discard the stems. Using a melon baller, remove the seeds and make a small, round cavity in each pear half.

Finely chop the pecans. Put the pecans on a large plate.

Shape each piece of goat cheese into a ball. Roll the balls in the pecans. Place one ball in each pear cavity.

Arrange the salad greens on plates. Place the pears on the salad greens. Sprinkle with any remaining pecans.

Put the vinegar in a small bowl. Add the sugar, whisking to dissolve.

Pour in the oil in a fine stream, whisking constantly until smooth. Drizzle over the pears.

PER SERVING
calories 117
total fat 6.0 g
saturated 1.5 g
trans 0.0 g
polyunsaturated 1.0 g
monounsaturated 3.0 g
cholesterol 3 mg
sodium 35 mg
carbohydrates 16 g
fiber 4 g
sugars 10 g
protein 2 g
dietary exchanges
1 fruit
1 fat

mixed fruit salad with raspberry vinaigrette

SERVES 8 · $1/2$ cup per serving
PREPARATION TIME · 10 minutes

Experiment with different varieties of apple and with seasonal fruit when you make this refreshing salad.

1 large Fuji or Granny Smith apple, thinly sliced

8 ounces strawberries, stemmed and thinly sliced

3 small plums, thinly sliced

2 tablespoons dried sweetened cherries or other dried fruit

$1^1/2$ to 2 tablespoons fat-free or light raspberry vinaigrette

In a medium bowl, toss together all the ingredients.

COOK'S TIP
In addition to varying the dried fruit, you can make flavor changes by substituting fruit nectar, such as apricot, or fat-free mango salad dressing for the raspberry vinaigrette.

PER SERVING
calories 44
total fat 0.0 g
saturated 0.0 g
trans 0.0 g
polyunsaturated 0.0 g
monounsaturated 0.0 g
cholesterol 0 mg
sodium 36 mg
carbohydrates 11 g
fiber 2 g
sugars 8 g
protein 1 g
dietary exchanges
$1/2$ fruit

peach fans on blackberry-lime sauce

SERVES 6 · ³/₄ cup per serving
PREPARATION TIME · 15 minutes
COOKING TIME · 1 to 2 minutes
CHILLING TIME · 30 minutes to 24 hours

As a first course or light dessert, this dish is a showpiece!

³/₄ cup all-fruit seedless blackberry spread (about 8 ounces)

2 tablespoons lime juice

¼ teaspoon grated peeled gingerroot (optional)

1¼ to 1½ pounds peaches

18 whole medium strawberries with stems (about 1 pint)

In a small saucepan over medium-high heat, heat the blackberry spread for 1 to 2 minutes, or until just melted, whisking constantly. Remove from the heat.

Whisk in the lime juice and gingerroot. Transfer to a small bowl. Cover and refrigerate for 30 minutes to 24 hours.

Peel and slice the peaches. Halve the strawberries lengthwise. If you cut the stem in half, too, you'll have a prettier presentation.

Spoon 2 tablespoons blackberry mixture onto the center of a salad or dessert plate. Rotate the plate to spread the sauce to about a 6-inch circle. Alternating peaches and strawberries, arrange the fruit accordion-style on the sauce. Repeat for each serving.

PER SERVING
calories 128
total fat 0.5 g
saturated 0.0 g
trans 0.0 g
polyunsaturated 0.0 g
monounsaturated 0.0 g
cholesterol 0 mg
sodium 1 mg
carbohydrates 32 g
fiber 2 g
sugars 25 g
protein 1 g
dietary exchanges 2 fruit

Pear Fans on Raspberry Sauce

Replace the blackberry spread with seedless raspberry spread and omit the lime juice. Replace the peaches with 2 large pears, and replace the strawberries with 3 peeled green kiwifruit, each cut lengthwise into sixths.

COOK'S TIP

You can slice peaches or pears up to 1 hour in advance. To prevent browning, stir in 1 to 1½ tablespoons lime juice. (Even though there's no lime juice in Pear Fans on Raspberry Sauce, you can treat the pears with some to keep them from turning brown.) Don't stir. Cover with plastic wrap and refrigerate. Too much lime juice will cause the fruit to "cook" and become mushy. Arrange the fruit slices immediately before serving.

orange-pineapple gelatin salad

SERVES 8 · ¹/₂ cup per serving
PREPARATION TIME · 10 minutes
COOKING TIME · 1 minute
CHILLING TIME · 4 hours

Buttermilk heightens the flavors of the fruit in this kid- and adult-pleasing salad or dessert.

1 8-ounce can crushed pineapple in its own juice, undrained

1 0.3-ounce box (4-serving size) sugar-free orange or mixed-fruit gelatin

1 11-ounce can mandarin oranges in water or juice, well drained

1 cup low-fat buttermilk

4 ounces frozen fat-free whipped topping, thawed in the refrigerator (about 1¹/₂ cups)

8 lettuce leaves (optional)

2 cups Bing cherries or seedless red grapes (about 12 ounces of either) (optional)

In a small saucepan, bring the pineapple with liquid to a boil over high heat, about 1 minute. Remove from the heat. Stir in the gelatin until completely dissolved, about 1 minute. Pour into an 8- or 9-inch square glass baking dish and put in the freezer for 5 to 8 minutes, or until beginning to set around the edges.

Stir in the oranges and buttermilk. Gently fold in the whipped topping until well blended.

Chill, covered, until set, about 4 hours. Cut into 8 pieces. Serve on the lettuce leaves. Garnish with the cherries.

PER SERVING
calories 70
total fat 0.5 g
saturated 0.0 g
trans 0.0 g
polyunsaturated 0.0 g
monounsaturated 0.0 g
cholesterol 1 mg
sodium 44 mg
carbohydrates 14 g
fiber 1 g
sugars 10 g
protein 2 g
dietary exchanges
1 carbohydrate

Lime-Pineapple Gelatin Salad

Substitute lime or lemon gelatin for the
orange or mixed-fruit gelatin, fat-free sour
cream for the buttermilk, and fat-free vanilla
yogurt for the whipped topping.

PER SERVING

calories 77
total fat 0.0 g
  saturated 0.0 g
  trans 0.0 g
  polyunsaturated 0.0 g
  monounsaturated 0.0 g
cholesterol 5 mg
sodium 39 mg
carbohydrates 16 g
  fiber 1 g
  sugars 11 g
protein 4 g
dietary exchanges
  1 carbohydrate

strawberry-mango salsa

SERVES 6 · $1/2$ cup per serving
PREPARATION TIME · 20 minutes

This exciting, inviting fruit salad is especially delicious served with grilled pork or chicken.

$1/4$ cup lime juice

2 tablespoons sugar

1 teaspoon grated peeled gingerroot

1 medium mango, diced, or 1 cup diced refrigerated or frozen mango slices, thawed

2 cups diced strawberries (about 1 pint)

1 to 2 tablespoons finely snipped fresh cilantro

1 medium fresh jalapeño, seeds and ribs discarded, finely chopped

In a medium bowl, whisk together the lime juice, sugar, and gingerroot.

Stir in the remaining ingredients. Serve at room temperature or cover and refrigerate for up to 1 hour. (Flavors are at their peak if the salad is served within 1 hour.)

PER SERVING
calories 60
total fat 0.5 g
saturated 0.0 g
trans 0.0 g
polyunsaturated 0.0 g
monounsaturated 0.0 g
cholesterol 0 mg
sodium 2 mg
carbohydrates 15 g
fiber 2 g
sugars 12 g
protein 1 g
dietary exchanges 1 fruit

Peach-Berry Salsa

Replace the strawberries with peaches, the mango with blueberries or raspberries, the lime juice with lemon juice, and the cilantro with mint. Omit the jalapeño.

PER SERVING
calories 58
total fat 0.0 g
saturated 0.0 g
trans 0.0 g
polyunsaturated 0.0 g
monounsaturated 0.0 g
cholesterol 0 mg
sodium 1 mg
carbohydrates 15 g
fiber 2 g
sugars 12 g
protein 1 g
dietary exchanges 1 fruit

COOK'S TIP ON HOT CHILE PEPPERS

Hot peppers—such as jalapeño, Anaheim, serrano, and poblano—contain oils that can burn your skin, lips, and eyes. Wear disposable gloves or wash your hands thoroughly with warm, soapy water immediately after handling such peppers.

barley and vegetable salad

SERVES 4 · heaping 1/2 cup per serving
PREPARATION TIME · 10 minutes
COOKING TIME · 10 to 12 minutes
STANDING TIME · 5 minutes
COOLING TIME · 5 minutes

Brimming with color and texture, this substantial side salad will keep for up to four days in the refrigerator.

1½ cups water
½ cup uncooked quick-cooking barley
¼ teaspoon salt
2 ounces fresh asparagus
¼ cup bottled roasted red bell peppers, drained
1 medium green onion, thinly sliced

½ cup shredded red cabbage
1 tablespoon crumbled feta cheese
2 teaspoons olive oil (extra-virgin preferred)
2 teaspoons lemon juice
½ teaspoon dried oregano, crumbled
½ teaspoon sugar

In a medium saucepan, bring the water to a boil over high heat. Stir in the barley and salt. Cook, covered, for 10 to 12 minutes, or until the barley is tender.

Meanwhile, trim the asparagus, discarding the trimmed portion. Cut the spears into 1-inch pieces. Drain and chop the roasted peppers.

Stir the asparagus into the cooked barley. Remove from the heat and let stand, covered, for 5 minutes. Drain any remaining liquid from the barley mixture. Let cool, uncovered, for 5 minutes.

In a large bowl, stir together the remaining ingredients. Stir in the barley mixture. Serve or cover and refrigerate until needed.

PER SERVING

calories 105
total fat 3.0 g
  saturated 1.0 g
  trans 0.0 g
  polyunsaturated 0.5 g
  monounsaturated 2.0 g
cholesterol 2 mg
sodium 186 mg
carbohydrates 17 g
  fiber 3 g
  sugars 2 g
protein 3 g
dietary exchanges
  1 starch
  ½ fat

COOK'S TIP ON BARLEY
Look for quick-cooking barley in the cereal section at the grocery store.

bulgur salad with avocado and tomatoes

SERVES 6 · $1/2$ cup per serving
PREPARATION TIME · 7 minutes
COOKING TIME · 9 minutes

Cooking bulgur with turmeric turns it a bright yellow that contrasts nicely with the red and green of this zesty salad.

1 cup water
$1/8$ to $1/4$ teaspoon ground turmeric
$1/2$ cup uncooked bulgur
1 medium avocado, diced
1 cup grape tomatoes, quartered
$1/4$ cup snipped fresh cilantro
1 teaspoon grated lemon zest

2 tablespoons lemon juice
2 teaspoons olive oil (extra-virgin preferred)
$1/2$ teaspoon bottled minced garlic or 1 medium garlic clove, minced
$1/8$ teaspoon salt
1 medium lemon, cut into 6 wedges

In a medium saucepan, bring the water and turmeric to a boil over high heat. Stir in the bulgur. Reduce the heat and simmer, covered, for 8 minutes, or until the bulgur is slightly firm and the water is almost evaporated. Pour into a fine-mesh strainer and run under cold water to cool completely. Shake off any excess liquid.

Meanwhile, in a medium bowl, gently toss together the remaining ingredients except the lemon wedges. Add the bulgur, tossing gently to combine. Serve with the lemon wedges to squeeze over all.

PER SERVING
calories 119
total fat 6.5 g
saturated 1.0 g
trans 0.0 g
polyunsaturated 1.0 g
monounsaturated 4.5 g
cholesterol 0 mg
sodium 58 mg
carbohydrates 15 g
fiber 5 g
sugars 2 g
protein 3 g
dietary exchanges
$1/2$ starch
1 vegetable
1 fat

herbed brown rice salad

SERVES 4 · ²/₃ cup per serving
PREPARATION TIME · 8 minutes
COOKING TIME · 12 minutes
COOLING TIME · 8 minutes

For a nice change from the typical pasta or potato salad—and a different way to enjoy brown rice—try this Mediterranean side salad with a bit of Mexican heat.

½ cup uncooked instant brown rice

½ medium red bell pepper, finely chopped

1 medium jalapeño, seeds and ribs discarded if desired, finely chopped

9 kalamata olives, coarsely chopped

1½ to 2 tablespoons cider vinegar

1 tablespoon olive oil (extra-virgin preferred)

1 tablespoon snipped fresh basil

½ teaspoon bottled minced garlic or 1 medium garlic clove, minced

¼ teaspoon finely snipped fresh rosemary (optional)

4 romaine lettuce leaves

In a medium saucepan, prepare the rice using the package directions, omitting the salt and margarine. Spoon in a thin layer on a sheet of aluminum foil or baking sheet to cool quickly, about 8 minutes.

Meanwhile, in a medium bowl, stir together the remaining ingredients except the lettuce.

Stir the cooled rice into the bell pepper mixture.

Place 1 lettuce leaf on each plate. Spoon the salad onto the lettuce.

PER SERVING

calories 105
total fat 6.0 g
  saturated 0.5 g
  trans 0.0 g
  polyunsaturated 1.0 g
  monounsaturated 4.5 g
cholesterol 0 mg
sodium 142 mg
carbohydrates 11 g
  fiber 1 g
  sugars 1 g
protein 1 g
dietary exchanges
  ½ starch
  1 fat

german potato salad

SERVES 6 · ½ cup per serving
PREPARATION TIME · 10 minutes

Making potato salad is a great way to use leftover Roasted Red and White Potatoes (page 278). This version uses caraway seeds and hot mustard for a German slant.

3 cups Roasted Red and White Potatoes, at room temperature or chilled

¼ cup chopped celery

2 tablespoons cider vinegar

2 teaspoons snipped fresh dillweed

¼ teaspoon caraway seeds

2 tablespoons fat-free sour cream

1 tablespoon light mayonnaise

½ to 1 teaspoon hot German mustard

In a medium bowl, stir together the potatoes, celery, vinegar, dillweed, and caraway seeds.

In a small bowl, whisk together the sour cream, mayonnaise, and mustard. Stir into the potato mixture.

PER SERVING
calories 94
total fat 1.5 g
saturated 0.0 g
trans 0.0 g
polyunsaturated 0.5 g
monounsaturated 0.5 g
cholesterol 2 mg
sodium 122 mg
carbohydrates 18 g
fiber 2 g
sugars 2 g
protein 2 g
dietary exchanges
1 starch

mexican potato salad

SERVES 6 · ¹/₂ cup per serving
PREPARATION TIME · 10 minutes

Make this creamy potato salad wild or mild, depending on your family's preference. Starting with already-cooked Roasted Red and White Potatoes (page 278) cuts your time in the kitchen to almost nothing!

3 cups Roasted Red and White Potatoes, at room temperature or chilled

3 medium green onions, chopped

2 tablespoons lime juice

2 teaspoons snipped fresh cilantro

2 teaspoons chopped canned jalapeño or green chiles, rinsed and drained (optional)

2 tablespoons fat-free plain yogurt

2 tablespoons fat-free sour cream

In a medium bowl, stir together the potatoes, green onions, lime juice, cilantro, and jalapeño.

In a small bowl, whisk together the yogurt and sour cream. Stir into the potato mixture.

PER SERVING
calories 94
total fat 1.0 g
saturated 0.0 g
trans 0.0 g
polyunsaturated 0.0 g
monounsaturated 0.5 g
cholesterol 1 mg
sodium 107 mg
carbohydrates 19 g
fiber 3 g
sugars 3 g
protein 3 g
dietary exchanges
1¹/₂ starch

edamame, salmon, and pasta salad

SERVES 4 · 1½ cups salad and 2 tablespoons dressing per serving
PREPARATION TIME · 12 to 15 minutes
COOKING TIME · 17 to 18 minutes

The lemon and dill vinaigrette is a wonderful complement to the flavors of this salad.

4 quarts water

1⅔ cups whole-wheat bow-tie pasta or macaroni (about 4½ ounces)

1 cup frozen shelled edamame

2 5-ounce cans pink salmon in water, drained, skin discarded, bones discarded if desired, flaked

1 medium rib of celery, chopped

½ medium red onion, chopped

½ medium red bell pepper, chopped

½ cup grape tomatoes

½ teaspoon grated lemon zest

¼ cup lemon juice

2½ tablespoons water

1 tablespoon honey

1½ teaspoons olive oil (extra-virgin preferred)

1 teaspoon dried dillweed, crumbled

¼ teaspoon pepper

⅛ teaspoon salt

8 lettuce leaves

In a large saucepan, bring the water to a boil over high heat. Add the pasta. Return to a boil and boil for 4 minutes. Stir in the edamame. Boil for 3 to 4 minutes, or until the pasta is just tender. Drain well in a colander.

Meanwhile, in a large bowl, stir together the salmon, celery, onion, bell pepper, and tomatoes.

Stir the pasta mixture into the salmon mixture.

In a small bowl, whisk together the remaining ingredients except the lettuce. Pour over the salad, tossing to coat.

Place 2 lettuce leaves on each plate. Spoon the salad onto the lettuce.

PER SERVING
calories 365
total fat 7.5 g
saturated 1.0 g
trans 0.0 g
polyunsaturated 1.5 g
monounsaturated 2.0 g
cholesterol 58 mg
sodium 375 mg
carbohydrates 46 g
fiber 5 g
sugars 10 g
protein 28 g
dietary exchanges
3 starch
3 lean meat

citrus pesto tuna

SERVES 4 · ½ cup tuna mixture and 2 lettuce leaves per serving
PREPARATION TIME · 10 minutes

You won't want to go back to traditional mayonnaise-based tuna salad after experiencing the fresh crispness of this citrusy version.

PESTO

⅓ cup tightly packed fresh basil (about ¾ ounce before removing stems)

½ teaspoon bottled minced garlic or 1 medium garlic clove

½ teaspoon dried oregano

2 teaspoons olive oil (extra-virgin preferred)

1 teaspoon lemon zest

2 tablespoons lemon juice

2 tablespoons orange juice

¼ teaspoon salt

¼ teaspoon pepper

• • •

1 medium rib of celery, chopped

1 medium green onion (green and white parts), chopped

12 ounces canned very low sodium chunk white albacore tuna, packed in water, drained and flaked

8 lettuce leaves

In a food processor or blender, pulse the basil, garlic, and oregano until finely chopped. Add the oil, lemon zest, lemon juice, orange juice, salt, and pepper, pulsing to blend.

In a medium bowl, gently stir together the celery, green onion, and tuna.

Pour in the pesto. Stir gently to combine. Spoon onto the lettuce leaves.

> **COOK'S TIP**
> This versatile tuna salad is equally good whether served on lettuce, spooned onto a tomato half, or used as a sandwich filling on low-sodium whole-grain bread.

PER SERVING
calories 144
total fat 5.0 g
saturated 1.0 g
trans 0.0 g
polyunsaturated 1.0 g
monounsaturated 2.5 g
cholesterol 36 mg
sodium 199 mg
carbohydrates 3 g
fiber 1 g
sugars 2 g
protein 21 g
dietary exchanges
3 lean meat

italian bean and tuna salad

SERVES 4 · 1¹/₂ cups per serving
PREPARATION TIME · 13 minutes

Flavors of the Mediterranean are blended in this simple, easy-to-love salad. Serve it as is or on lettuce.

2 15-ounce cans no-salt-added cannellini beans or reduced-sodium Great Northern beans, rinsed and drained

2 5- or 6-ounce cans very low sodium white tuna packed in water, drained

¹/₂ to 1 cup finely chopped red onion

¹/₄ cup plus 2 tablespoons snipped fresh parsley or 2 tablespoons chopped fresh basil

¹/₄ cup to ¹/₄ cup plus 2 tablespoons balsamic vinegar

2 tablespoons olive oil (extra-virgin preferred)

¹/₂ teaspoon pepper

In a medium bowl, stir together the beans, tuna, onion, parsley, and vinegar.

Drizzle with the oil. Sprinkle with the pepper.

island shrimp salad

SERVES 4 · about 1½ cups salad and 2 to 3 ounces shrimp per serving
PREPARATION TIME · 20 minutes
MARINATING TIME · 10 minutes
COOKING TIME · 3 to 4 minutes

Island breezes are sure to stir, even in winter, when you serve this salad.

1 tablespoon dark or light brown sugar

1 teaspoon ground allspice

1 teaspoon garlic powder

1 teaspoon black pepper

¼ teaspoon cayenne

¼ teaspoon salt

2 tablespoons fresh lime juice

1 tablespoon light or dark molasses

1 teaspoon olive oil and 2 teaspoons olive oil, divided use

1 pound raw medium shrimp, peeled, rinsed and patted dry

Cooking spray

5 cups very lightly packed torn salad greens

½ medium red bell pepper, diced

1 8-ounce can pineapple tidbits in their own juice, drained, 2 tablespoons juice reserved

1 tablespoon cider vinegar

2 teaspoons honey

In a medium bowl, stir together the brown sugar, allspice, garlic powder, black pepper, cayenne, and salt. Whisk in the lime juice, molasses, and 1 teaspoon olive oil. Add the shrimp and toss to coat well. Cover and refrigerate for 10 minutes.

Meanwhile, preheat the broiler. Lightly spray the broiler pan with cooking spray.

Let the marinade drip off the shrimp. Place the shrimp in a single layer in the broiler pan.

Broil about 4 inches from the heat for 2 minutes. Turn over and broil for 1 to 2 minutes, or until the shrimp are pink and cooked through.

Meanwhile, in a salad bowl, gently toss the salad greens, bell pepper, and pineapple.

In a small bowl, whisk together the vinegar, honey, reserved pineapple juice, and remaining 2 teaspoons oil. Drizzle over the salad greens. Toss to combine. Top with the shrimp.

PER SERVING
calories 138
total fat 1.0 g
saturated 0.5 g
trans 0.0 g
polyunsaturated 0.5 g
monounsaturated 0.0 g
cholesterol 168 mg
sodium 362 mg
carbohydrates 13 g
fiber 2 g
sugars 11 g
protein 19 g
dietary exchanges
1 carbohydrate
3 very lean meat

chicken and grapefruit salad

SERVES 4 · 2¹/₂ cups per serving
PREPARATION TIME · 15 minutes
COOKING TIME · 8 minutes

A mildly spicy vinaigrette tops mixed salad greens, soy-brushed chicken, and tangy grapefruit.

SALAD

1 teaspoon canola or corn oil

4 boneless, skinless chicken breast halves (about 4 ounces each), all visible fat discarded

1 tablespoon soy sauce (lowest sodium available)

8 cups mixed salad greens

1 cup grapefruit sections

¹/₂ cup thinly sliced red onion (about 2 ounces)

DRESSING

²/₃ cup grapefruit juice

1¹/₂ tablespoons honey

2 teaspoons cider vinegar

¹/₂ teaspoon crushed red pepper flakes

In a large nonstick skillet, heat the oil over medium-high heat, swirling to coat the bottom. Cook the chicken for 3 minutes. Brush the tops with half the soy sauce. Turn over. Cook for 4 minutes, or until the chicken is no longer pink in the center. Using a clean brush, brush the tops with the remaining soy sauce. Transfer to a plate and let cool slightly.

Meanwhile, arrange the salad greens on plates. Top each serving with the grapefruit and onion.

Cut the chicken into thin strips. Arrange on the salads.

In a small bowl, whisk together the dressing ingredients. Spoon over the salads.

PER SERVING
calories 221
total fat 3.0 g
saturated 0.5 g
trans 0.0 g
polyunsaturated 1.0 g
monounsaturated 1.0 g
cholesterol 66 mg
sodium 201 mg
carbohydrates 20 g
fiber 3 g
sugars 16 g
protein 30 g
dietary exchanges
1 fruit
1 vegetable
3 very lean meat

asian chicken and wild rice salad

SERVES 4 · 1¹/₄ cups per serving
PREPARATION TIME · 10 minutes
COOKING TIME · 8 minutes
COOLING TIME · 8 minutes

planned-
overs

If you can keep a secret, no one will guess that this delectable salad uses leftovers from Apricot-Barbecue Chicken Chunks (page 141) as a key ingredient.

1 7-ounce package instant white and wild rice, seasoning packet discarded

3 tablespoons soy sauce (lowest sodium available)

1¹/₂ tablespoons sugar

2 teaspoons plain rice vinegar

¹/₄ teaspoon crushed red pepper flakes, or to taste

2 cups cooked chicken from Apricot-Barbecue Chicken Chunks

1 large red or green bell pepper, chopped

1 8-ounce can sliced water chestnuts, rinsed, drained, and chopped

4 lettuce leaves (optional)

Prepare the rice using the package directions, omitting the salt, margarine, and seasoning packet. Spread the cooked rice on a baking sheet in a thin layer. Put on a cooling rack and let cool for 8 minutes, stirring occasionally.

Meanwhile, in a large bowl, whisk together the soy sauce, sugar, vinegar, and red pepper flakes. Add the chicken, bell pepper, and water chestnuts, tossing to coat.

Stir the cooled rice into the chicken mixture. Serve on the lettuce.

PER SERVING

calories 420
total fat 2.0 g
  saturated 0.5 g
  trans 0.0 g
  polyunsaturated 0.5 g
  monounsaturated 0.5 g
cholesterol 66 mg
sodium 478 mg
carbohydrates 67 g
  fiber 3 g
  sugars 21 g
protein 32 g
dietary exchanges
  2 starch
  1 vegetable
  1 carbohydrate
  2¹/₂ very lean meat

COOK'S TIP ON RICE VINEGAR

When shopping for rice vinegar, read the label carefully. If it says "Seasoned Rice Vinegar," the product may have a lot of salt added. Mild and slightly sweet, plain rice vinegar contains no sodium.

southwestern chicken salad

SERVES 6 · 1 cup per serving
PREPARATION TIME · 20 minutes
MICROWAVE TIME · 4 to 5 minutes
or
COOKING TIME · 17 minutes

Here's a new twist on chicken salad. Serve this one with baked tortilla chips on lettuce-lined plates, garnished with jalapeño rings.

CHICKEN SALAD

4 boneless, skinless chicken breast halves (about 4 ounces each), all visible fat discarded

½ medium red bell pepper

½ medium green bell pepper

¼ to ½ medium red onion

1 15-ounce can no-salt-added black beans, rinsed and drained

1 cup diced peeled jícama

½ cup snipped fresh cilantro

½ medium fresh jalapeño, seeds and ribs discarded, minced (optional)

DRESSING

3 tablespoons cider vinegar

2 tablespoons olive oil (extra-virgin preferred)

2 tablespoons orange juice

1 teaspoon ground cumin

½ teaspoon chili powder

½ teaspoon cayenne

½ teaspoon salt

If using a microwave oven, put the chicken in a 9-inch microwaveable pie plate. Cover with wax paper and microwave on 100 percent power (high) for 4 to 5 minutes, turning once halfway through. For stovetop cooking, in a large skillet, bring ½ inch water to a simmer. Cook the chicken, covered, for 15 minutes, or until the chicken is barely pink in the center. Set aside to finish cooking and to let cool.

Meanwhile, dice the bell peppers and onion. Transfer to a large bowl.

Stir in the remaining chicken salad ingredients.

PER SERVING
calories 204
total fat 6.5 g
saturated 1.0 g
trans 0.0 g
polyunsaturated 1.0 g
monounsaturated 4.0 g
cholesterol 42 mg
sodium 42 mg
carbohydrates 16 g
fiber 5 g
sugars 4 g
protein 20 g
dietary exchanges
1 starch
2½ lean meat

In a small bowl, whisk together the dressing ingredients until the salt is dissolved. Pour over the salad mixture.

Chop the chicken. Add to the salad mixture, tossing well. Serve or cover and refrigerate until needed.

COOK'S TIP ON JÍCAMA

Jícama (HEE-kah-mah) is firm and barely sweet, like a fresh water chestnut. Its texture is somewhat applelike, but its flavor is much milder. A crunchy addition to raw vegetable platters, jícama is a refreshing dipper. Peel and slice or chop—that's it.

TIME-SAVER Use 2 to 3 cups of chopped skinless leftover chicken cooked without salt instead of microwaving or poaching the chicken breast halves.

salad greens with chicken, mandarin oranges, and asian vinaigrette

SERVES 4 · 2½ cups salad and 3 ounces chicken per serving
PREPARATION TIME · 12 to 15 minutes
COOKING TIME · 7 minutes

express

A small amount of intensely flavored dressing goes a long way in this brilliantly colored salad.

4 boneless, skinless chicken breast halves (about 4 ounces each), all visible fat discarded

1 teaspoon soy sauce and 2 teaspoons soy sauce (lowest sodium available), divided use

¼ cup plus 1½ teaspoons plain rice vinegar

3 tablespoons honey or dark brown sugar

1 tablespoon toasted sesame oil

¼ to ½ teaspoon crushed red pepper flakes, or to taste

8 cups lightly packed torn salad greens

2 11-ounce cans mandarin oranges in water or juice, drained

½ cup thinly sliced red onion, separated into rings and halved

In a large nonstick skillet, cook the chicken over medium-high heat for 3 minutes. Brush the tops with 1 teaspoon soy sauce. Turn over and cook for 4 minutes, or until no longer pink in the center.

Meanwhile, in a small bowl, whisk together the vinegar, honey, oil, red pepper flakes, and remaining 2 teaspoons soy sauce.

Thinly slice or dice the chicken.

In a salad bowl, toss together the salad greens, mandarin oranges, red onion, and chicken. Drizzle with the dressing. Toss again.

PER SERVING
calories 273
total fat 5.0 g
saturated 1.0 g
trans 0.0 g
polyunsaturated 2.0 g
monounsaturated 1.5 g
cholesterol 66 mg
sodium 207 mg
carbohydrates 29 g
fiber 4 g
sugars 24 g
protein 29 g
dietary exchanges
1 fruit
1 carbohydrate
3 lean meat

COOK'S TIP ON SESAME OIL
Be sure to use toasted sesame oil (also called Asian sesame oil) in this recipe because it has more flavor than regular sesame oil. Toasted sesame oil also is darker and more fragrant.

thai beef salad

SERVES 4 · 1 cup per serving
PREPARATION TIME · 20 minutes

Turn leftover roast beef such as from Tuscan Braised Beef (page 172) into a taste adventure by adding Thai-style dressing.

SALAD

8 Boston lettuce leaves

12 ounces cooked beef from Tuscan Braised Beef or other cooked lean roast beef, cut into 1 x ½-inch strips

1 small cucumber, peeled and diced

½ small red onion, thinly sliced

Pepper to taste

DRESSING

2 tablespoons lime juice

1 tablespoon sugar

1 tablespoon no-salt-added tomato paste

1 tablespoon fish sauce

1 tablespoon canola or corn oil

1 teaspoon bottled minced garlic or 2 medium garlic cloves, minced

¼ teaspoon crushed red pepper flakes

● ● ●

1½ tablespoons snipped fresh cilantro (optional)

Arrange the lettuce leaves on salad plates.

In a medium bowl, stir together the beef, cucumber, and onion. Sprinkle with the pepper.

In a small bowl, whisk together the dressing ingredients. Stir into the beef mixture. Arrange on the lettuce. Sprinkle with the cilantro.

COOK'S TIP ON FISH SAUCE

Thin and usually brown, fish sauce is a condiment made from salted, fermented fish, most often anchovies. Its flavor and odor are pungent, so a little goes a long way. Thai fish sauce, *nam pla,* is milder than its Vietnamese counterpart, *nuoc mam* or *nuoc cham.* Check the Asian section of the supermarket for these sauces.

PER SERVING

calories 195
total fat 6.0 g
  saturated 1.5 g
  trans 0.0 g
  polyunsaturated 1.0 g
  monounsaturated 3.5 g
cholesterol 48 mg
sodium 482 mg
carbohydrates 8 g
  fiber 1 g
  sugars 5 g
protein 26 g
dietary exchanges
  ½ carbohydrate
  3 lean meat

beef salad with vinaigrette dressing

SERVES 4 · 1 cup per serving
PREPARATION TIME · 15 minutes

Here's an interesting lunch or light supper salad that uses cooked eye-of-round roast, such as leftovers from Tuscan Braised Beef (page 172), and your choice of two dressings. You can even use leftovers of the leftovers tomorrow—any extra salad makes a great filling for sandwiches.

SALAD

3 cups lightly packed arugula or mixed baby greens (about 3 ounces)

12 ounces cooked roast from Tuscan Braised Beef or other thinly sliced cooked and chilled eye-of-round roast

1/2 small red onion, thinly sliced

1 teaspoon capers, drained

1/8 teaspoon salt

Pepper to taste

VINAIGRETTE DRESSING

3 tablespoons balsamic vinegar

1/4 teaspoon Dijon mustard

1/4 teaspoon bottled minced garlic or 1 small garlic clove, minced

1 tablespoon olive oil (extra-virgin preferred)

Stack the arugula leaves on a cutting board. Cut them crosswise at 1-inch intervals. Or chop the baby greens. Arrange on salad plates.

Cut the beef slices into 1 x 1/2-inch strips. Arrange on the arugula. Sprinkle with the remaining salad ingredients.

In a small bowl, whisk together the vinegar, mustard, and garlic. Slowly whisk in the oil. Pour over the salad.

PER SERVING
calories 181
total fat 6.0 g
saturated 1.5 g
trans 0.0 g
polyunsaturated 0.5 g
monounsaturated 3.5 g
cholesterol 48 mg
sodium 237 mg
carbohydrates 5 g
fiber 1 g
sugars 3 g
protein 26 g
dietary exchanges
1/2 carbohydrate
3 lean meat

Beef Salad with Horseradish Dressing

Prepare the salad as directed on page 92, substituting 4 medium radishes, thinly sliced, for the red onion and capers. Instead of the vinaigrette dressing, whisk together ½ cup fat-free plain yogurt; 1 tablespoon light mayonnaise; 1 teaspoon grated onion or onion juice, or to taste, and 1 to 1½ teaspoons bottled white horseradish, drained.

COOK'S TIP ON BEEF YIELD

Beef shrinks about 25 percent when it cooks. To get 12 ounces of cooked meat, start with 1 pound.

vegetarian taco salad

SERVES 4 · 3 cups per serving

PREPARATION TIME · 10 minutes

Such a simple meal and such a great taste! The fresh and tangy blend is wonderful by itself or with whatever additions you have on hand. Check your refrigerator for tomatoes, bell peppers, chiles, or corn to add to this versatile salad.

1 15-ounce can no-salt-added black beans, rinsed and drained

¼ to ½ cup salsa and ¼ to ½ cup salsa (lowest sodium available), divided use

8 cups chopped lettuce

8 ounces baked tortilla chips (lowest sodium available) (about 2½ cups), slightly crushed

¾ to 1 cup shredded fat-free Cheddar or Monterey Jack cheese (3 to 4 ounces)

¼ cup low-fat sour cream

In a small bowl, stir together the beans with ¼ to ½ cup salsa. Mash slightly with a potato masher or fork.

To assemble, put the lettuce on plates. Sprinkle with the chips. Spread the bean mixture over each serving. Top with the Cheddar, remaining ¼ to ½ cup salsa, and a dollop of sour cream.

PER SERVING
calories 403
total fat 3.0 g
saturated 0.5 g
trans 0.0 g
polyunsaturated 1.0 g
monounsaturated 0.5 g
cholesterol 7 mg
sodium 450 mg
carbohydrates 74 g
fiber 10 g
sugars 8 g
protein 22 g
dietary exchanges
4½ starch
1 vegetable
2 very lean meat

COOK'S TIP

If you have 10 extra minutes, make Mexican Bean Dip (page 39) and use 1 cup of it instead of the canned black beans.

fresh herb couscous salad

SERVES 8 · 1½ cups per serving
PREPARATION TIME · 15 minutes
COOLING TIME · 15 minutes

The fresh herbs in this salad add an exotic flavor that's reminiscent of Mediterranean favorites.

2 cups uncooked whole-wheat couscous

¼ cup chopped walnuts

½ teaspoon salt

3 cups boiling water

1 medium or large tomato

1 medium cucumber

½ cup chopped mixed fresh herbs (such as chives, parsley, and basil)

¼ to ½ cup chopped fresh mint

¼ cup lemon juice

¼ cup olive oil (extra-virgin preferred)

½ teaspoon bottled minced garlic or 1 medium garlic clove, minced

In a large bowl, stir together the couscous, walnuts, and salt. Pour the boiling water over the mixture, stirring to combine. Let cool for about 15 minutes.

Meanwhile, chop the tomato. Peel, seed, and chop the cucumber. Add to the cooled couscous with the remaining ingredients. Stir together. Serve at room temperature or cover and refrigerate until needed.

PER SERVING
calories 305
total fat 10.5 g
saturated 1.5 g
trans 0.0 g
polyunsaturated 3.0 g
monounsaturated 5.5 g
cholesterol 0 mg
sodium 154 mg
carbohydrates 48 g
fiber 8 g
sugars 1 g
protein 9 g
dietary exchanges
3 starch
2 fat

orzo salad with green peas and artichokes

SERVES 6 · 1 cup per serving
PREPARATION TIME · 8 to 10 minutes
COOKING TIME · 15 minutes

This pleasant pasta salad is even tastier the second day. Enjoy it as an entrée for six or a side dish for twelve.

6 ounces uncooked orzo

3/4 cup pine nuts

1 1/2 cups frozen green peas, thawed

1/3 cup finely chopped fresh basil (about 1 ounce before removing stems) or 2 tablespoons dried, crumbled

3 tablespoons cider vinegar

1 14.5-ounce can artichoke quarters, drained and cut in half lengthwise

1 7.2-ounce bottle roasted red bell peppers, drained and chopped

1 2.5-ounce can sliced black olives, drained

1/4 cup snipped fresh parsley (Italian, or flat-leaf, preferred) (optional)

2 teaspoons olive oil (extra-virgin preferred)

1/8 teaspoon salt

Pepper to taste

Prepare the orzo using the package directions, omitting the salt and oil. Pour into a colander and rinse under cold running water for 30 seconds to stop the cooking process and cool quickly. Drain well.

Meanwhile, in a medium skillet, dry-roast the pine nuts over medium-high heat for 1 to 2 minutes, or until just fragrant, stirring frequently. Remove from the skillet so they don't burn.

In a large bowl, stir together the peas, basil, and vinegar. Add the artichokes, bell peppers, olives, and parsley, tossing well.

Add the orzo, oil, salt, and pepper to the artichoke mixture, tossing well. Serve or cover and refrigerate for up to 24 hours to serve chilled.

TIME-SAVER To bring water to a boil quickly, start with hot tap water and cover the pot.

PER SERVING
calories 264
total fat 11.0 g
saturated 1.5 g
trans 0.0 g
polyunsaturated 3.5 g
monounsaturated 5.0 g
cholesterol 0 mg
sodium 382 mg
carbohydrates 35 g
fiber 4 g
sugars 5 g
protein 10 g
dietary exchanges
2 starch
1 vegetable
1/2 very lean meat
2 fat

seafood

Catfish with Cornmeal-Mustard Topping

Catfish with Chunky Creole Sauce

Fish Bundles

Five-Flavor Fish

Orange Roughy with Bok Choy and Cherry Tomatoes

Chutney Salmon

Salmon Sorrento

Honey-Mustard Salmon

Lemony Salmon Fettuccine

Scrod Veracruz

Citrus Sole

Sole Mozzarella

Portuguese Fish Fillets

Pan-Seared Tilapia with Fresh Fruit Salsa

Tilapia with Artichokes and Sun-Dried Tomatoes

Ginger Grilled Trout

Grilled Tuna Niçoise

Grilled Tuna with Garlic

Hawaiian-Style Tuna

Tuna Casserole with Broccoli and Water Chestnuts

Scallops Provençal

Pan-Blackened Scallops over Lemon Rice

Shrimp Marsala

Mixed Kebabs

Spanish Shrimp

catfish with cornmeal-mustard topping

SERVES 4 · 3 ounces fish per serving
PREPARATION TIME · 8 minutes
COOKING TIME · 15 minutes

express *no shopping required*

This easy, no-mess weeknight dish simply requires spreading a bit of mustard over catfish fillets, sprinkling them lightly with a garlicky paprika-cornmeal mixture, and popping them in the oven.

Cooking spray

4 catfish fillets (about 4 ounces each), rinsed and patted dry

2 teaspoons yellow mustard

2 tablespoons yellow cornmeal

1/2 teaspoon paprika

1/4 teaspoon garlic powder

1/8 teaspoon salt

1 to 2 tablespoons finely snipped fresh parsley

8 to 12 drops red hot-pepper sauce (optional)

Preheat the oven to 450°F.

Line a baking sheet with aluminum foil. Lightly spray the foil with cooking spray. Place the fish on the foil so the fillets don't touch. Spread the mustard over the tops.

In a small bowl, stir together the cornmeal, paprika, and garlic powder. Sprinkle over the fish.

Bake for 15 minutes, or until the fish flakes easily when tested with a fork. Remove from the oven. Sprinkle with the salt, and then with the parsley and hot-pepper sauce.

PER SERVING
calories 127
total fat 3.5 g
saturated 1.0 g
trans 0.0 g
polyunsaturated 1.0 g
monounsaturated 1.0 g
cholesterol 66 mg
sodium 151 mg
carbohydrates 4 g
fiber 1 g
sugars 0 g
protein 19 g
dietary exchanges
3 very lean meat

catfish with chunky creole sauce

SERVES 4 · 3 ounces fish and ¼ cup sauce per serving
PREPARATION TIME · 10 minutes
COOKING TIME · 30 to 32 minutes

This mildly seasoned fish with its medley of Creole veggies is wonderful over steamed brown rice.

CHUNKY CREOLE SAUCE

1 tablespoon light tub margarine

1 large tomato (about 8 ounces), chopped

1 cup chopped green bell pepper

¾ cup thinly sliced celery (about 1½ medium ribs)

½ cup chopped onion

1 teaspoon bottled minced garlic or 2 medium garlic cloves, minced

½ teaspoon dried thyme, crumbled, or 2 tablespoons finely snipped fresh parsley

½ teaspoon Worcestershire sauce (lowest sodium available)

¼ teaspoon sugar

• • •

4 catfish or other mild fillets (about 4 ounces each), rinsed and patted dry

⅛ teaspoon salt

In a large nonstick skillet, melt the margarine over medium-high heat, swirling to coat the bottom. When the margarine is bubbly, stir in the remaining sauce ingredients. Bring to a boil. Reduce the heat and simmer, covered, for 22 minutes, or until the celery is tender. Pour into a medium bowl.

Place the fish in the skillet, trying not to overlap the fillets. Pour the sauce over the fish. Cook, uncovered, for 6 to 8 minutes, or until the fish flakes easily when tested with a fork. Sprinkle with the salt.

PER SERVING
calories 144
total fat 4.5 g
saturated 1.0 g
trans 0.0 g
polyunsaturated 1.5 g
monounsaturated 1.5 g
cholesterol 66 mg
sodium 172 mg
carbohydrates 5 g
fiber 1 g
sugars 4 g
protein 19 g
dietary exchanges
1 vegetable
3 lean meat

fish bundles

SERVES 4 · 3 ounces fish per serving
PREPARATION TIME · 10 minutes
COOKING TIME · 15 minutes

When the French cook en papillote, *they steam the food in cooking parchment. Here we use aluminum foil to provide the same results. Both preparation and cleanup are super quick.*

Cooking spray

4 fish fillets, such as mahi-mahi (about 4 ounces each), rinsed and patted dry

1 teaspoon bottled chopped garlic or 2 medium garlic cloves, chopped

1/2 teaspoon salt

1/2 teaspoon crushed red pepper flakes

8 or 12 fresh basil leaves

4 medium Italian plum (Roma) tomatoes, cored and cut crosswise into 1/4-inch slices

1/4 cup dry white wine (regular or nonalcoholic)

Preheat the oven to 375°F or preheat the grill on medium.

Tear off four sheets of aluminum foil, each about 12 x 10 inches. Fold each sheet in half, make a crease, then open again. Lightly spray with cooking spray. Place a fillet on one half of each sheet. Sprinkle each fillet with the garlic, salt, and red pepper flakes. Top with the basil and tomatoes. Pour 1 tablespoon wine over each serving. Fold the foil over the fish. Tightly fold up the foil to enclose the fish.

Bake or grill for about 15 minutes, or until the fish flakes easily when tested with a fork. When unfolding the foil, be careful not to get a steam burn. Slide the contents of each packet onto a plate.

PER SERVING
calories 119
total fat 1.0 g
saturated 0.0 g
trans 0.0 g
polyunsaturated 0.0 g
monounsaturated 0.0 g
cholesterol 83 mg
sodium 395 mg
carbohydrates 3 g
fiber 1 g
sugars 2 g
protein 22 g
dietary exchanges
3 very lean meat

five-flavor fish

SERVES 4 · 3 ounces fish per serving
PREPARATION TIME · 5 minutes
COOKING TIME · 10 to 12 minutes

This basic fish dish is so easy to prepare that it's just about foolproof.

Olive oil spray
1 teaspoon ground cumin
1 teaspoon chili powder
1/2 teaspoon garlic powder
1/2 teaspoon onion powder

1/2 teaspoon dried thyme, crumbled
4 mild fish fillets, such as orange
  roughy (about 4 ounces each),
  rinsed and patted dry

Preheat the oven to 425°F. Heavily spray a 13 x 9 x 2-inch glass
baking dish with olive oil spray.

In a small bowl, stir together the remaining ingredients except
the fish. Sprinkle on both sides of the fish,
pressing gently so the mixture adheres.
Put the fish in a single layer in the baking
dish.

Bake for 10 to 12 minutes, or until the fish
flakes easily when tested with a fork.

PER SERVING
calories 96
total fat 1.0 g
saturated 0.0 g
trans 0.0 g
polyunsaturated 0.0 g
monounsaturated 0.5 g
cholesterol 68 mg
sodium 66 mg
carbohydrates 1 g
fiber 0 g
sugars 0 g
protein 20 g
dietary exchanges
3 very lean meat

COOK'S TIP ON ORANGE ROUGHY
Orange roughy is usually frozen, then sent to the
grocery store and thawed. If you refreeze and rethaw
it, the texture will be harmed.

orange roughy with bok choy and cherry tomatoes

SERVES 4 · 3 ounces fish and ¾ cup sauce per serving
PREPARATION TIME · 15 minutes
COOKING TIME · 18 to 25 minutes

Bok choy is traditionally used in stir-fry dishes, but rules can be broken! This recipe incorporates the crispy white stalks and spinachlike leaves into a creamy sauce that's accented with cherry tomatoes and served over poached fish. Elegant enough for company and easy enough to enjoy once a week.

1 teaspoon canola or corn oil

½ medium onion, thinly sliced

4 mild fish fillets, such as orange roughy (about 4 ounces each), rinsed and patted dry

½ cup fat-free, low-sodium chicken broth

½ cup dry white wine (regular or nonalcoholic)

⅛ teaspoon pepper

1 small bunch bok choy (12 to 16 ounces)

1 cup cherry tomatoes

1½ tablespoons all-purpose flour

3 tablespoons water

¼ cup fat-free sour cream, at room temperature

In a large skillet, heat the oil over medium-high heat, swirling to coat the bottom. Cook the onion for about 3 minutes, or until soft, stirring occasionally.

Add the fish, broth, wine, and pepper to the skillet. Bring to a simmer, still over medium-high heat. Reduce the heat and simmer, covered, for 8 to 10 minutes, or until the fish flakes easily when tested with a fork.

Meanwhile, trim and discard the ends of the bok choy stalks. Slice the stalks crosswise into ¼-inch pieces. Transfer to a small bowl. Cut the bok choy leaves crosswise into thin strips. Transfer to a separate small bowl. Halve the tomatoes. Add to the bok choy leaves. Set aside.

PER SERVING
calories 157
total fat 2.5 g
saturated 0.0 g
trans 0.0 g
polyunsaturated 0.5 g
monounsaturated 1.0 g
cholesterol 71 mg
sodium 149 mg
carbohydrates 11 g
fiber 2 g
sugars 5 g
protein 23 g
dietary exchanges
2 vegetable
3 very lean meat

Put the flour in a small bowl. Add the water, whisking to dissolve. Set aside.

When the fish is done, use a slotted spatula or slotted spoon to transfer to a platter. Cover with aluminum foil to keep warm. (The fish will continue to cook slightly as it stands.)

Add the bok choy stalks to the skillet. Increase the heat to medium high and bring to a simmer. Simmer for 1 to 2 minutes, or until tender-crisp, stirring occasionally.

Stir in the flour mixture. Cook for 1 to 2 minutes, or until thick and bubbly, stirring occasionally. Reduce the heat to low.

Add the bok choy leaves and tomatoes. Cook for 1 to 2 minutes, or until the leaves are tender and the mixture cools slightly, stirring occasionally. Remove from the heat (leave the stove on).

Stir in the sour cream. Return to the heat and cook for 1 to 2 minutes, or until warmed through, stirring occasionally. Spoon over the fish.

COOK'S TIP ON BOK CHOY

To make slicing bok choy easier, stack the leaves and roll them up together, starting from a long side. Slice the roll crosswise into thin strips.

chutney salmon

SERVES 4 · 3 ounces fish per serving
PREPARATION TIME · 5 minutes
COOKING TIME · 20 minutes

A fragrant aroma will fill your kitchen while the chutney bakes over the salmon, ensuring moist and tender fillets every time.

Cooking spray

4 salmon fillets with skin (about 5 ounces each), rinsed and patted dry

¼ teaspoon garlic powder

½ cup mango chutney (any variety)

1 teaspoon dried parsley, crumbled

½ teaspoon ground cumin

Preheat the oven to 350°F. Line a baking sheet with aluminum foil. Lightly spray the foil with cooking spray.

Place the fish with the skin side down on the baking sheet. Sprinkle the garlic powder over the fish.

Spoon the chutney into a small bowl, cutting any large fruit pieces. Stir in the parsley and cumin. Spread over the top side of the fish.

Bake for 20 minutes, or until the fish is cooked to the desired doneness.

PER SERVING
calories 234
total fat 5.5 g
saturated 1.0 g
trans 0.0 g
polyunsaturated 2.0 g
monounsaturated 1.5 g
cholesterol 81 mg
sodium 111 mg
carbohydrates 14 g
fiber 1 g
sugars 12 g
protein 31 g
dietary exchanges
1 carbohydrate
4 lean meat

COOK'S TIP

If you can find mango chutney with ginger, it is particularly good in this dish.

salmon sorrento

SERVES 4 · 3 ounces fish per serving
PREPARATION TIME · 10 minutes
COOKING TIME · 24 to 27 minutes

With its thick, colorful sauce, this dish provides a way to dress up salmon without covering up its natural flavor.

1 tablespoon olive oil

5 medium Italian plum (Roma) tomatoes, diced

6 medium black olives, coarsely chopped

6 medium green olives, coarsely chopped

3 tablespoons lemon juice

2 tablespoons chopped fresh parsley (Italian, or flat-leaf, preferred)

1 tablespoon capers, drained

1½ teaspoons bottled minced garlic or 3 medium garlic cloves, thinly sliced

Pepper to taste

1 1-pound salmon fillet, rinsed and patted dry

In a large skillet, heat the oil over medium-high heat, swirling to coat the bottom. Stir in all the ingredients except the salmon. Bring to a boil over medium-high heat, 2 to 3 minutes. Reduce the heat to medium. Cook for 5 minutes, or until the mixture is reduced by about one-third, stirring occasionally.

Using a spoon, push the sauce to one side and place the fish in the skillet. Spoon the sauce over the fish. Cook, covered, for 15 to 17 minutes, or until the fish is cooked to the desired doneness.

PER SERVING

calories 193
total fat 8.5 g
  saturated 1.5 g
  trans 0.0 g
  polyunsaturated 2.0 g
  monounsaturated 4.5 g
cholesterol 59 mg
sodium 317 mg
carbohydrates 5 g
  fiber 1 g
  sugars 2 g
protein 24 g
dietary exchanges
  1 vegetable
  3 lean meat

honey-mustard salmon

SERVES 6 · 3 ounces fish per serving
PREPARATION TIME · 5 minutes
COOKING TIME · 6 minutes

This dish is elegant enough for company, quick enough for a "desperation dinner," and convenient enough for any cook. You can put it together at the last minute or assemble it in the morning so it's ready to cook when you are.

Cooking spray

2 tablespoons snipped fresh dillweed or 1 teaspoon dried, crumbled

2 tablespoons Dijon mustard

1 tablespoon honey

6 salmon fillets with skin (about 5 ounces each), rinsed and patted dry

If grilling, lightly spray the grill rack with cooking spray. If broiling, lightly spray a baking sheet with cooking spray. Preheat the grill on high or preheat the broiler.

In a small bowl, whisk together the dillweed, mustard, and honey. Brush over the flesh side of the fish.

Put the fish with the skin side down on the grill or baking sheet. Grill or broil about 6 inches from the heat for about 6 minutes, or until the fish is cooked to the desired doneness.

PER SERVING

calories 149
total fat 4.5 g
  saturated 0.5 g
  trans 0.0 g
  polyunsaturated 1.5 g
  monounsaturated 1.0 g
cholesterol 59 mg
sodium 179 mg
carbohydrates 4 g
  fiber 0 g
  sugars 3 g
protein 23 g
dietary exchanges
  3 lean meat

lemony salmon fettuccine

SERVES 4 · 1½ cups per serving
PREPARATION TIME · 10 minutes
COOKING TIME · 15 to 19 minutes

This quick dish tastes so rich and flavorful!

5 ounces dried whole-grain fettuccine

11 ounces fresh asparagus, trimmed and cut into 1- to 1¼-inch pieces

½ cup fat-free milk

⅓ cup light tub cream cheese

⅓ cup fat-free sour cream

2 5-ounce cans pink salmon in water, drained, skin discarded, bones discarded if desired, flaked

¼ cup shredded or grated Parmesan cheese and 1 tablespoon shredded or grated Parmesan cheese, divided use

3 tablespoons lemon juice

¼ teaspoon pepper

2 tablespoons snipped fresh parsley (Italian, or flat-leaf, preferred)

Prepare the fettuccine using the package directions, omitting the salt and oil. Stir in the asparagus for the last 4 minutes of the cooking time. Drain well in a colander.

Meanwhile, in a medium saucepan, whisk together the milk, cream cheese, and sour cream. Cook over low heat for 3 to 4 minutes, or until the cream cheese is melted and the mixture is smooth, whisking frequently.

Stir in the salmon, ¼ cup Parmesan, lemon juice, and pepper. Cook for 2 to 3 minutes, or until hot, stirring occasionally.

In a large bowl, stir together the pasta and salmon mixture. Sprinkle with the remaining 1 tablespoon Parmesan, then with the parsley.

COOK'S TIP

For a change of pace, replace the asparagus with other fresh or frozen vegetables, adding them during the last 3 to 5 minutes of boiling time for the pasta. If you have some leftover vegetables that would go well with the salmon and pasta combo, you could heat them to add instead.

PER SERVING
calories 340
total fat 9.0 g
saturated 4.0 g
trans 0.0 g
polyunsaturated 1.5 g
monounsaturated 2.5 g
cholesterol 80 mg
sodium 517 mg
carbohydrates 37 g
fiber 6 g
sugars 7 g
protein 29 g
dietary exchanges
2½ starch
3 lean meat

scrod veracruz

SERVES 4 · 3 ounces fish per serving
PREPARATION TIME · 5 minutes
COOKING TIME · 15 to 20 minutes

Some like it hot, so here's the perfect spicy fish dish. While it bakes, you'll have time to prepare corn on the cob and steamed zucchini.

Cooking spray

4 mild fish fillets, such as scrod (about 4 ounces each), rinsed and patted dry

½ cup salsa (lowest sodium available)

2 tablespoons plain dry bread crumbs

2 tablespoons shredded low-fat Monterey Jack or low-fat mozzarella cheese

Preheat the oven to 375°F. Lightly spray a 12 x 8 x 2-inch baking pan with cooking spray.

Put the fish in the pan. Top with the salsa, bread crumbs, and Monterey Jack.

Bake for 15 to 20 minutes, or until the fish flakes easily when tested with a fork.

PER SERVING
calories 127
total fat 1.5 g
saturated 0.5 g
trans 0.0 g
polyunsaturated 0.5 g
monounsaturated 0.5 g
cholesterol 51 mg
sodium 223 mg
carbohydrates 4 g
fiber 0 g
sugars 1 g
protein 22 g
dietary exchanges
½ carbohydrate
3 very lean meat

citrus sole

SERVES 4 · 3 ounces fish per serving
PREPARATION TIME · 5 minutes
COOKING TIME · 18 to 20 minutes

Orange marmalade brings a completely different taste to an already wonderful combination of seafood and citrus juices.

Cooking spray

2 tablespoons lemon juice

2 tablespoons lime juice

1½ tablespoons all-fruit orange
   marmalade

4 mild fish fillets, such as sole
(about 4 ounces each), rinsed
and patted dry

Preheat the oven to 375°F. Lightly spray a 12 x 8 x 2-inch baking pan with cooking spray.

In a small bowl, stir together the lemon and lime juices and orange marmalade. Using a basting brush, coat both sides of the fish with the mixture. Transfer the fish to the pan.

Bake for 18 to 20 minutes, or until the fish flakes easily when tested with a fork.

PER SERVING
calories 110
total fat 1.0 g
saturated 0.5 g
trans 0.0 g
polyunsaturated 0.5 g
monounsaturated 0.0 g
cholesterol 53 mg
sodium 82 mg
carbohydrates 5 g
fiber 0 g
sugars 3 g
protein 19 g
dietary exchanges
½ carbohydrate
3 very lean meat

sole mozzarella

SERVES 4 · 3 ounces fish per serving
PREPARATION TIME · 15 minutes
COOKING TIME · 9 minutes

To prepare this Italian specialty with a fraction of the usual saturated fat and cholesterol, just use egg substitute and low-fat mozzarella cheese. It's as simple as that.

³/₄ cup egg substitute

³/₄ cup plain dry bread crumbs

4 mild thin fish fillets, such as sole (about 4 ounces each), rinsed and patted dry

Cooking spray

12 ounces canned no-salt-added tomato sauce

½ teaspoon bottled minced garlic or 1 medium garlic clove, minced

¼ teaspoon dried Italian seasoning, crumbled

⅓ cup shredded low-fat mozzarella cheese (about 1½ ounces)

1 tablespoon snipped fresh parsley (Italian, or flat-leaf, preferred)

Pour the egg substitute into a shallow medium bowl. Put the bread crumbs on a plate. Cut a piece of wax paper about 12 inches long. Set the bowl, plate, and wax paper in a row assembly-line fashion.

Dip one piece of fish in the egg substitute, turning to coat. Dip in the bread crumbs, turning to coat and shaking off any excess. Put the fish on the wax paper. Repeat with the remaining fish.

Lightly spray a large skillet with cooking spray. Heat over medium heat. Place the fish in the skillet. Cook for 3 minutes. Turn over. Cook for 2 minutes. Reduce the heat to low.

In a medium bowl, stir together the tomato sauce, garlic, and Italian seasoning. Pour over the fish. Cook, covered, for 2 minutes.

Sprinkle with the mozzarella and cook, covered, for 2 minutes, or until the fish flakes easily when tested with a fork. Sprinkle with the parsley.

PER SERVING
calories 248
total fat 2.5 g
saturated 0.5 g
trans 0.0 g
polyunsaturated 1.0 g
monounsaturated 0.5 g
cholesterol 56 mg
sodium 416 mg
carbohydrates 23 g
fiber 3 g
sugars 6 g
protein 33 g
dietary exchanges
1 starch
1 vegetable
3½ very lean meat

portuguese fish fillets

SERVES 4 · 3 ounces fish per serving
PREPARATION TIME · 10 minutes
COOKING TIME · 10 to 20 minutes

Green spinach and red tomato contrast handsomely with white-flesh fillets in this dish. Microwave potatoes to round out the meal.

Olive oil spray

1 10-ounce package frozen chopped spinach, thawed, drained well, and squeezed dry

4 mild fish fillets, such as tilapia (about 4 ounces each), rinsed and patted dry

¼ teaspoon salt

Pepper to taste

1 medium tomato, thinly sliced

1 small onion, sliced into thin rings

1 tablespoon olive oil

1 tablespoon red wine vinegar

1 tablespoon lemon juice

Preheat the oven to 400°F. Lightly spray an 11 x 7 x 1½-inch baking pan with cooking spray.

Spread the spinach in the pan. Place the fish on the spinach. Sprinkle with the salt and pepper. Top with the tomato and onion. Drizzle with the oil, vinegar, and lemon juice.

Bake for 10 to 20 minutes, or until the fish flakes easily when tested with a fork.

PER SERVING
calories 177
total fat 6.0 g
saturated 1.5 g
trans 0.0 g
polyunsaturated 1.0 g
monounsaturated 3.0 g
cholesterol 57 mg
sodium 259 mg
carbohydrates 7 g
fiber 3 g
sugars 3 g
protein 26 g
dietary exchanges
1 vegetable
3 lean meat

pan-seared tilapia with fresh fruit salsa

SERVES 4 · 3 ounces fish and ¼ cup fruit salsa per serving
PREPARATION TIME · 10 minutes
COOKING TIME · 4 to 5 minutes

A colorful trio of fresh fruits, coupled with the spiciness of jalapeño pepper, enlivens the flavor of mild tilapia.

FRUIT SALSA

½ cup cubed fresh pineapple (about ¼-inch cubes) or 8-ounce can pineapple tidbits in their own juice, drained

½ medium green kiwifruit, peeled and chopped

3 or 4 medium strawberries, hulled and chopped

½ medium fresh jalapeño, seeds and ribs discarded, minced

1 tablespoon snipped fresh cilantro

1 tablespoon lime juice

TILAPIA

1 teaspoon canola or corn oil

4 tilapia or other mild fish fillets (about 4 ounces each), rinsed and patted dry

½ teaspoon chili powder

⅛ teaspoon salt

⅛ teaspoon pepper

1 tablespoon lime juice

In a medium bowl, gently toss together the salsa ingredients. Set aside.

In a large skillet, heat the oil over medium-high heat, swirling to coat the bottom. Place the fish in a single layer in the skillet. Sprinkle with the chili powder. Cook for 2 minutes. Turn the fish over. Sprinkle with the salt and pepper. Cook for 2 to 3 minutes, or until the fish is lightly browned and flakes easily when tested with a fork. Using a wide spatula, transfer to a platter.

Drizzle the fish with the remaining 1 tablespoon lime juice. Spoon the fruit salsa down the center of the fish.

PER SERVING
calories 142
total fat 3.5 g
saturated 1.0 g
trans 0.0 g
polyunsaturated 1.0 g
monounsaturated 1.5 g
cholesterol 57 mg
sodium 136 mg
carbohydrates 6 g
fiber 1 g
sugars 4 g
protein 23 g
dietary exchanges
½ fruit
3 very lean meat

tilapia with artichokes and sun-dried tomatoes

SERVES 4 · 3 ounces fish per serving
PREPARATION TIME · 10 minutes
COOKING TIME · 12 to 14 minutes

Tilapia, a farm-raised fish, has a very delicate flavor, similar to that of sole. In this recipe, tilapia combines superbly with white wine, sun-dried tomatoes, and artichoke hearts for a dish fit for almost any occasion.

1 tablespoon all-purpose flour

4 mild fish fillets, such as tilapia (about 4 ounces each), rinsed and patted dry

2 tablespoons olive oil

1 teaspoon bottled chopped garlic or 2 medium garlic cloves, chopped

1/2 cup dry white wine (regular or nonalcoholic)

1/2 cup fat-free evaporated milk

1/4 cup plus 2 tablespoons lemon juice

1/2 9-ounce package frozen artichoke hearts, thawed and patted dry

4 dry-packed sun-dried tomato halves, chopped

Pepper to taste

Sprinkle the flour on both sides of the fish.

In a large skillet, heat the oil over medium heat, swirling to coat the bottom. Cook the fish for 3 minutes. Turn over. Cook for 2 minutes. Sprinkle with the garlic. Cook for 1 minute.

Increase the heat to high. Gently stir in the remaining ingredients. Cook for 6 to 8 minutes, or until the fish flakes easily when tested with a fork and the sauce is the desired consistency, stirring occasionally.

PER SERVING
calories 252
total fat 9.0 g
saturated 2.0 g
trans 0.0 g
polyunsaturated 1.5 g
monounsaturated 5.5 g
cholesterol 58 mg
sodium 116 mg
carbohydrates 12 g
fiber 3 g
sugars 5 g
protein 27 g
dietary exchanges
1 vegetable
1/2 carbohydrate
3 lean meat

ginger grilled trout

SERVES 4 · 3 ounces fish per serving
PREPARATION TIME · 10 minutes
COOKING TIME · 4 to 6 minutes

Fresh ginger and garlic are perfect seasonings for grilled trout.

Cooking spray

2 tablespoons plain rice vinegar

1 tablespoon soy sauce (lowest sodium available)

1 tablespoon canola or corn oil

1 tablespoon grated peeled gingerroot

1 tablespoon snipped fresh Italian (flat-leaf) parsley and 1 tablespoon snipped fresh Italian (flat-leaf) parsley, divided use

1 teaspoon bottled minced garlic or 2 medium garlic cloves, minced

2 8- to 9-ounce trout fillets with skin, rinsed and patted dry

Lightly spray the grill rack with cooking spray. Preheat the grill on medium high.

In a small bowl, stir together the rice vinegar, soy sauce, and oil. Remove and set aside 1 tablespoon of the mixture. Brush the remaining mixture over both sides of each fillet. (It helps keep the skin side from sticking to the grill rack.)

In the same small bowl, stir together the gingerroot, 1 tablespoon parsley, and garlic. Sprinkle over the flesh side of the fish.

Place the fish with the skin side down on the grill. Grill for 4 to 6 minutes, or until the fish flakes easily when tested with a fork. Using a wide spatula, remove the fish from the grill. Place the fish with the skin side up on a platter. Discard the skin. Cut each fillet in half. Drizzle with the reserved 1 tablespoon rice vinegar mixture. Garnish with the remaining 1 tablespoon parsley.

PER SERVING
calories 149
total fat 5.0 g
saturated 1.0 g
trans 0.0 g
polyunsaturated 1.5 g
monounsaturated 2.0 g
cholesterol 67 mg
sodium 134 mg
carbohydrates 1 g
fiber 0 g
sugars 0 g
protein 24 g
dietary exchanges
3 lean meat

grilled tuna niçoise

SERVES 4 · 1½ cups per serving
PREPARATION TIME · 15 minutes
COOKING TIME · 15 to 20 minutes

Here's a warm version of the popular French salade niçoise. Très bien!

Olive oil spray

4 4-ounce red potatoes, cut crosswise into ⅛-inch slices

1 9-ounce package frozen French-style green beans

¼ teaspoon salt

1 pound tuna steaks (about ¾ inch thick), rinsed and patted dry

1 tablespoon olive oil

1 teaspoon dried basil, crumbled

¼ to ½ teaspoon pepper

8 cherry tomatoes, halved

12 medium or 16 small yellow teardrop tomatoes, halved, or 2 medium yellow tomatoes, diced

2 large hard-cooked eggs, whites chopped and yolks discarded

2 teaspoons capers, drained

Preheat the oven to 400°F. Preheat the grill on medium high.

Lightly spray a baking sheet with olive oil spray. Place the potato slices in a single layer on the baking sheet. Lightly spray the tops of the potatoes with olive oil spray.

Bake for 12 to 15 minutes, or until tender and lightly browned.

Meanwhile, prepare the green beans using the package directions, omitting the salt and margarine. Drain well in a colander. Transfer to a medium bowl. Stir in the salt. Cover to keep warm.

Brush one side of the fish with the oil. Sprinkle with half the basil and half the pepper. Repeat on the other side.

Grill the fish for 3 to 5 minutes on each side, or until cooked to the desired doneness. Cut into 4 pieces.

To assemble, arrange the potato slices on plates. Top with the green beans. Stack the fish on top. Serve the tomatoes, egg whites, and capers on the side or sprinkled over the fish.

PER SERVING
calories 263
total fat 5.0 g
saturated 1.0 g
trans 0.0 g
polyunsaturated 1.0 g
monounsaturated 2.5 g
cholesterol 49 mg
sodium 314 mg
carbohydrates 26 g
fiber 4 g
sugars 5 g
protein 29 g
dietary exchanges
1 starch
2 vegetable
3 lean meat

grilled tuna with garlic

SERVES 4 · 3 ounces fish per serving
PREPARATION TIME · 10 minutes
COOKING TIME · 5 to 15 minutes

With the texture of steak and the benefits of fish, tuna is a true winner. So is this easy, easy dish. Grill some fresh vegetables at the same time, slice some tomatoes, and call the family to dinner.

2 medium garlic cloves

1 1-pound tuna steak, rinsed and patted dry

Olive oil spray

1 medium lemon, cut into 4 wedges (optional)

Preheat the grill on medium high.

Cut each garlic clove lengthwise into 5 or 6 slices.

Put the fish on a flat surface. With the tip of a sharp knife, make one short, 1/4-inch-deep cut in the fish for each slice of garlic. With your thumb, insert a garlic slice into each cut.

Lightly spray both sides of the fish with olive oil spray. Place on the grill. Don't pat or move the fish until it's ready to turn, 3 minutes for medium rare to 10 minutes for well done. Turn over. Cook for about 2 minutes for medium rare to about 5 minutes for well done. Serve with the lemon wedges.

PER SERVING
calories 121
total fat 1.0 g
saturated 0.5 g
trans 0.0 g
polyunsaturated 0.5 g
monounsaturated 0.0 g
cholesterol 49 mg
sodium 40 mg
carbohydrates 1 g
fiber 0 g
sugars 0 g
protein 26 g
dietary exchanges
3 very lean meat

COOK'S TIP

Vary the flavor of this dish by sprinkling a fresh herb, such as rosemary or dillweed, or some coarsely ground pepper over the tuna before grilling it.

hawaiian-style tuna

SERVES 4 · 2 cups per serving
PREPARATION TIME · 10 minutes
COOKING TIME · 17 to 20 minutes

With its rainbow of colors, this all-in-one dinner looks and tastes great.

1 cup uncooked instant brown rice

1 tablespoon olive oil

1 medium green bell pepper, diced

1 medium red bell pepper, diced

1 medium yellow bell pepper, diced

1 large red onion, diced

1 pound tuna, rinsed and patted dry

1 8-ounce can pineapple chunks in their own juice, undrained

6 ounces pineapple juice

1 teaspoon ground ginger

1 teaspoon soy sauce (lowest sodium available)

Prepare the rice using the package directions, omitting the salt and margarine.

Meanwhile, in a large skillet, heat the oil over medium-high heat, swirling to coat the bottom. Cook the bell peppers and onion, covered, for 10 to 12 minutes, or until they begin to soften, stirring frequently.

Cut the fish into 1-inch strips. When the bell peppers and onion are ready, add the fish, undrained pineapple, and pineapple juice to the skillet. Cook, uncovered, for 4 to 7 minutes, or until the fish is the desired doneness.

Reduce the heat to low. Stir in the rice, ginger, and soy sauce. Cook, uncovered, for 2 minutes or until heated through.

PER SERVING
calories 333
total fat 5.5 g
saturated 1.0 g
trans 0.0 g
polyunsaturated 1.0 g
monounsaturated 3.0 g
cholesterol 51 mg
sodium 90 mg
carbohydrates 40 g
fiber 4 g
sugars 16 g
protein 30 g
dietary exchanges
1 starch
1 fruit
2 vegetable
3 lean meat

scallops provençal

SERVES 4 · 1 cup per serving
PREPARATION TIME · 10 minutes
COOKING TIME · 9 to 14 minutes

 express

This recipe is a great example of how to prepare a classic French dinner in minutes and in only one pan.

1 tablespoon olive oil

1 medium to large zucchini, diced

1 teaspoon bottled minced garlic or 2 medium garlic cloves, finely chopped

1/4 teaspoon dried thyme, crumbled

Pepper to taste

1 pound bay or sea scallops, rinsed and patted dry

10 to 12 cherry tomatoes, halved

1/3 cup dry white wine (regular or nonalcoholic)

In a 12-inch skillet or a Dutch oven, heat the oil over medium-high heat, swirling to coat the bottom. Cook the zucchini, garlic, thyme, and pepper for 5 to 8 minutes, or until the zucchini is tender-crisp, stirring occasionally.

Gently stir the scallops, tomatoes, and wine into the zucchini mixture. Cook for 3 to 4 minutes for bay scallops or 4 to 5 minutes for sea scallops, or until the scallops have turned white and the zucchini is tender, stirring occasionally.

PER SERVING
calories 161
total fat 4.5 g
saturated 0.5 g
trans 0.0 g
polyunsaturated 0.5 g
monounsaturated 2.5 g
cholesterol 37 mg
sodium 192 mg
carbohydrates 7 g
fiber 1 g
sugars 2 g
protein 20 g
dietary exchanges
1 vegetable
3 lean meat

pan-blackened scallops over lemon rice

SERVES 4 · 1½ cups per serving
PREPARATION TIME · 10 minutes
COOKING TIME · 10 to 12 minutes

If you love spicy food, this dish is for you. The combination of blackening spice and chutney will tantalize your taste buds.

1 cup uncooked instant brown rice

3 tablespoons lemon juice

1 pound sea scallops, rinsed and patted dry

1 tablespoon olive oil

1½ teaspoons blackening spice and 1½ teaspoons blackening spice, divided use

½ teaspoon white pepper and ½ teaspoon white pepper, divided use

¼ cup frozen peas

2 tablespoons chutney

Prepare the rice using the package directions, omitting the salt and margarine and adding the lemon juice to the water.

Put the scallops in a medium bowl. Add the oil, stirring well to coat. Sprinkle with 1½ teaspoons blackening spice and ½ teaspoon pepper. Stir.

Heat a large nonstick skillet over high heat. Cook the scallops for 3 minutes, or until slightly firm, without stirring. Sprinkle with the remaining 1½ teaspoons blackening spice and ½ teaspoon pepper. Turn over. Cook for 3 to 5 minutes, or until white, without stirring.

Meanwhile, prepare the peas using the package directions, omitting the salt and margarine.

Spoon the rice onto plates. Sprinkle with the peas. Spoon the scallops over the rice. Top with the chutney.

PER SERVING
calories 239
total fat 5.0 g
saturated 0.5 g
trans 0.0 g
polyunsaturated 1.0 g
monounsaturated 3.0 g
cholesterol 37 mg
sodium 200 mg
carbohydrates 26 g
fiber 2 g
sugars 4 g
protein 22 g
dietary exchanges
1 starch
½ carbohydrate
3 lean meat

shrimp marsala

SERVES 4 · 1 cup per serving
PREPARATION TIME · 8 minutes
COOKING TIME · 8 to 10 minutes

Shrimp Marsala has it all—savory aroma, the rich flavors of wine and mushrooms, and company-pretty looks. A baked potato and steamed asparagus go well with this dish.

2 tablespoons all-purpose flour

1 pound raw colossal shrimp, peeled, rinsed and patted dry

1 tablespoon olive oil

5 ounces presliced fresh button mushrooms

½ cup marsala wine

Fresh parsley, snipped (optional)

Sprinkle the flour over the shrimp, shaking off the excess.

In a large skillet, heat the oil over medium-high heat, swirling to coat the bottom. Cook the shrimp for 2 minutes. Turn over.

Stir in the mushrooms and marsala. Increase the heat to high and cook for 5 to 7 minutes, or until the sauce has thickened to a consistency almost like melted caramels, stirring occasionally. Sprinkle with the parsley.

PER SERVING
calories 184
total fat 4.5 g
saturated 0.5 g
trans 0.0 g
polyunsaturated 1.0 g
monounsaturated 2.5 g
cholesterol 168 mg
sodium 198 mg
carbohydrates 8 g
fiber 1 g
sugars 3 g
protein 20 g
dietary exchanges
½ carbohydrate
3 lean meat

mixed kebabs

SERVES 4 · 1 kebab per serving
PREPARATION TIME · 10 minutes
MARINATING TIME · 5 to 10 minutes
COOKING TIME · 6 to 8 minutes

Whether your family craves Italian, Tex-Mex, or Asian food tonight, this simple standby with its triple combination of meat and seafood and its choice of marinades will come to your rescue.

ITALIAN MARINADE

2 teaspoons balsamic vinegar

1 teaspoon dried oregano, crumbled

1 teaspoon bottled minced garlic or 2 medium garlic cloves, minced

1 teaspoon olive oil

or

TEX-MEX MARINADE

2 teaspoons lime juice

1 teaspoon bottled minced garlic or 2 medium garlic cloves, minced

1 teaspoon canola or corn oil

1/2 teaspoon garlic powder

or

ASIAN MARINADE

2 teaspoons soy sauce (lowest sodium available)

1 teaspoon bottled minced garlic or 2 medium garlic cloves, minced

1 teaspoon canola or corn oil

1/2 teaspoon toasted sesame oil

KEBABS

12 raw peeled shrimp (about 6 ounces), rinsed and patted dry

5 ounces boneless, skinless chicken breasts, all visible fat discarded, cut into 3/4-inch cubes

5 ounces boneless sirloin steak, all visible fat discarded, cut into 1-inch cubes

ITALIAN KEBABS	TEX-MEX KEBABS	ASIAN KEBABS
PER SERVING	PER SERVING	PER SERVING
calories 124	calories 124	calories 124
total fat 2.5 g	total fat 2.5 g	total fat 2.5 g
saturated 1.0 g	saturated 1.0 g	saturated 1.0 g
trans 0.0 g	trans 0.0 g	trans 0.0 g
polyunsaturated 0.5 g	polyunsaturated 0.5 g	polyunsaturated 0.5 g
monounsaturated 1.0 g	monounsaturated 1.0 g	monounsaturated 1.0 g
cholesterol 104 mg	cholesterol 104 mg	cholesterol 104 mg
sodium 114 mg	sodium 114 mg	sodium 179 mg
carbohydrates 0 g	carbohydrates 0 g	carbohydrates 0 g
fiber 0 g	fiber 0 g	fiber 0 g
sugars 0 g	sugars 0 g	sugars 0 g
protein 24 g	protein 24 g	protein 24 g
dietary exchanges	dietary exchanges	dietary exchanges
3 very lean meat	3 very lean meat	3 very lean meat

In a large shallow glass dish, stir together the ingredients for your choice of marinade. Add the shrimp, chicken, and steak, turning to coat. Cover and refrigerate for 5 to 10 minutes.

Meanwhile, preheat the grill on medium high.

Remove the shrimp, chicken, and steak from the marinade, letting any excess drip off. Discard the marinade. Thread the kebab ingredients alternately on four 10-inch metal skewers.

Grill the kebabs for 3 to 4 minutes on each side, or until the shrimp turns pink and is cooked through, the chicken is no longer pink in the center, and the steak is the desired doneness.

COOK'S TIP

If you want your steak cubes well done, use ¾-inch cubes. The 1-inch size will give you medium-well in this recipe.

TIME-SAVER Buy preskewered kebabs at the supermarket. Be sure to choose the leanest ones.

spanish shrimp

SERVES 4 · 1¼ cups per serving
PREPARATION TIME · 10 minutes
COOKING TIME · 23 to 24 minutes

The aroma of this dish will attract your family to the table. Serve the colorful entrée over rice—perhaps topped with a dollop of fat-free sour cream—so you can enjoy every bit of the sauce.

1½ tablespoons olive oil

3 cups frozen red, yellow, and green bell pepper strips or 1 medium red bell pepper, 1 medium yellow bell pepper, and 1 medium green bell pepper, cut into 1-inch strips

2 medium yellow or white onions (Spanish preferred), each cut into eighths

1 teaspoon bottled chopped garlic or 2 medium garlic cloves, chopped

8 ounces raw medium shrimp, peeled, rinsed and patted dry

¼ cup lime juice

1 tablespoon snipped fresh cilantro

¼ teaspoon crushed red pepper flakes, or to taste

In a large skillet, heat the oil over medium heat, swirling to coat the bottom. Cook the bell peppers, onions, and garlic for 15 minutes, stirring occasionally.

Stir in the remaining ingredients. Cook for 7 to 8 minutes, or until the shrimp turns pink, stirring frequently.

PER SERVING
calories 135
total fat 5.0 g
saturated 1.0 g
trans 0.0 g
polyunsaturated 0.5 g
monounsaturated 3.5 g
cholesterol 84 mg
sodium 105 mg
carbohydrates 12 g
fiber 2 g
sugars 8 g
protein 10 g
dietary exchanges
2 vegetable
1½ lean meat

poultry

Honey-Mustard Chicken with
Couscous and Peas

Greek Chicken

Southwestern-Style Roasted Chicken

Crispy Chicken with Creamy Gravy

Roasted Chicken Breasts with
Garlic Gravy

Skillet Chicken with Capers and
White Wine

Sun-Dried Tomato Pesto Chicken
and Pasta
*Basil-Parmesan Pesto Chicken
and Pasta*

Border Chicken

Grilled Chicken with Green Chiles
and Cheese

Italian Grilled Chicken

Barbecued Chicken Dijon

Chicken and Brown Rice Lettuce
Wraps

Apricot-Barbecue Chicken Chunks

Chicken Chili

Spicy Honey-Kissed Chicken

Chicken and Shrimp Stir-Fry

Chicken and Vegetable Stir-Fry
Italian Stir-Fry

Chicken Creole on the Run

Lemon Chicken with Asparagus
and Pasta

Curried Chicken and Cauliflower

Chicken Biryani

Bell Pepper Chicken and Noodles

Creamed Chicken and Vegetables
Creamed Tuna and Vegetables

Lemongrass Chicken with Snow Peas
and Jasmine Rice

Chicken Fajita Pasta with Chipotle
Alfredo Sauce

Sour Cream Chicken Enchilada
Casserole

Grilled Turkey Cutlets with
Pineapple

Turkey Cutlets with Two Sauces

Turkey Breast with Cranberry Sage
Stuffing

Turkey and Broccoli Stir-Fry
Vegetarian Stir-Fry

Italian Bean Stew with Turkey
and Ham

honey-mustard chicken with couscous and peas

SERVES 4 · 3 ounces chicken and 1 cup couscous and peas per serving
PREPARATION TIME · 10 minutes
COOKING TIME · 9 to 10 minutes
STANDING TIME · 5 minutes

express · no shopping required

Dijon mustard, honey, and cumin might seem to be an unlikely combination, but this dish will win raves every time.

Cooking spray

1 tablespoon Dijon mustard

2 teaspoons honey

4 boneless, skinless chicken breast halves (about 4 ounces each), all visible fat discarded, pounded to about 1/2 inch thick

8 ounces frozen green peas

3/4 cup fat-free, low-sodium chicken broth

1/2 cup water

1/2 teaspoon ground cumin

3/4 cup uncooked whole-wheat couscous

Preheat the broiler. Lightly spray the broiler pan with cooking spray.

In a small bowl, stir together the mustard and honey. Brush about half the mixture over one side of the chicken.

Broil the chicken about 4 inches from the heat for 3 minutes. Turn the chicken over. Using a clean brush, brush with the remaining mustard mixture. Broil for 3 to 4 minutes, or until the chicken is lightly browned on the outside and no longer pink on the inside.

Meanwhile, in a medium saucepan, stir together the remaining ingredients except the couscous. Cook, covered, over medium-high heat until the water comes to a boil. Stir in the couscous. Remove from the heat. Let stand, covered, for 5 minutes. Fluff with a fork.

Serve the chicken over the couscous mixture.

PER SERVING
calories 356
total fat 3.0 g
saturated 0.5 g
trans 0.0 g
polyunsaturated 0.5 g
monounsaturated 0.5 g
cholesterol 66 mg
sodium 244 mg
carbohydrates 47 g
fiber 9 g
sugars 7 g
protein 37 g
dietary exchanges
3 starch
3 very lean meat

greek chicken

SERVES 4 · 3 ounces chicken and ⅓ cup bulgur mixture per serving
PREPARATION TIME · 5 minutes
COOKING TIME · 26 to 32 minutes

You'll think you're at a taverna on the Mediterranean Sea when you bite into this chicken. It's packed with flavor from lemon, feta cheese, oregano, and kalamata olives.

Olive oil spray

4 boneless, skinless chicken breast halves (about 4 ounces each), all visible fat discarded

1 14.5-ounce can fat-free, low-sodium chicken broth, divided use

⅓ cup water

½ teaspoon (heaping) dried oregano, crumbled

½ teaspoon grated lemon zest

1¼ teaspoons lemon juice

⅛ teaspoon pepper

⅔ cup uncooked bulgur

8 kalamata olives, thinly sliced

1 tablespoon plus 1 teaspoon crumbled feta cheese

Lightly spray a large, deep skillet or Dutch oven with olive oil spray. Cook the chicken over medium-high heat for 2 to 3 minutes on each side, or until lightly browned. (The chicken will not be done.)

Add 1 cup broth, the water, oregano, lemon zest, lemon juice, and pepper. Bring to a simmer, 1 to 2 minutes. Reduce the heat and simmer, covered, for 10 minutes, or until the chicken is no longer pink in the center. Transfer the chicken to a plate.

Stir in the bulgur and remaining ¾ cup broth. Return the chicken to the skillet. Increase the heat to medium high and bring to a boil, covered, 1 to 2 minutes. Reduce the heat and simmer, covered, for 12 to 15 minutes, or until the bulgur is tender.

Serve sprinkled with the olives and feta.

PER SERVING
calories 240
total fat 4.5 g
saturated 1.0 g
trans 0.0 g
polyunsaturated 0.5 g
monounsaturated 2.0 g
cholesterol 69 mg
sodium 260 mg
carbohydrates 19 g
fiber 5 g
sugars 0 g
protein 31 g
dietary exchanges
1½ starch
3 very lean meat

southwestern-style roasted chicken

SERVES 4 · 3 ounces chicken per serving (plus 12 ounces chicken reserved)
PREPARATION TIME · 12 minutes
COOKING TIME · 25 to 28 minutes

planned-overs

Although these highly seasoned chicken breasts are delicious on their own, they also make a fine foundation for a variety of other dishes, such as Sour Cream Chicken Enchilada Casserole (page 160).

Cooking spray
1½ teaspoons ground cumin
¾ teaspoon chili powder
¼ teaspoon dried oregano, crumbled
⅛ teaspoon salt

8 boneless, skinless chicken breast halves (about 4 ounces each), all visible fat discarded
1 large shallot, very thinly sliced
4 sprigs fresh cilantro, finely snipped
1 to 1½ tablespoons lime juice

Preheat the oven to 350°F. Lightly spray a 13 x 9 x 2-inch glass dish with cooking spray.

In a small bowl, stir together the cumin, chili powder, oregano, and salt. Put the chicken in the glass dish. Rub the chili powder mixture into the chicken. Sprinkle with the shallot and cilantro. Pour the lime juice over the chicken. Lightly spray the chicken with cooking spray.

Bake for 25 to 28 minutes, or until the chicken is no longer pink in the center. Using a slotted spoon, transfer 4 breast halves to an airtight container and refrigerate for use in Sour Cream Chicken Enchilada Casserole. Serve the remaining chicken breast halves.

PER SERVING
calories 129
total fat 1.5 g
saturated 0.5 g
trans 0.0 g
polyunsaturated 0.5 g
monounsaturated 0.5 g
cholesterol 66 mg
sodium 114 mg
carbohydrates 1 g
fiber 0 g
sugars 0 g
protein 26 g
dietary exchanges
3 very lean meat

crispy chicken with creamy gravy

SERVES 4 · 3 ounces chicken and ¼ cup gravy per serving
PREPARATION TIME · 10 minutes
COOKING TIME · 11 to 14 minutes

express

For comfort food sure to please, try this cracker-coated chicken. You may want to make extra gravy to top mashed potatoes.

2 tablespoons all-purpose flour and 1 tablespoon all-purpose flour, divided use

¼ cup egg substitute

¼ cup unsalted cracker crumbs (about 7 crackers)

1 teaspoon salt-free all-purpose seasoning blend

4 boneless, skinless chicken breast halves (about 4 ounces each), all visible fat discarded, lightly flattened

Cooking spray

1 tablespoon canola or corn oil

½ cup bottled fat-free chicken gravy

½ cup fat-free milk

Put 2 tablespoons flour and the egg substitute in separate shallow bowls. In a third shallow bowl, stir together the cracker crumbs and seasoning blend. Set the bowls in a row, assembly-line fashion.

Working with 1 piece of chicken at a time, dip in the flour, turning to coat. Dip in the egg substitute, letting any excess drip off. Dip in the cracker crumb mixture, turning to coat. Lightly spray both sides with cooking spray.

In a large nonstick skillet, heat the oil over medium heat, swirling to coat the bottom. Cook the chicken with the meaty side down for 4 to 5 minutes, or until browned on the bottom. Turn over. Cook for 4 to 5 minutes, or until the chicken is no longer pink in the center. Transfer to plates.

In the same skillet, whisk together the gravy, milk, and remaining 1 tablespoon flour. Cook over medium heat until thick and bubbly, 2 to 3 minutes, whisking occasionally. Spoon over the chicken.

PER SERVING
calories 219
total fat 6.5 g
saturated 1.0 g
trans 0.0 g
polyunsaturated 4.5 g
monounsaturated 3.0 g
cholesterol 66 mg
sodium 285 mg
carbohydrates 12 g
fiber 0 g
sugars 2 g
protein 27 g
dietary exchanges
1 starch
3 lean meat

roasted chicken breasts with garlic gravy

SERVES 4 · 3 ounces chicken and scant ½ cup gravy per serving
PREPARATION TIME · 15 minutes
MICROWAVE TIME · 1 minute
COOKING TIME · 22 minutes

This yummy chicken and gravy combination goes well with just about any side dish.

Cooking spray
2 large, plump whole garlic bulbs
1 tablespoon olive oil
4 boneless, skinless chicken breast halves (about 4 ounces each), all visible fat discarded
1 teaspoon dried thyme, crumbled

¼ teaspoon pepper
¼ teaspoon salt and ¼ teaspoon salt, divided use
1 tablespoon all-purpose flour
2 cups fat-free, low-sodium chicken broth

Preheat the oven to 400°F. Lightly spray a rimmed baking sheet with cooking spray.

Cut about ¼ inch off the top of the garlic bulbs to create a flat top and expose the middle cloves. Put on a microwaveable plate. Microwave on 100 percent power (high) for 1 minute. Separate the cloves of garlic and peel off the skins (they should slip off very easily). Heap the garlic on the baking sheet. Drizzle the garlic with the oil. Spread the garlic toward the edges, leaving the middle of the baking sheet empty.

Sprinkle both sides of the chicken with the thyme, pepper, and ¼ teaspoon salt. Put the chicken in the middle of the baking sheet.

Bake for 20 minutes, or until the chicken is no longer pink in the center. If the smaller garlic cloves go beyond the golden stage before the chicken is done, put them in a large skillet. Transfer the cooked chicken to plates. Add the rest of the garlic to the skillet. Using the back of a spoon or fork, crush the garlic. Stir in the remaining ¼ teaspoon salt.

PER SERVING	
calories 187	
total fat 6.0 g	
saturated 1.0 g	
trans 0.0 g	
polyunsaturated 1.0 g	
monounsaturated 3.5 g	
cholesterol 63 mg	
sodium 378 mg	
carbohydrates 7 g	
fiber 1 g	
sugars 0 g	
protein 25 g	
dietary exchanges	
½ carbohydrate	
3 lean meat	

Put the flour in a small bowl. Pour in the broth, whisking to dissolve. Stir into the garlic mixture. Bring to a boil over medium heat, stirring constantly and continuing to break up the garlic. When the sauce thickens and boils, about 2 minutes, pour over the chicken.

COOK'S TIP ON ROASTED GARLIC

Roasted garlic has a creamy, mild flavor. It's versatile and tastes so good you may want to roast one or two heads when you're using the oven. Keep roasted garlic on hand as a low-calorie substitute for margarine to spread on bread or use to thicken sauces.

skillet chicken with capers and white wine

SERVES 4 · 3 ounces chicken and 1 tablespoon sauce per serving
PREPARATION TIME · 6 minutes
COOKING TIME · 10 to 12 minutes
STANDING TIME · 3 minutes

Bursting with flavor, this super-fast entrée features chicken that is cooked, then "marinated" for a few minutes in a light but richly seasoned sauce.

1 teaspoon dried Italian seasoning, crumbled

1 teaspoon dried oregano, crumbled

1/2 teaspoon pepper (coarsely ground preferred)

4 boneless, skinless chicken breast halves (about 4 ounces each), all visible fat discarded

1 teaspoon olive oil and 2 teaspoons olive oil, divided use

1/4 cup dry white wine (regular or nonalcoholic)

3 tablespoons capers, drained

1 teaspoon grated lemon zest

2 teaspoons lemon juice

1/2 teaspoon bottled minced garlic or 1 medium garlic clove, minced

1/4 teaspoon dried rosemary, crushed

Sprinkle the Italian seasoning, oregano, and pepper on both sides of the chicken. Using your fingertips, lightly press the seasonings so they adhere.

In a large nonstick skillet, heat 1 teaspoon oil over medium-high heat, swirling to coat the bottom. Cook the chicken for 4 to 5 minutes on each side, or until no longer pink in the center.

Meanwhile, in a small bowl, stir together the wine, capers, lemon zest, lemon juice, garlic, rosemary, and remaining 2 teaspoons oil.

PER SERVING
calories 170
total fat 5.0 g
saturated 1.0 g
trans 0.0 g
polyunsaturated 0.5 g
monounsaturated 3.0 g
cholesterol 66 mg
sodium 266 mg
carbohydrates 1 g
fiber 1 g
sugars 0 g
protein 27 g
dietary exchanges
3 lean meat

When the chicken is done, pour in the wine mixture. Bring to a boil and boil for 30 seconds, or until the sauce is reduced slightly. Remove from the heat. Turn the chicken pieces several times to coat evenly. Cover and let stand for 3 minutes to absorb flavors. Transfer the chicken to plates, leaving the sauce in the skillet.

Stir the sauce, scraping to release any browned bits. Spoon the sauce over the chicken.

sun-dried tomato pesto chicken and pasta

SERVES 4 · 3 ounces chicken and 1 cup pasta per serving
PREPARATION TIME · 10 minutes
COOKING TIME · 12 minutes

This fantastically easy recipe utilizes bottled sun-dried tomato pesto to cut your prep time.

1 teaspoon canola or corn oil

4 boneless, skinless chicken breast halves (about 4 ounces each), all visible fat discarded

¼ cup bottled sun-dried tomato pesto

2 tablespoons water

2 tablespoons dry red wine (regular or nonalcoholic)

1½ tablespoons dried basil, crumbled

1 tablespoon balsamic vinegar

¼ teaspoon salt

9 ounces refrigerated angel hair pasta (lowest fat and sodium available)

Using the package directions for the pasta, put hot tap water into a pot and bring to a boil, covering the pot so the water boils faster.

In a large nonstick skillet, heat the oil over medium-high heat, swirling to coat the bottom. Cook the chicken for 2 minutes on each side.

Meanwhile, in a small bowl, whisk together the remaining ingredients except the pasta. Pour over the chicken. Reduce the heat and simmer, covered, for 5 to 7 minutes, or until the chicken is no longer pink in the center.

When the water for the pasta comes to a boil, add the pasta and cook using the package directions, omitting any salt and oil. Don't overcook. Drain well in a colander.

Serve the chicken on the pasta. Spoon the pesto sauce over all.

PER SERVING
calories 381
total fat 9.0 g
saturated 1.0 g
trans 0.0 g
polyunsaturated 0.5 g
monounsaturated 1.0 g
cholesterol 67 mg
sodium 441 mg
carbohydrates 39 g
fiber 3 g
sugars 3 g
protein 34 g
dietary exchanges
2½ starch
3 lean meat

Basil-Parmesan Pesto Chicken and Pasta

Replace the sun-dried tomato pesto with basil-Parmesan pesto, the dry red wine with dry white wine, and the balsamic vinegar with lemon juice

border chicken

SERVES 4 · 3 ounces chicken, 1/2 cup rice, and 2/3 cup sauce per serving
PREPARATION TIME · 15 minutes
COOKING TIME · 23 to 25 minutes

Celebrate flavors of the Yucatán with this chicken dish, which is served on brown rice colored with turmeric.

1 14.5-ounce can no-salt-added diced tomatoes, undrained

1 tablespoon lime juice

1/2 1- to 1 1/2-ounce package taco seasoning mix

1 teaspoon sugar and 1/2 teaspoon sugar, divided use

1/2 teaspoon dried oregano, crumbled

1/2 teaspoon red hot-pepper sauce

4 boneless, skinless chicken breast halves (about 4 ounces each), all visible fat discarded

3/4 cup uncooked instant brown rice

1/4 teaspoon turmeric

1 tablespoon olive oil (extra-virgin preferred)

1 tablespoon snipped fresh cilantro

In a medium bowl, stir together the tomatoes with liquid, lime juice, taco seasoning, 1 teaspoon sugar, oregano, and hot-pepper sauce.

Put the chicken in a Dutch oven. Pour the tomato mixture over the chicken. Bring to a boil over high heat. Stir. Reduce the heat and simmer, covered, for 20 minutes, stirring occasionally. For a slightly thicker sauce, remove the cover after about 10 minutes.

Meanwhile, prepare the rice using the package directions, omitting the salt and margarine and adding the turmeric.

When the chicken is done, stir in the oil and remaining 1/2 teaspoon sugar.

Spoon the rice onto the center of a platter. Arrange the chicken around the edge. Pour the sauce over the chicken. Sprinkle with the cilantro.

PER SERVING
calories 261
total fat 5.5 g
saturated 1.0 g
trans 0.0 g
polyunsaturated 1.0 g
monounsaturated 3.0 g
cholesterol 66 mg
sodium 390 mg
carbohydrates 23 g
fiber 3 g
sugars 5 g
protein 29 g
dietary exchanges
1 carbohydrate
1 vegetable
3 lean meat

grilled chicken with green chiles and cheese

SERVES 4 · 3 ounces chicken per serving
PREPARATION TIME · 6 minutes
COOKING TIME · 8 to 10 minutes

Break out of a plain-chicken rut with this southwestern-style dish. The only way it could be easier would be for the dish to prepare itself!

Olive oil spray

4 boneless, skinless chicken breast halves (about 4 ounces each), all visible fat discarded

1 teaspoon chili powder

¼ cup canned diced green chiles, rinsed if desired, drained

¼ cup shredded low-fat Cheddar cheese (about 1 ounce)

Preheat the grill on medium high.

Spray one side of the chicken with the olive oil spray. Sprinkle with half the chili powder. Turn over. Repeat.

Grill the chicken with the smooth side down for 4 to 5 minutes. Turn over. Spread the green chiles on the chicken. Sprinkle with the Cheddar. Grill for 4 to 5 minutes, or until the chicken is no longer pink in the center.

PER SERVING
calories 138
total fat 3.0 g
saturated 1.0 g
trans 0.0 g
polyunsaturated 0.5 g
monounsaturated 1.0 g
cholesterol 64 mg
sodium 159 mg
carbohydrates 1 g
fiber 1 g
sugars 0 g
protein 25 g
dietary exchanges
3 very lean meat

italian grilled chicken

SERVES 4 · 3 ounces chicken per serving
PREPARATION TIME · 10 minutes
COOKING TIME · 8 to 10 minutes

express · no shopping required

So few ingredients, so much flavor! This super-easy, super-quick entrée definitely belongs in your repertoire.

Olive oil spray

4 boneless, skinless chicken breast halves (about 4 ounces each), all visible fat discarded

1 teaspoon dried oregano, crumbled

1 teaspoon olive oil

1 thinly sliced medium bell pepper, any color

1 thinly sliced medium onion

2 tablespoons shredded or grated Parmesan cheese

Preheat the grill on medium high.

Spray one side of the chicken with the olive oil spray. Sprinkle with half the oregano. Turn over. Repeat.

Grill the chicken for 8 to 10 minutes, or until the chicken is no longer pink in the center, turning halfway through.

Meanwhile, in a medium skillet, heat 1 teaspoon olive oil over medium-high heat, swirling to coat the bottom. Cook the bell pepper and onion for about 3 minutes, or until tender, stirring occasionally. Spoon over the cooked chicken. Sprinkle with the Parmesan.

PER SERVING
calories 160
total fat 4.5 g
saturated 1.5 g
trans 0.0 g
polyunsaturated 0.5 g
monounsaturated 2.0 g
cholesterol 65 mg
sodium 99 mg
carbohydrates 5 g
fiber 1 g
sugars 3 g
protein 24 g
dietary exchanges
1 vegetable
3 lean meat

barbecued chicken dijon

SERVES 4 · 3 ounces chicken per serving
PREPARATION TIME · 8 minutes
COOKING TIME · 9 to 11 minutes

Barbecued chicken reaches a new level with the addition of rosemary and flavored mustard.

Olive oil spray

4 boneless, skinless chicken breast halves (about 4 ounces each), all visible fat discarded

1 teaspoon dried rosemary, crushed

¼ cup barbecue sauce (lowest sodium available)

1 teaspoon flavored Dijon mustard, such as horseradish, orange, or honey

Preheat the grill on medium high.

Spray one side of the chicken with the olive oil spray. Sprinkle with half the rosemary. Turn over. Repeat.

Grill the chicken for 8 to 10 minutes, or until no longer pink in the center, turning once halfway through.

Meanwhile, in a small bowl, stir together the barbecue sauce and mustard.

When the chicken is done, brush one side with the barbecue sauce mixture. Grill with that side down for 30 seconds. Brush the top side with the barbecue sauce mixture. Turn over. Grill for 30 seconds.

PER SERVING
calories 150
total fat 3.0 g
saturated 0.5 g
trans 0.0 g
polyunsaturated 0.5 g
monounsaturated 1.0 g
cholesterol 63 mg
sodium 104 mg
carbohydrates 7 g
fiber 0 g
sugars 5 g
protein 23 g
dietary exchanges
½ carbohydrate
3 very lean meat

chicken and brown rice lettuce wraps

SERVES 4 · 2 wraps per serving
PREPARATION TIME · 18 minutes
COOKING TIME · 14 to 16 minutes

Crisp, crunchy romaine leaves enclose warm chicken and brown rice for an Asian entrée that you'll want to add to your go-to list.

1 cup uncooked instant brown rice
1/2 cup preshredded carrots
1 teaspoon toasted sesame oil
1 pound boneless, skinless chicken breasts halves, all visible fat discarded, finely diced

3 medium green onions, sliced
1 medium rib of celery, thinly sliced
2 tablespoons soy sauce (lowest sodium available)
1 tablespoon hoisin sauce
8 medium romaine leaves

In a medium saucepan, prepare the rice using the package directions, omitting the salt and oil and adding the carrots to the boiling water when you add the rice. When the rice is cooked, remove the pan from the heat.

Meanwhile, heat the sesame oil in a medium nonstick skillet over medium-high heat. Cook the chicken for 4 to 6 minutes, or until no longer pink in the center, stirring occasionally.

Stir the remaining ingredients except the romaine into the rice mixture. Stir in the chicken. Spoon the mixture down the center of each romaine leaf and roll loosely. Place with the seam side down on plates. Serve immediately for the best texture.

PER SERVING

calories 247
total fat 3.5 g
  saturated 0.5 g
  trans 0.0 g
  polyunsaturated 1.0 g
  monounsaturated 1.0 g
cholesterol 66 mg
sodium 316 mg
carbohydrates 22 g
  fiber 3 g
  sugars 3 g
protein 29 g
dietary exchanges
  1 1/2 starch
  3 very lean meat

COOK'S TIP

Instead of rolling the filling in romaine leaves, try serving it on about 4 cups chopped romaine or packaged angel hair slaw.

apricot-barbecue chicken chunks

SERVES 4 · ½ cup per serving (plus 2 cups
  chicken reserved)
PREPARATION TIME · 5 minutes
COOKING TIME · 6 to 7 minutes

*Here's the answer when you have to have a kid-pleasing entrée in next to
no time. This recipe even gives you a bonus—planned-overs to use in
Asian Chicken and Wild Rice Salad (page 87).*

Cooking spray

2 pounds boneless, skinless chicken
  breasts or turkey breast
  tenderloins, all visible fat
  discarded, cut into bite-size
  pieces

½ cup barbecue sauce (lowest
  sodium available)

½ cup all-fruit apricot or plum
  spread

1 teaspoon ground ginger
  (optional)

Lightly spray a large skillet with cooking
spray. Cook the chicken over medium-high
heat for 3 to 4 minutes, or until tender and no
longer pink in the center, stirring occasionally.

Stir in the barbecue sauce, apricot spread,
and ginger. Cook for about 3 minutes, or until
heated through, stirring constantly. Refrigerate half the chicken (2 cups) in an airtight
container for use in Asian Chicken and Wild
Rice Salad. Serve the remaining chicken.

PER SERVING
calories 195
total fat 1.5 g
saturated 0.5 g
trans 0.0 g
polyunsaturated 0.5 g
monounsaturated 0.5 g
cholesterol 66 mg
sodium 179 mg
carbohydrates 17 g
fiber 0 g
sugars 14 g
protein 26 g
dietary exchanges
1 carbohydrate
3 very lean meat

chicken chili

SERVES 4 · 1½ cups per serving
PREPARATION TIME · 12 to 14 minutes
COOKING TIME · 23 minutes

Comforting, spicy, and oh-so-good describe this hearty dish.

Cooking spray

1 pound boneless, skinless chicken breasts, all visible fat discarded, cut into ¾-inch cubes

1½ cups chopped onion

½ cup chopped green bell pepper

½ to 1 medium fresh jalapeño, seeds and ribs discarded, minced

1 15-ounce can reduced-sodium Great Northern beans, rinsed and drained

1 14.5-ounce can fat-free, low-sodium chicken broth

1 4-ounce can diced green chiles, drained

1 cup water

1 cup frozen whole-kernel corn

2 to 3 teaspoons ground cumin

2 teaspoons dried oregano, crumbled

1 teaspoon garlic powder

⅛ teaspoon salt

3 tablespoons snipped fresh cilantro

Lightly spray a large saucepan with cooking spray. Cook the chicken over medium-high heat for 2 minutes, stirring frequently.

Stir in the onions, bell pepper, and jalapeño. Cook for 3 minutes, stirring frequently.

Stir in the remaining ingredients except the cilantro. Bring to a boil, covered, still on medium high, about 3 minutes. Reduce the heat to low and cook, covered, for 15 minutes.

Stir in the cilantro just before serving.

PER SERVING
calories 285
total fat 2.0 g
saturated 0.5 g
trans 0.0 g
polyunsaturated 0.5 g
monounsaturated 0.5 g
cholesterol 66 mg
sodium 390 mg
carbohydrates 32 g
fiber 7 g
sugars 7 g
protein 35 g
dietary exchanges
1½ starch
2 vegetable
3½ very lean meat

Slow-Cooker Method

In a 3½- to 4-quart slow cooker, combine all the ingredients except the cilantro (no need to cook the chicken, onion, and peppers first). Cook, covered, on low for 5 to 7 hours or on high for 2½ to 3 hours. Stir in the cilantro just before serving.

 TIME-SAVER Cutting chicken breasts or other boneless meats is quick and easy if they are very cold or even partially frozen (about 30 minutes in the freezer).

spicy honey-kissed chicken

SERVES 4 · 1 cup per serving
PREPARATION TIME · 5 minutes
COOKING TIME · 5 to 8 minutes

express · no shopping required

Cumin, sage, and ginger spice up the rub that gives this chicken its distinctive flavor.

RUB

1 teaspoon ground cumin
1/2 teaspoon dried sage
1/2 teaspoon ground ginger
1/2 teaspoon salt
1/4 to 1/2 teaspoon pepper

CHICKEN

1 pound boneless, skinless chicken breasts, all visible fat discarded
1 tablespoon canola or corn oil
3 tablespoons lemon juice
1 tablespoon honey
1 tablespoon soy sauce (lowest sodium available)

In a small bowl, stir together the rub ingredients. Using your fingertips, lightly press the rub all over the chicken. Cut the chicken into strips about 1/2 inch wide.

In a large nonstick skillet, heat the oil over medium-high heat, swirling to coat the bottom. Cook the chicken for 3 to 5 minutes, or until nearly cooked through, stirring frequently.

Meanwhile, in a small bowl, whisk together the lemon juice, honey, and soy sauce.

Stir the lemon juice mixture into the chicken. Increase the heat to high and cook for 1 to 2 minutes, or until the chicken is no longer pink in the center.

PER SERVING
calories 181
total fat 5.0 g
saturated 0.5 g
trans 0.0 g
polyunsaturated 1.5 g
monounsaturated 2.5 g
cholesterol 66 mg
sodium 463 mg
carbohydrates 6 g
fiber 0 g
sugars 5 g
protein 27 g
dietary exchanges
1/2 carbohydrate
3 lean meat

chicken and shrimp stir-fry

SERVES 4 · 1 cup per serving
PREPARATION TIME · 10 minutes
COOKING TIME · 8 minutes

Snow peas paired with either chicken or shrimp is a classic Asian combination. When you can't decide which you'd prefer, try this recipe, which gives you both.

2 teaspoons canola or corn oil

2 teaspoons bottled chopped garlic or 4 medium garlic cloves, chopped

1/2 teaspoon crushed red pepper flakes

9 ounces raw large shrimp, peeled, rinsed and patted dry

2 boneless, skinless chicken breast halves (about 4 ounces each), all visible fat discarded, cut crosswise into 1/4-inch strips

8 ounces fresh or frozen snow peas, trimmed if fresh

1/2 teaspoon salt

In a large nonstick skillet, heat the oil over medium-high heat, swirling to coat the bottom. Cook the garlic and red pepper flakes for about 30 seconds, or until the garlic is aromatic.

Stir in the shrimp and chicken. Increase the heat to high. Cook for about 2 minutes, stirring constantly.

If using fresh snow peas, cook the chicken and shrimp for 2 more minutes before adding the peas. Cook, uncovered, for 2 minutes with the peas. If using frozen snow peas, add to the chicken and shrimp and cook, covered, for 2 minutes. Uncover and cook for 2 minutes, or until the chicken is no longer pink in the center and the shrimp is pink and cooked through.

Stir in the salt.

PER SERVING

calories 157
total fat 3.5 g
  saturated 0.5 g
  trans 0.0 g
  polyunsaturated 1.0 g
  monounsaturated 2.0 g
cholesterol 127 mg
sodium 439 mg
carbohydrates 5 g
  fiber 2 g
  sugars 2 g
protein 25 g
dietary exchanges
  1 vegetable
  3 very lean meat

COOK'S TIP
Using salt near the end of preparation heightens the flavors without adding too much sodium.

chicken and vegetable stir-fry

SERVES 4 · 1 heaping cup per serving
PREPARATION TIME · 10 minutes
COOKING TIME · 9 to 11 minutes

This basic stir-fry recipe gives you many options. You can choose between the Asian and Italian flavorings (see Italian Stir-Fry on page 147), and you can vary the meat by replacing the chicken with round steak, pork chops or tenderloin, firm-fleshed fish, bay scallops, or tofu. Save even more time by using precut vegetables or frozen mixed vegetables (no need to thaw before cooking). Even if you make only half this recipe, you'll probably want to make the entire amount of sauce.

SAUCE

2 tablespoons water

1 tablespoon bottled stir-fry sauce (lowest sodium available)

1 teaspoon cornstarch

• • •

1 teaspoon canola or corn oil

1 pound boneless, skinless chicken breasts, all visible fat discarded, thinly sliced

1 cup broccoli florets, cut into 1-inch pieces

½ cup sliced red bell pepper

½ cup thinly sliced carrot

½ cup canned baby corn, rinsed, drained, and cut into bite-size pieces

2 medium green onions, sliced

1 teaspoon bottled minced garlic or 2 medium garlic cloves, minced

In a small bowl, whisk together the sauce ingredients. Set aside.

In a wok or large skillet, heat the oil over medium-high heat, swirling to coat the bottom. Cook the chicken for 3 to 4 minutes, or until no longer pink in the center, stirring occasionally.

Add the remaining ingredients. Cook for 3 to 4 minutes, or until the vegetables are tender-crisp, stirring frequently.

Push the chicken mixture aside, making a well in the center of the wok. Pour the sauce into the well. Stir the chicken mixture into the sauce. Cook for 1 to 2 minutes, or until the sauce has thickened, stirring occasionally.

PER SERVING
calories 179
total fat 3.0 g
saturated 0.5 g
trans 0.0 g
polyunsaturated 0.5 g
monounsaturated 1.0 g
cholesterol 66 mg
sodium 208 mg
carbohydrates 8 g
fiber 3 g
sugars 3 g
protein 28 g
dietary exchanges
½ carbohydrate
3 very lean meat

Italian Stir-Fry

SERVES 4 · 1¼ cups per serving

Prepare as directed on page 146 except replace the sauce mixture with 3 tablespoons fat-free, low-sodium chicken broth, 1 teaspoon cornstarch, and ½ teaspoon dried oregano, crumbled; replace the canola or corn oil with olive oil; and replace the carrot and corn with ½ cup sliced fresh asparagus and ½ cup sliced zucchini. Add 1 medium-sliced Italian plum (Roma) tomato when adding the chicken mixture.

chicken creole on the run

SERVES 4 · 1 cup per serving
PREPARATION TIME · 10 minutes
COOKING TIME · 25 to 26 minutes
STANDING TIME · 15 minutes (optional)

Enjoy this soup-stew as is or, for a one-dish meal, ladle it over brown rice. Pass the hot-pepper sauce, please!

1 teaspoon olive oil and 2 teaspoons olive oil (extra-virgin preferred), divided use

12 ounces boneless, skinless chicken breasts, all visible fat discarded, cut into bite-size pieces

1 14.5-ounce can no-salt-added stewed tomatoes, undrained

1 cup fat-free, low-sodium chicken broth

1 cup diced green bell pepper

1 cup frozen cut okra, thawed

2 medium dried bay leaves

1 teaspoon sugar

1 teaspoon Worcestershire sauce (lowest sodium available)

1/2 teaspoon dried thyme, crumbled

1/4 teaspoon Louisiana hot-pepper sauce or red hot-pepper sauce

1/4 cup snipped fresh parsley

1/2 teaspoon salt

In a large nonstick skillet, heat 1 teaspoon oil over medium-high heat, swirling to coat the bottom. Cook the chicken for 2 to 3 minutes, or until barely pink in the center, stirring frequently. Transfer to a plate.

In the same skillet, stir together the tomatoes with liquid, broth, bell pepper, okra, bay leaves, sugar, Worcestershire sauce, thyme, and hot-pepper sauce. Bring to a boil over medium-high heat, about 2 minutes. Reduce the heat and simmer, covered, for 20 minutes, or until the okra is tender and the mixture has thickened slightly, breaking up any large pieces of tomato near the end of cooking. Remove from the heat. Discard the bay leaves.

Stir in the parsley, salt, remaining 2 teaspoons oil, and chicken with any accumulated juices. If time allows, cover and let stand for 15 minutes so the flavors blend thoroughly.

PER SERVING
calories 176
total fat 4.5 g
saturated 1.0 g
trans 0.0 g
polyunsaturated 0.5 g
monounsaturated 2.5 g
cholesterol 49 mg
sodium 394 mg
carbohydrates 11 g
fiber 3 g
sugars 7 g
protein 22 g
dietary exchanges
2 vegetable
2 1/2 lean meat

lemon chicken with asparagus and pasta

SERVES 4 · 1½ cups per serving
PREPARATION TIME · 12 minutes
COOKING TIME · 21 to 23 minutes

Nothing brings out the flavor of fresh asparagus better than lemon. Here the two combine with whole-grain bow-tie pasta, mushrooms, and chicken chunks for a delightful one-dish meal.

4½ ounces uncooked whole-grain bow-tie pasta (about 1⅔ cups)

2 teaspoons olive oil

8 ounces fresh asparagus, trimmed and cut into 1½-inch pieces

3 ounces presliced fresh button mushrooms

1 medium green onion (green and white parts), chopped, and 1 medium green onion (green and white parts), chopped, divided use

1 pound boneless, skinless chicken breasts, all visible fat discarded, cut into ¾-inch cubes

1 cup fat-free, low-sodium chicken broth

2 tablespoons lemon juice

¼ teaspoon pepper

⅛ teaspoon salt

2 tablespoons shredded or grated Parmesan cheese

Prepare the pasta using the package directions, omitting the salt and oil. Drain well in a colander.

Meanwhile, in a large skillet, heat the oil over medium-high heat, swirling to coat the bottom. Cook the asparagus, mushrooms, and 1 green onion for 3 minutes, stirring frequently.

Stir in the chicken. Cook for 4 minutes, stirring frequently.

Stir in the broth, lemon juice, pepper, and salt. Cook, covered, for 3 minutes, or until the chicken is no longer pink in the center and the vegetables are tender-crisp.

Stir the pasta into the chicken mixture. Cook for 1 minute, or until heated through. Sprinkle with the remaining 1 green onion and the Parmesan.

PER SERVING

calories 331
total fat 5.0 g
  saturated 1.0 g
  trans 0.0 g
  polyunsaturated 1.0 g
  monounsaturated 2.5 g
cholesterol 68 mg
sodium 210 mg
carbohydrates 37 g
  fiber 5 g
  sugars 3 g
protein 36 g
dietary exchanges
  2½ starch
  3 very lean meat

curried chicken and cauliflower

SERVES 4 · 1 cup per serving
PREPARATION TIME · 15 minutes
COOKING TIME · 14 to 19 minutes

Turn ordinary chicken and cauliflower into a flavor sensation with curry powder and tangy yogurt. Serve over couscous, noodles, or rice.

1 teaspoon canola or corn oil

¼ cup frozen chopped onion or ½ medium onion, thinly sliced

1 teaspoon bottled minced garlic or 2 medium garlic cloves, minced

1 pound boneless, skinless chicken breasts, all visible fat discarded, cut into ¾-inch cubes

1 medium cauliflower, separated into bite-size pieces (about 2 cups)

1 cup fat-free, low-sodium chicken broth

1 teaspoon curry powder

¼ teaspoon salt

¼ teaspoon turmeric (optional)

⅛ teaspoon pepper

3 tablespoons all-purpose flour

¼ cup water

½ cup fat-free plain yogurt

In a large nonstick skillet, heat the oil over medium-high heat, swirling to coat the bottom. Cook the onion and garlic for about 3 minutes, or until the onion is soft, stirring occasionally. Push to one side of the skillet.

Add the chicken to the middle of the skillet. Cook for 4 to 5 minutes, or until no longer pink in the center, stirring occasionally (only the chicken).

Add the cauliflower, broth, curry powder, salt, turmeric, and pepper. Stir to incorporate the chicken, onion, and garlic. Increase the heat to high and bring to a boil. Reduce the heat to medium low. Cook, covered, for 5 to 6 minutes, or until the cauliflower is tender. Increase the heat to medium high.

PER SERVING
calories 195
total fat 3.0 g
saturated 0.5 g
trans 0.0 g
polyunsaturated 0.5 g
monounsaturated 1.0 g
cholesterol 66 mg
sodium 274 mg
carbohydrates 11 g
fiber 2 g
sugars 4 g
protein 30 g
dietary exchanges
½ carbohydrate
1 vegetable
3 very lean meat

Put the flour in a small bowl. Add the water, whisking to dissolve. Pour into the skillet and cook, uncovered, for 2 to 3 minutes, or until the mixture is thickened, stirring occasionally. Reduce the heat to low.

Spoon a small amount of warm chicken mixture into a small bowl. Stir in the yogurt. Stir into the skillet. Cook, uncovered, for 1 to 2 minutes, or until warmed through, stirring occasionally.

chicken biryani

SERVES 4 · scant 1½ cups per serving
PREPARATION TIME · 12 to 14 minutes
COOKING TIME · 36 minutes

Known as a festive, regal dish in India and Pakistan, biryani is packed with flavor. Don't be scared off by the long list of ingredients. The dish really is quick and easy to prepare.

1 cup water and 2 tablespoons water, divided use

⅔ cup uncooked basmati rice

⅔ cup preshredded carrots

2 teaspoons canola or corn oil

1 pound boneless, skinless chicken breasts, all visible fat discarded, cut into strips about 2 x ¼ inch

1 cup chopped onion

2 teaspoons grated peeled gingerroot

1 teaspoon bottled minced garlic or 2 medium garlic cloves, minced

2 teaspoons ground cumin

½ teaspoon ground cardamom

½ teaspoon ground cloves

½ teaspoon turmeric

¼ teaspoon black pepper

¼ teaspoon cayenne

1 cup frozen green peas

1 cup fat-free, low-sodium chicken broth

⅛ teaspoon salt

1 tablespoon cornstarch

In a medium saucepan, bring 1 cup water to a boil. Stir in the rice and carrots. Cook using the package directions, omitting the salt and margarine.

Meanwhile, in another medium saucepan, heat the oil over medium-high heat, swirling to coat the bottom. Cook the chicken, onion, gingerroot, and garlic for 3 minutes, stirring frequently.

In a small bowl, stir together the cumin, cardamom, cloves, turmeric, black pepper, and cayenne. Sprinkle over the chicken. Cook for 2 minutes, stirring frequently.

PER SERVING
calories 331
total fat 4.5 g
saturated 0.5 g
trans 0.0 g
polyunsaturated 1.0 g
monounsaturated 2.0 g
cholesterol 66 mg
sodium 221 mg
carbohydrates 40 g
fiber 4 g
sugars 5 g
protein 32 g
dietary exchanges
2 starch
2 vegetable
3 very lean meat

Stir in the peas, broth, and salt. Cook, covered, until the mixture comes to a boil, about 2 minutes. Reduce the heat to low and cook, covered, for 10 minutes, or until the chicken is no longer pink in the center and the vegetables are tender.

Pour the remaining 2 tablespoons water into a cup. Add the cornstarch, whisking to dissolve. Stir into the chicken mixture. Increase the heat to medium. Cook for about 2 minutes, or until the mixture is bubbly and slightly thickened, stirring constantly. Serve over the rice.

COOK'S TIP

For a spicier, more authentic biryani, stir an additional ¼ teaspoon cayenne into the chicken mixture just before spooning over the rice.

bell pepper chicken and noodles

SERVES 4 · heaping 1¾ cups per serving

PREPARATION TIME · 15 minutes

COOKING TIME · 18 minutes

STANDING TIME · 15 minutes (optional)

all-in-one · no shopping required

Although this dish is delicious if served immediately, the chicken and noodles absorb even more flavors if the mixture has time to stand for a while.

Cooking spray

12 ounces chicken tenders, all visible fat discarded

1 cup fat-free, low-sodium chicken broth

¼ cup no-salt-added ketchup and 1½ tablespoons no-salt-added ketchup, divided use

1 teaspoon dried oregano, crumbled

½ teaspoon salt and ¼ teaspoon salt, divided use

3 cups frozen chopped green bell pepper; 2 large green bell peppers, thinly sliced; or 1 large green bell pepper and 2 poblano chiles, thinly sliced

2 cups frozen chopped onion or 1 large onion, thinly sliced (yellow preferred)

1 14.5-ounce can no-salt-added diced tomatoes, undrained

4 ounces dried no-yolk noodles

Lightly spray a Dutch oven with cooking spray. Cook the chicken over medium-high heat for 3 minutes, stirring frequently.

Meanwhile, in a small bowl, whisk together the broth, ¼ cup ketchup, oregano, and ½ teaspoon salt.

Increase the heat to high. Stir in the bell pepper, onion, tomatoes with liquid, noodles, and broth mixture. Bring to a boil. Reduce the heat and simmer, covered, for 13 minutes, stirring occasionally. Remove from the heat.

Stir in the remaining 1½ tablespoons ketchup and remaining ¼ teaspoon salt. Let stand for about 15 minutes to absorb flavors, if desired.

PER SERVING
calories 283
total fat 1.5 g
saturated 0.5 g
trans 0.0 g
polyunsaturated 0.5 g
monounsaturated 0.5 g
cholesterol 49 mg
sodium 577 mg
carbohydrates 39 g
fiber 4 g
sugars 14 g
protein 26 g
dietary exchanges
1½ starch
3 vegetable
2½ very lean meat

creamed chicken and vegetables

SERVES 4 · 1 cup per serving
PREPARATION TIME · 5 minutes
COOKING TIME · 20 minutes

This simple dish is as pleasing to the eyes as it is to the palate. Savor it as is or over whole-grain toast or rice.

3 cups frozen mixed peas, carrots, baby corn, and snow peas or mixed peas and carrots

1 10-ounce can low-fat condensed cream of chicken soup (lowest sodium available)

1/2 cup bottled or canned mushrooms, drained

8 ounces frozen cooked diced skinless chicken breast pieces, cut into about 1-inch cubes

1/3 cup fat-free, low-sodium chicken broth or water

1/2 teaspoon dried tarragon, crumbled

1/4 teaspoon pepper

In a medium saucepan, stir together all the ingredients. Cook, covered, over medium heat for 20 minutes, or until the vegetables are tender and the mixture is completely heated, stirring occasionally.

PER SERVING

calories 207
total fat 4.0 g
  saturated 1.5 g
  trans 0.0 g
  polyunsaturated 1.0 g
  monounsaturated 1.0 g
cholesterol 51 mg
sodium 475 mg
carbohydrates 19 g
  fiber 3 g
  sugars 6 g
protein 22 g
dietary exchanges
  1 1/2 starch
  2 very lean meat

Creamed Tuna and Vegetables

Substitute two 5-ounce cans very low sodium white or light tuna in water, drained and flaked, for the chicken.

PER SERVING

calories 182
total fat 2.5 g
  saturated 0.5 g
  trans 0.0 g
  polyunsaturated 0.5 g
  monounsaturated 0.5 g
cholesterol 33 mg
sodium 474 mg
carbohydrates 19 g
  fiber 3 g
  sugars 6 g
protein 22 g
dietary exchanges
  1 1/2 starch
  2 1/2 very lean meat

lemongrass chicken with snow peas and jasmine rice

SERVES 4 · 1 cup chicken mixture and ½ cup rice per serving
PREPARATION TIME · 5 minutes
COOKING TIME · 20 to 25 minutes

Transform leftover cooked chicken into a dish that will delight the senses with color, texture, aroma, and flavor. Lemongrass, Thai red curry paste, and coconut (our heart-healthy recipe uses coconut extract) are the popular Thai ingredients that do the trick.

¾ cup uncooked jasmine rice

1½ cups water and 2 cups water, divided use

1 stalk lemongrass or 1 teaspoon grated lemon zest

2 cups fat-free, low-sodium chicken broth

2 cups diced cooked skinless chicken, cooked without salt (3 to 4 ounces)

3 ounces snow peas, trimmed and cut into thin strips

2 medium green onions, thinly sliced

1 tablespoon Thai red curry paste

½ teaspoon coconut extract

Prepare the rice using the package directions, except use 1½ cups water and omit the salt and margarine.

Meanwhile, trim and discard about 6 inches from the slender tip end of the lemongrass stalk. Remove the outer layer of the leaves from the bottom part of the stalk. Carefully cut the stalk in half lengthwise. Put in a large saucepan (don't add the lemon zest yet if using).

Add the broth, remaining 2 cups water, and chicken to the pan. Bring to a boil over high heat. Reduce the heat to medium low. Cook, covered, for 6 to 8 minutes, or until the mixture has a lemon flavor. Don't stir. Discard the lemongrass.

Add the remaining ingredients (if you are using lemon zest instead of lemongrass, add it now). Cook for 1 to 2 minutes, or until the snow peas are tender-crisp, stirring occasionally. Serve over the rice.

PER SERVING
calories 206
total fat 3.0 g
saturated 1.0 g
trans 0.0 g
polyunsaturated 0.5 g
monounsaturated 1.0 g
cholesterol 60 mg
sodium 161 mg
carbohydrates 17 g
fiber 1 g
sugars 2 g
protein 24 g
dietary exchanges
1 starch
3 very lean meat

COOK'S TIP ON LEMONGRASS

Lemongrass is an herb that often is used in Thai cooking. Although the outer leaves and tops are too tough and fibrous to eat, they can be cooked to provide lemony flavor and an appealing fragrance without the acidity of fresh lemon. Chop or slice the lower part of the stem, the only edible part, for use in a variety of chicken and seafood dishes.

COOK'S TIP ON THAI RED CURRY PASTE

Made of fresh chile peppers, herbs, and spices, Thai red curry paste is very hot and aromatic. The hotter the chile pepper used (Thai bird's eye is among the hottest), the hotter the chile paste; check the ingredients and make your selection accordingly. Among the many other ingredients that may be included in the paste are cinnamon, coriander seeds, cumin seeds, galangal or fresh ginger, garlic, kaffir lime leaves, lemongrass, onion, shrimp paste, turmeric, and vinegar.

chicken fajita pasta
with chipotle alfredo sauce

SERVES 4 · heaping 1¾ cups per serving
PREPARATION TIME · 10 minutes
COOKING TIME · 26 to 30 minutes

all-in-one

Buy marinated chicken fajita meat at the grocery store, choosing the one with the lowest sodium, or marinate chicken tenders in a low-sodium fajita marinade. You can even use leftover cooked chicken or lean beef. Warm it with the pasta and sauce.

8 ounces dried rigatoni

8 ounces uncooked marinated chicken fajita meat, all visible fat discarded

1 teaspoon olive oil

2 cups frozen bell pepper strips or 1 large green bell pepper and 1 large red bell pepper, thinly sliced

¾ cup frozen chopped onion or 1 large onion, thinly sliced

¾ cup fat-free evaporated milk

1 teaspoon bottled chipotle sauce

⅛ teaspoon pepper

¼ cup sliced black olives, drained

1 medium tomato (yellow preferred), cut into 8 wedges

Prepare the pasta using the package directions, omitting the salt and oil. Drain well in a colander. Return to the pan and turn off the heat. Set aside.

Meanwhile, thinly slice the chicken.

In a large nonstick skillet, heat the oil over medium-high heat, swirling to coat the bottom. Cook the bell peppers and onion for about 3 minutes, or until tender, stirring occasionally. Push to one side of the skillet.

Add the chicken and cook until browned, stirring occasionally (just the chicken). Stir to incorporate the bell pepper mixture. Cook until the chicken is no longer pink in the center, 6 to 8 minutes total, stirring occasionally.

Meanwhile, in a small bowl, stir together the evaporated milk, chipotle sauce, and pepper.

PER SERVING
calories 347
total fat 3.5 g
saturated 0.5 g
trans 0.0 g
polyunsaturated 0.5 g
monounsaturated 1.5 g
cholesterol 20 mg
sodium 397 mg
carbohydrates 56 g
fiber 3 g
sugars 11 g
protein 22 g
dietary exchanges
3 starch
2 vegetable
2 very lean meat

Stir the chicken mixture and the evaporated milk mixture into the cooked pasta. Cook over low heat for 1 to 2 minutes, or until warmed, stirring occasionally.

Garnish with the olives and tomato.

COOK'S TIP ON CHIPOTLE SAUCE

Dried chipotle (chih-POHT-lay) peppers add great smoky flavor to many dishes, such as soups, salsas, and beans. However, rehydrating the peppers takes some time. To quickly add that spicy-smoky flavor to your favorite dish, use bottled chipotle sauce. Find it in the condiment or Mexican section of your grocery store.

sour cream chicken enchilada casserole

SERVES 6 · 1½ cups per serving
PREPARATION TIME · 12 minutes
COOKING TIME · 19 to 22 minutes

Create this mouthwatering favorite with the extra chicken you saved from Southwestern-Style Roasted Chicken (page 128). Serve with pinto beans and slaw.

Cooking spray

SAUCE

1¼ cups fat-free, low-sodium chicken broth

1 tablespoon plus 1 teaspoon cornstarch

½ teaspoon ground cumin

⅛ teaspoon pepper

4 ounces fat-free brick cream cheese

½ cup salsa (lowest sodium available)

12 6-inch corn tortillas, halved

¾ cup fat-free sour cream

2 teaspoons lime juice

¼ teaspoon chili powder

● ● ●

12 ounces cooked skinless chicken breast from Southwestern-Style Roasted Chicken, chopped (about 3 cups)

Preheat the oven to 350°F. Lightly spray a 13 x 9 x 2-inch baking dish with cooking spray.

In a small saucepan, whisk together the sauce ingredients. Bring to a simmer over medium-high heat. Cook for 1 to 2 minutes, or until the mixture is thick and bubbly, whisking constantly.

In a medium nonstick skillet, combine the chicken, cream cheese, and salsa. Cook over medium-low heat for 5 to 6 minutes, or until the mixture is warmed through and the cream cheese is melted, stirring occasionally.

Meanwhile, on a baking sheet, put the tortillas in a single layer.

PER SERVING
calories 216
total fat 2.0 g
saturated 0.5 g
trans 0.0 g
polyunsaturated 0.5 g
monounsaturated 0.5 g
cholesterol 52 mg
sodium 372 mg
carbohydrates 23 g
fiber 2 g
sugars 4 g
protein 24 g
dietary exchanges
1½ starch
3 very lean meat

Bake the tortillas for 5 minutes, or until slightly crisp on the edges and somewhat soft in the center.

Pour $\frac{1}{2}$ cup sauce into the baking dish. Spread to cover the bottom. Top with half the tortillas. Spread the chicken mixture over the sauce. Top with the remaining tortillas. Pour the remaining sauce over the tortillas.

Bake, covered, for 10 minutes, or until warmed through.

Meanwhile, in a small bowl, whisk together the sour cream and lime juice. After 10 minutes, spread the mixture over the casserole. Bake, uncovered, for 1 to 2 minutes, or until the topping is slightly warm. Sprinkle with the chili powder.

grilled turkey cutlets with pineapple

SERVES 4 · 3 ounces turkey and 1 pineapple ring per serving
PREPARATION TIME · 10 minutes
MARINATING TIME · 10 minutes to 8 hours
COOKING TIME · 8 to 10 minutes

Try these citrus-flavored cutlets with sweet potatoes sprinkled with nutmeg. If you double the recipe except the pineapple slices, you'll have enough turkey for Turkey Tortilla Soup (page 54), too.

2 tablespoons lime juice

1 tablespoon orange-flavored liqueur or orange juice

2 teaspoons canola or corn oil

½ teaspoon dried oregano, crumbled

¼ teaspoon pepper

1 pound skinless turkey breast, all visible fat discarded, sliced into cutlets ½ inch thick

4 slices pineapple canned in their own juice, drained

In a large shallow glass dish, stir together the lime juice, liqueur, oil, oregano, and pepper. Add the turkey, turning to coat. Refrigerate, covered, for 10 minutes to 8 hours, turning occasionally if marinating more than 10 minutes.

Preheat the grill on medium high.

Discard the marinade. Grill the turkey for 4 to 5 minutes on each side, or until no longer pink in the center, turning once. Transfer to a platter.

Meanwhile, grill the pineapple slices for 1 minute on each side. Place on the turkey.

PER SERVING
calories 149
total fat 1.0 g
saturated 0.5 g
trans 0.0 g
polyunsaturated 0.5 g
monounsaturated 0.0 g
cholesterol 73 mg
sodium 53 mg
carbohydrates 8 g
fiber 1 g
sugars 7 g
protein 26 g
dietary exchanges
½ fruit
3 very lean meat

COOK'S TIP

To make cutlets from a turkey breast, use a sharp knife and slice the turkey at a slight angle into ½-inch cutlets.

turkey cutlets with two sauces

SERVES 4 · 3 ounces turkey, 1 cup spaghetti, and ¼ cup sauce per serving
PREPARATION TIME · 10 minutes
COOKING TIME · 1 hour to 1 hour 3 minutes

Can't decide whether you prefer spaghetti sauce or Alfredo sauce? With this double-sauced casserole, you get to enjoy both.

8 ounces dried whole-grain spaghetti

Olive oil spray

¾ cup fat-free, low-sodium chicken broth

1 pound turkey cutlets or strips, all visible fat discarded

¼ cup panko (Japanese bread crumbs)

½ cup fat-free meatless spaghetti sauce (lowest sodium available)

½ cup light Alfredo sauce

Prepare the pasta using the package directions, omitting the salt and oil.

Meanwhile, preheat the oven to 375°F. Lightly spray a 1½-quart shallow baking dish or 13 x 9 x 2-inch baking dish with olive oil spray.

Spread the pasta in the dish. Pour the broth over the pasta. Place the turkey in one layer over the pasta. Sprinkle with the panko. Lightly spray with olive oil spray.

Bake, covered, for 35 minutes. Pour the spaghetti sauce over the casserole. Pour the Alfredo sauce over the spaghetti sauce. Bake, uncovered, for 8 to 10 minutes, or until the sauce is warmed through and the turkey is no longer pink in the center.

PER SERVING
calories 398
total fat 5.5 g
saturated 2.5 g
trans 0.0 g
polyunsaturated 1.0 g
monounsaturated 0.5 g
cholesterol 76 mg
sodium 365 mg
carbohydrates 50 g
fiber 8 g
sugars 4 g
protein 38 g
dietary exchanges
3½ starch
3 very lean meat

turkey breast with cranberry sage stuffing

SERVES 6 · 3 ounces turkey and ¼ cup gravy per serving
PREPARATION TIME · 15 minutes
COOKING TIME · 55 minutes to 1 hour

You may want to prepare this meal quite often—not just for the holidays—when you see how easy it is.

STUFFING

1 medium rib of celery, diced

1 leek (white part only) or ½ small onion, diced

½ 6-inch whole-wheat pita, torn into small pieces

½ cup dried sweetened cranberries

¼ cup fat-free, low-sodium chicken broth

1 teaspoon dried sage

⅛ teaspoon pepper

● ● ●

1 1½-pound boneless, skinless turkey breast, butterflied, all visible fat discarded

1 tablespoon canola or corn oil

2 cups fat-free, low-sodium chicken broth

¼ cup all-purpose flour

½ cup water

In a medium bowl, stir together the stuffing ingredients.

If your butcher wouldn't butterfly the turkey breast, cut it lengthwise down the center, *almost* in half; don't cut completely through it. Lay it out flat between two pieces of plastic wrap. Using the smooth side of a meat mallet or a heavy pan, lightly flatten the turkey, being careful not to tear the meat.

Spoon the stuffing down the middle of the turkey. Roll the turkey around the stuffing. Tie at 2-inch intervals with kitchen twine.

Preheat the oven to 350°F.

In a Dutch oven, heat the oil over medium-high heat, swirling to coat the bottom. Brown the turkey for 2 minutes on each side. Pour 2 cups broth over the turkey.

PER SERVING
calories 231
total fat 4.5 g
saturated 1.0 g
trans 0.0 g
polyunsaturated 1.0 g
monounsaturated 2.0 g
cholesterol 68 mg
sodium 130 mg
carbohydrates 18 g
fiber 1 g
sugars 9 g
protein 29 g
dietary exchanges
1 carbohydrate
3 lean meat

Bake, covered, for 45 to 50 minutes, or until the turkey is no longer pink and the internal temperature reaches 170°F. Transfer the turkey to a carving board, leaving the liquid in the Dutch oven. Let the turkey rest while you make the gravy.

Bring the broth to a boil over medium-high heat.

Meanwhile, put the flour in a small bowl. Pour in the water, whisking to dissolve. Whisk into the boiling broth. Cook for 3 to 4 minutes, or until the gravy is thick and bubbly, whisking frequently. Remove from the heat.

Slice the turkey into 6 pieces. Serve with the gravy.

COOK'S TIP ON MESH

Kitchen twine is a great way to secure roasts and help them keep their shape while cooking. Butchers use a similar product that is stringlike and stretchy, and with a bit of maneuvering, can easily cover a roast. Many butchers will sell—or perhaps even give—you a small amount of mesh to use at home. For large quantities, check restaurant supply or specialty stores.

turkey and broccoli stir-fry

SERVES 4 · 1 cup per serving
PREPARATION TIME · 15 minutes
COOKING TIME · 12 minutes

Both the turkey supper and the vegetarian version are good over brown rice. Add a cup of soup or a fruit salad to round out the meal.

2 tablespoons soy sauce and 1 tablespoon soy sauce (lowest sodium available), divided use

1 tablespoon dry sherry

12 ounces turkey scallopine (thinly sliced turkey breast) or boneless, skinless chicken breast halves, all visible fat discarded

Pepper to taste

3 tablespoons lemon juice

1/4 cup water and 1/4 cup water (plus more as needed), divided use

1 tablespoon sugar

1 tablespoon cornstarch

2 medium green onions, minced

1 medium fresh jalapeño, seeds and ribs discarded, minced, or crushed red pepper flakes to taste (optional)

1 tablespoon bottled minced garlic or 6 medium garlic cloves, minced

1 tablespoon minced peeled gingerroot

1 1/2 teaspoons canola or corn oil and 1 1/2 teaspoons canola or corn oil, divided use

1 pound broccoli florets

In a medium bowl, whisk together 2 tablespoons soy sauce and the sherry for the marinade.

Cut the turkey across the short side into slivers about 1/4 inch wide and 2 inches long. Stir into the soy sauce marinade. Season with the pepper. Set aside.

In a small bowl, whisk together the lemon juice, 1/4 cup water, sugar, and remaining 1 tablespoon soy sauce. Whisk in the cornstarch. Set aside.

In a separate small bowl, stir together the green onions, jalapeño, garlic, and gingerroot.

PER SERVING
calories 197
total fat 5.0 g
saturated 0.5 g
trans 0.0 g
polyunsaturated 1.5 g
monounsaturated 2.5 g
cholesterol 51 mg
sodium 377 mg
carbohydrates 14 g
fiber 3 g
sugars 5 g
protein 23 g
dietary exchanges
1 vegetable
1/2 carbohydrate
2 1/2 lean meat

Heat a 12-inch skillet (cast-iron preferred), a wok, or a Dutch oven over high heat for a full minute. Add 1½ teaspoons oil, swirling to coat the bottom. Stir in half the turkey. Cook for 2 minutes, or until it starts becoming opaque, stirring constantly. Transfer to a serving bowl. Repeat with the remaining 1½ teaspoons oil and turkey, plus any remaining marinade.

Stir the green onion mixture, broccoli, and remaining ¼ cup water into the skillet. Cook, covered, for 3 minutes.

Stir the lemon juice mixture to disperse the cornstarch. Stir this mixture and the turkey into the skillet. Cook for 2 minutes, stirring constantly. Stir in more water to thin the sauce if necessary.

Vegetarian Stir-Fry

Omit 2 tablespoons soy sauce, the sherry, turkey, and pepper. Beat ½ cup egg substitute with ¼ teaspoon salt. Chop 4 medium green onions. In a 12-inch skillet (cast-iron preferred), a wok, or a Dutch oven, heat 1 tablespoon canola or corn oil over high heat, swirling to coat the bottom. Cook the green onions for a few seconds, stirring constantly. Add the egg substitute mixture. Cook until softly set (no stirring needed). Transfer to a plate. Continue as directed above, replacing the turkey with the egg substitute mixture.

PER SERVING

calories 148
total fat 7.5 g
  saturated 0.5 g
  trans 0.0 g
  polyunsaturated 2.0 g
  monounsaturated 4.5 g
cholesterol 0 mg
sodium 341 mg
carbohydrates 16 g
  fiber 4 g
  sugars 7 g
protein 6 g
dietary exchanges
  1 vegetable
  ½ carbohydrate
  ½ lean meat
  1 fat

COOK'S TIP ON STIR-FRYING

Old-fashioned cast-iron skillets are excellent for stir-frying. Black metal absorbs heat well, and the iron will hold onto the heat after you add the meat and vegetables.

italian bean stew with turkey and ham

SERVES 4 · 2 cups per serving
PREPARATION TIME · 5 minutes
COOKING TIME · 19 to 21 minutes

This bubbling stew incorporates the basics of a traditional Italian dish called ribollita, *but it takes much less time to prepare. A savory way to use leftover ham, the stew is just right for warming up before the Friday-night football game.*

1 tablespoon olive oil

1 pound ground skinless turkey breast

1 teaspoon fennel seeds, crushed if desired (optional)

2 15-ounce cans no-salt-added navy beans, rinsed and drained

3 cups fat-free, low-sodium chicken broth

1 9-ounce package frozen Italian green beans

1 cup diced lower-sodium, low-fat ham (4 ounces)

1 teaspoon bottled minced garlic or 2 medium garlic cloves, minced

1/2 teaspoon dried thyme, crumbled

1/2 teaspoon dried oregano, crumbled

1/4 teaspoon pepper

In a Dutch oven, heat the oil over medium-high heat, swirling to coat the bottom. Cook the turkey and fennel seeds for 6 to 8 minutes, or until the turkey is no longer pink, stirring occasionally to turn and break up the turkey.

Stir in the remaining ingredients. Increase the heat to high and bring to a boil. Reduce the heat to medium low. Cook, covered, for 10 minutes, or until the green beans are tender, stirring occasionally.

PER SERVING
calories 402
total fat 5.0 g
saturated 1.0 g
trans 0.0 g
polyunsaturated 0.5 g
monounsaturated 3.0 g
cholesterol 82 mg
sodium 345 mg
carbohydrates 38 g
fiber 10 g
sugars 9 g
protein 46 g
dietary exchanges
2 1/2 starch
5 very lean meat

meats

Beef Tenderloin with Mixed Baby Greens

Tuscan Braised Beef

Round Steak with Sour Cream Gravy

Grilled Sirloin with Honey-Mustard Marinade

Burgundy Beef Stew

Orange-Marinated Flank Steak

Glazed Beef Strips with Sugar Snap Peas

Beef with Rice Noodles and Vegetables

Picante Cube Steaks

Taco-Rubbed Flank Steak

Flank Steak Burritos

Minute Steaks with Sherry-Mushroom Sauce

Ultimate Steak Sandwich

No-Chop Stew

Cranberry-Topped Meat Loaf

Middle Eastern Spiced Beef

Mediterranean Beef and Rice

Cheddar Jack Chili Mac

Asian Beef and Brown Rice Stir-Fry

Cajun Skillet Supper

Blue Cheese Beef and Fries

Beef and Caramelized Onion on Hot French Bread

Blackberry Pork with Mixed Rice and Broccoli

Parmesan Pork Medallions

Roasted Lemon Pork with Cinnamon Sweet Potatoes

Orange Sesame Pork

Cook's-Choice Fried Rice

Red-Hot Pork Stir-Fry
Red-Hot Chicken Stir-Fry

Asian Pork Stir-Fry

Rosemary Braised Pork Chops
Celery-Sage Pork Chops

Sweet-and-Sour Black-Eyed Peas with Ham

Ham and Hash Brown Casserole

Smoked Sausage Skillet Supper

beef tenderloin with mixed baby greens

SERVES 4 · 3 ounces beef and 1 cup mixed baby greens per serving
PREPARATION TIME · 15 minutes
COOKING TIME · 25 to 27 minutes

A quick sauce of beef broth, balsamic vinegar, and caramelized brown bits left from cooking the tenderloin tops a stack of baby greens, garlic toast, and sliced beef—an elegant presentation.

GARLIC TOASTS

4 1-ounce slices French bread
  (about ¾ inch thick)

Olive oil spray

1 teaspoon bottled minced garlic
  or 2 medium garlic cloves,
  minced

SAUCE

½ cup fat-free, no-salt-added beef
  broth

½ cup water

¼ cup balsamic vinegar

2 tablespoons light brown sugar

¼ teaspoon pepper

• • •

1 teaspoon olive oil

1 1-pound beef tenderloin, all
  visible fat discarded, sliced
  crosswise into 4 pieces

4 cups loosely packed mixed baby
  greens or baby spinach leaves

Preheat the oven to 375°F.

Put the bread slices on a small baking sheet. Lightly spray both sides of the bread with olive oil spray. Spread the garlic over the tops.

Bake for 10 minutes, or until the bread is toasted and lightly golden. Let cool on a cooling rack. (The garlic toasts can be prepared ahead and refrigerated for up to three days in an airtight container.)

Meanwhile, in a small bowl, whisk together the sauce ingredients. Set aside.

In a large skillet (preferably not nonstick), heat the oil over medium-high heat, swirling to coat the bottom. Cook the beef for 5 minutes. Turn over (a flexible metal spatula works well). Cook for 4 to 6 minutes, or until the beef

PER SERVING
calories 294
total fat 6.5 g
saturated 2.5 g
trans 0.0 g
polyunsaturated 0.5 g
monounsaturated 3.5 g
cholesterol 57 mg
sodium 270 mg
carbohydrates 28 g
fiber 2 g
sugars 11 g
protein 28 g
dietary exchanges
1 starch
1 carbohydrate
3 lean meat

reaches the desired doneness (5 minutes on each side for medium-rare to medium). Remove the beef from the skillet. Immediately add the sauce mixture to the skillet. Using a spoon, scrape to dislodge any browned bits. Increase the heat to high and cook without stirring for 5 minutes, or until the mixture is reduced by half.

While the beef cooks, arrange the salad greens on plates, mounding slightly in the center. Gently place a garlic toast on each mound. Carefully place the beef on the garlic toast. Just before serving, pour the sauce over each serving of beef and greens.

COOK'S TIP ON DEGLAZING

The secret to many a great sauce is those crunchy bits left in the pan after the meat or vegetables are browned. To incorporate their rich, caramelized flavor into the sauce, deglaze the pan: Add a liquid and reduce the sauce either by boiling it at a high temperature without stirring or by thickening it, such as with a mixture of flour or cornstarch and water. A nonstick pan is not a good choice when making sauces and gravies by deglazing because no browned bits will stick to it.

tuscan braised beef

SERVES 4 · 3 ounces beef per serving (plus 12 ounces beef reserved)

PREPARATION TIME · 10 minutes

COOKING TIME · 2½ to 3 hours

or

SLOW-COOKER TIME · 4 to 5 hours on high or 8 to 10 hours on low

STANDING TIME · 10 to 15 minutes (both methods)

planned-overs

A taste of Italy, this tender roast gets a robust herb rub, then is left to bake or cook in the slow cooker. Among the recipes we've included for using the planned-over portion are Thai Beef Salad (page 91), Beef Salad with Vinaigrette or Horseradish Dressing (page 92), and Blue Cheese Beef and Fries (page 201).

RUB

1 tablespoon dried rosemary, crushed

2 teaspoons bottled minced roasted or raw garlic or 4 medium roasted or raw garlic cloves, minced

1 teaspoon dried sage

1 teaspoon grated lemon zest

¼ teaspoon salt

¼ teaspoon pepper

● ● ●

1 2-pound eye-of-round roast, all visible fat discarded

2 cups fat-free, no-salt-added beef broth

3 tablespoons all-purpose flour

⅓ cup water

Preheat the oven to 350°F.

In a small bowl, stir together the rub ingredients. Using a pastry brush or your hands, brush or rub the mixture over the roast. Put the roast in an ungreased Dutch oven. Pour the broth around the roast.

Cover the Dutch oven with aluminum foil. Put a lid over the foil. Bake for 2½ to 3 hours, or until the roast is tender or registers an internal temperature of 140°F to 150°F for medium, 155°F to 165°F for medium-well, or 170°F to 185°F for well-done on a meat or instant-read thermometer. Transfer to a carving board, leaving the liquid in the pot. Cover the roast with aluminum foil. Let stand for 10 to 15 minutes before carving.

PER SERVING
calories 154
total fat 2.5 g
saturated 1.0 g
trans 0.0 g
polyunsaturated 0.0 g
monounsaturated 1.0 g
cholesterol 48 mg
sodium 144 mg
carbohydrates 5 g
fiber 0 g
sugars 0 g
protein 26 g
dietary exchanges
½ starch
3 very lean meat

Bring the reserved liquid to a simmer over medium-high heat.

Meanwhile, put the flour in a small bowl. Add the water, whisking to dissolve. Whisk the mixture into the simmering broth. Cook for 2 to 3 minutes, or until thick and bubbly, whisking occasionally. Refrigerate half the roast (12 ounces) in an airtight container for use in Thai Beef Salad, Beef Salad with Vinaigrette or Horseradish Dressing, or Blue Cheese Beef and Fries. Serve the gravy over the remaining roast.

Slow-Cooker Method

Apply the rub mixture to the roast as directed on page 172. Put the roast in a 3$^{1}/_{2}$- to 4-quart slow cooker and pour in the beef broth. Cook, covered, on high for 4 to 5 hours or on low for 8 to 10 hours, or until the roast is tender. When the roast is done, remove from the slow cooker and let stand as directed. To make the gravy, pour the liquid from the slow cooker into a medium saucepan. Thicken with the flour mixture as directed.

COOK'S TIP ON LEAN MEAT

Sometimes lean cuts of meat, such as eye-of-round roast, can become dry while cooking. To keep this from happening, cover your pot with aluminum foil, then with the lid.

round steak with sour cream gravy

SERVES 4 · 3 ounces steak per serving
PREPARATION TIME · 20 minutes
COOKING TIME · 1 hour 7 minutes to 1 hour 10 minutes

This comforting steak casserole is slightly sweet and savory at the same time.

Cooking spray

STEAK

1/3 cup all-purpose flour

1 teaspoon ground chipotle chile powder

1/2 teaspoon pepper

1/4 teaspoon salt

1 pound boneless top round steak, slightly flattened with a meat mallet, quartered, all visible fat discarded

2 teaspoons canola or corn oil

1/2 cup chopped onion

1 teaspoon bottled minced garlic or 2 medium garlic cloves, minced

GRAVY

3/4 cup water

1/2 cup low-fat sour cream

2 1/2 tablespoons cornstarch

2 tablespoons firmly packed light brown sugar

1/2 teaspoon chipotle pepper sauce or red hot-pepper sauce

Preheat the oven to 300°F. Lightly spray a 1 1/2-quart glass baking dish (11 x 7 or 8 inches) with cooking spray.

In a shallow bowl, stir together the flour, chipotle chile powder, pepper, and salt. Dip one piece of steak in the flour mixture, turning to coat. Gently shake off the excess flour. Put the steak on a plate. Repeat with the remaining steak.

In a nonstick skillet large enough to hold the steaks in a single layer, heat the oil over medium-high heat, swirling to coat the bottom. Cook the steaks for 2 to 3 minutes on each side, or until lightly browned, being careful when turning so the coating does not stick to the skillet. Transfer the steaks to the baking dish.

PER SERVING
calories 281
total fat 6.5 g
saturated 2.0 g
trans 0.0 g
polyunsaturated 1.0 g
monounsaturated 3.0 g
cholesterol 58 mg
sodium 227 mg
carbohydrates 25 g
fiber 1 g
sugars 10 g
protein 28 g
dietary exchanges
1 1/2 starch
3 lean meat

In the same skillet, cook the onion over medium-high heat for about 3 minutes, or until soft, stirring frequently. Remove from the heat. Stir in the garlic. Spoon over the steaks.

In a small bowl, whisk together all the gravy ingredients until smooth. Pour over the steaks.

Bake for 1 hour, or until the steaks are tender.

COOK'S TIP ON ROUND STEAK

Pounding less tender cuts of meat, such as round steak, with the waffle side of a meat mallet breaks down the meat fibers, increasing the tenderness.

grilled sirloin with honey-mustard marinade

SERVES 4 · 3 ounces beef per serving (plus 12 ounces beef reserved)
PREPARATION TIME · 10 minutes
MARINATING TIME · 24 to 48 hours
COOKING TIME · 15 minutes
STANDING TIME · 10 minutes (optional)

planned-overs   no shopping required

This steak is ideal for entertaining outdoors, and you get a bonus—enough meat to make another meal, such as Beef and Caramelized Onion on Hot French Bread (page 202).

MARINADE

⅓ cup yellow mustard

¼ cup honey

1 to 2 teaspoons crushed red pepper flakes

1 teaspoon cider vinegar

● ● ●

2 pounds boneless top sirloin steak, all visible fat discarded

Cooking spray

In a large glass casserole dish, whisk together the marinade ingredients until well blended. Reserve ¼ cup marinade in a small nonmetallic container. Add the steak to the remaining marinade, turning to coat. Cover the casserole dish and small container and refrigerate for 24 to 48 hours, turning the steak occasionally.

Lightly spray a grill rack with cooking spray. Preheat the grill and grill rack on medium high.

Drain the steak, discarding the marinade in the casserole dish.

Cook the steak, covered, for 5 minutes. Turn over. Baste with 2 tablespoons reserved marinade. Cook for 5 minutes. Turn over. Using a clean basting brush, baste with the remaining marinade. Cook for 5 minutes, or until the desired doneness. Let stand for 10 minutes for easier slicing. Cut diagonally into strips.

PER SERVING
calories 173
total fat 6.0 g
saturated 2.5 g
trans 0.0 g
polyunsaturated 0.5 g
monounsaturated 3.0 g
cholesterol 61 mg
sodium 167 mg
carbohydrates 4 g
fiber 0 g
sugars 4 g
protein 25 g
dietary exchanges
3 lean meat

Refrigerate half the steak (about 12 ounces) in an airtight container for use in Beef and Caramelized Onion on Hot French Bread. Serve the remaining steak.

COOK'S TIP

Freeze ¼ cup marinade in one airtight freezer container and the steak and remaining marinade in another airtight freezer container. The time it takes to freeze and thaw is the marinating time.

burgundy beef stew

SERVES 6 · 1¹/₂ cups per serving
PREPARATION TIME · 20 minutes
COOKING TIME · 37 minutes
STANDING TIME · 10 minutes

An almost-effortless dish, this stew requires no peeling and little or no cutting!

2 cups water

1 6-ounce can no-salt-added tomato paste

1 1-ounce package dried onion soup mix

2 tablespoons dry red wine (regular or nonalcoholic) (optional)

2 teaspoons dried oregano, crumbled

1¹/₂ teaspoons soy sauce (lowest sodium available)

¹/₂ teaspoon sugar

Cooking spray

1 pound boneless sirloin steak, all visible fat discarded, cut into 1-inch pieces

1 16-ounce package frozen stew vegetables

2 cups chopped green bell peppers

1 10-ounce package frozen cut green beans

Pepper to taste

In a medium bowl, whisk together the water, tomato paste, soup mix, wine, oregano, soy sauce, and sugar.

Lightly spray a Dutch oven with cooking spray. Heat over high heat until very hot. Brown the steak for 2 to 3 minutes, stirring frequently.

Stir in the stew vegetables, bell peppers, green beans, and tomato paste mixture. Bring to a boil. Reduce the heat and simmer, covered, for 30 minutes, stirring occasionally. Remove from the heat.

Cut the potatoes from the stew vegetables in half. Stir the stew. Sprinkle with the pepper. Let stand, covered, for 10 minutes so the flavors blend.

TIME-SAVER Ask your butcher to trim and cut the steak while you finish shopping.

PER SERVING
calories 209
total fat 3.5 g
saturated 1.5 g
trans 0.0 g
polyunsaturated 0.0 g
monounsaturated 1.5 g
cholesterol 40 mg
sodium 495 mg
carbohydrates 23 g
fiber 3 g
sugars 8 g
protein 20 g
dietary exchanges
1 starch
2 vegetable
2¹/₂ very lean meat

orange-marinated flank steak

SERVES 4 · 3 ounces beef and 1 tablespoon sauce per serving
PREPARATION TIME · 5 minutes
COOKING TIME · 9 to 11 minutes
MARINATING TIME · 8 to 48 hours
STANDING TIME · 3 minutes

no
shopping
required

Here's the recipe to turn to when you want to spend your time with your family or friends, not in the kitchen. Just refrigerate lean flank steak in a lively orange marinade for up to 48 hours, then quickly grill indoors or out.

2 teaspoons grated orange zest

1/3 cup orange juice

2 tablespoons sugar

2 tablespoons soy sauce (lowest sodium available)

2 tablespoons balsamic vinegar

1 tablespoon Worcestershire sauce (lowest sodium available)

1/2 teaspoon crushed red pepper flakes

1 1-pound flank steak, all visible fat discarded

Cooking spray

In a medium glass dish, whisk together the orange zest, orange juice, sugar, soy sauce, vinegar, Worcestershire sauce, and red pepper flakes until the sugar is dissolved. Add the steak, turning to coat. Cover and refrigerate for 8 to 48 hours, turning occasionally.

Remove the steak from the dish, reserving the marinade.

Lightly spray a grill pan or grill rack with cooking spray. Heat the pan over medium-high heat or preheat the grill on medium high. Cook the steak for 4 to 5 minutes on each side, or until the desired doneness. Transfer to a cutting board and let stand for 3 minutes. Thinly slice on the diagonal.

Meanwhile, in a medium nonstick skillet, bring the marinade to a boil over medium-high heat. Boil for 3 minutes, or until reduced to 1/4 cup. Drizzle over the steak.

PER SERVING

calories 209
total fat 6.5 g
  saturated 3.0 g
  trans 0.0 g
  polyunsaturated 0.5 g
  monounsaturated 3.0 g
cholesterol 48 mg
sodium 244 mg
carbohydrates 11 g
  fiber 0 g
  sugars 10 g
protein 24 g
dietary exchanges
  1/2 carbohydrate
  3 lean meat

glazed beef strips with sugar snap peas

SERVES 4 · 1 cup per serving
PREPARATION TIME · 20 minutes
MARINATING TIME · 10 minutes to 12 hours
COOKING TIME · 11 to 14 minutes

This recipe boasts a Japanese marinade and a slightly sweet glaze. Like many other Asian stir-fries, it goes well over steamed brown rice.

MARINADE

1/4 cup chopped onion or 2 medium green onions, thinly sliced

2 tablespoons sake or dry white wine (regular or nonalcoholic)

1 teaspoon wasabi powder (optional)

1 teaspoon soy sauce (lowest sodium available)

1/4 teaspoon ground ginger or 1 teaspoon grated peeled gingerroot

1 pound boneless sirloin steak, all visible fat discarded, cut into thin strips

1/4 cup fat-free, no-salt-added beef broth

1 1/2 tablespoons light brown sugar

1 tablespoon teriyaki sauce (lowest sodium available)

2 teaspoons canola or corn oil

2 cups fresh or frozen sugar snap peas (8 ounces), trimmed if fresh

1 teaspoon sesame seeds (optional)

• • •

In a medium bowl, stir together the marinade ingredients.

Add the steak, stirring to coat. Cover and refrigerate for 10 minutes to 12 hours, stirring occasionally if marinating more than 10 minutes.

In a small bowl, stir together the broth, brown sugar, and teriyaki sauce. Set aside.

In a large nonstick skillet, heat the oil over medium-high heat, swirling to coat the bottom. Cook the steak with any remaining marinade for 3 to 4 minutes, or until browned, stirring occasionally.

PER SERVING

calories 229
total fat 7.0 g
  saturated 2.0 g
  trans 0.0 g
  polyunsaturated 1.0 g
  monounsaturated 3.5 g
cholesterol 60 mg
sodium 175 mg
carbohydrates 11 g
  fiber 2 g
  sugars 8 g
protein 27 g
dietary exchanges
  1/2 starch
  3 lean meat

Stir in the broth mixture. Cook for 6 to 7 minutes, stirring occasionally.

Stir in the peas. Cook for 1 to 2 minutes, or until most of the liquid is gone and the steak is glazed, stirring occasionally. Sprinkle with the sesame seeds.

COOK'S TIP

Also known as Japanese horseradish, wasabi is available in paste and powder. Both pack a powerful pungency, so add wasabi in small amounts. The powder form of this light green condiment is usually mixed with water or other liquids.

beef with rice noodles and vegetables

SERVES 6 · 1¼ cups per serving
PREPARATION TIME · 15 minutes
COOKING TIME · 10 to 11 minutes

Cubes of beef are browned and simmered with colorful vegetables and thin noodles in this tasty, soupy Asian stew.

1 teaspoon canola or corn oil

1 pound boneless sirloin steak, all visible fat discarded, cut into ¾-inch cubes

2 cups presliced fresh button mushrooms (about 8 ounces)

1 medium carrot, cut into thin strips

1 teaspoon bottled minced garlic or 2 medium garlic cloves, minced

2 cups fat-free, no-salt-added beef broth

1 cup asparagus pieces, about ½ inch long

1 tablespoon soy sauce (lowest sodium available)

¼ teaspoon chili oil

6 ounces frozen leaf spinach or collard greens

2 ounces dried rice noodles or dried whole-grain angel hair pasta

½ teaspoon toasted sesame oil

1 medium lime, cut into wedges (optional)

In a Dutch oven, heat the oil over medium-high heat, swirling to coat the bottom. Cook the steak for 2 minutes, or until brown, stirring occasionally.

Stir in the mushrooms, carrot, and garlic. Cook for 1 minute, stirring occasionally.

Stir in the broth, asparagus, soy sauce, and chili oil. Increase the heat to high and bring to a boil, 1 to 2 minutes.

Stir in the spinach, rice noodles, and sesame oil. Reduce the heat to low. Cook, covered, for 5 minutes, or until the noodles are tender. Using tongs, transfer the noodles to soup bowls. Ladle the broth and vegetables on top. Serve with the lime wedges to squeeze over the mixture.

PER SERVING
calories 174
total fat 4.5 g
saturated 1.5 g
trans 0.0 g
polyunsaturated 0.5 g
monounsaturated 2.0 g
cholesterol 40 mg
sodium 182 mg
carbohydrates 12 g
fiber 2 g
sugars 2 g
protein 21 g
dietary exchanges
½ starch
1 vegetable
2½ lean meat

picante cube steaks

SERVES 4 · 3 ounces cube steak and about ½ cup tomato sauce per serving
PREPARATION TIME · 8 minutes
COOKING TIME · 31 to 44 minutes

While the steak is simmering, prepare instant brown rice to serve with the sweet and spicy sauce. Round out the meal with tossed salad or your favorite green vegetable.

Cooking spray

4 cube steaks (about 4 ounces each)

1 14.5-ounce can no-salt-added diced tomatoes

½ cup chopped onion

3 tablespoons lime juice

1½ teaspoons bottled minced garlic or 3 medium garlic cloves, minced

1 medium fresh jalapeño, seeds and ribs discarded, diced

1 teaspoon ground cumin

2 tablespoons snipped fresh cilantro

Lightly spray a large skillet with cooking spray. Cook the steaks over medium-high heat for 2 to 3 minutes on each side, or until browned.

Stir in the remaining ingredients except the cilantro. Bring to a simmer, still over medium-high heat, and simmer for 2 to 3 minutes. Reduce the heat and simmer, covered, for 25 to 35 minutes, or until the steaks are tender.

Sprinkle with the cilantro.

PER SERVING
calories 164
total fat 2.5 g
saturated 1.0 g
trans 0.0 g
polyunsaturated 0.0 g
monounsaturated 1.0 g
cholesterol 54 mg
sodium 94 mg
carbohydrates 9 g
fiber 2 g
sugars 5 g
protein 26 g
dietary exchanges
2 vegetable
3 very lean meat

COOK'S TIP

Cube steaks are not the same as steak cubes. Rather, the steaks are smallish, thin pieces of round steak that have been run through a tenderizer.

taco-rubbed flank steak

SERVES 6 · 3 ounces beef per serving (plus 6 ounces beef reserved)
PREPARATION TIME · 10 minutes
COOKING TIME · 10 to 30 minutes

To add lots of flavor and no fat to meats, rub them with a spice rub. Make the rub mild to extra-spicy, depending on the level of heat you like best. Use leftovers from this recipe for Flank Steak Burritos (page 186) or Cook's-Choice Fried Rice (page 210).

Cooking spray

RUB

2 tablespoons chili powder

2 teaspoons ground cumin

1 teaspoon dried oregano,
   crumbled

1/2 teaspoon salt

1/2 teaspoon sugar

1/4 to 1 teaspoon cayenne

● ● ●

1 medium lime, halved

1 2-pound flank steak, all visible fat
   discarded

Lightly spray a grill rack or broiler rack and pan with cooking spray. Preheat the grill on high or preheat the broiler.

In a small bowl, stir together the rub ingredients.

Squeeze the lime over both sides of the steak. Rub into the steak. Spoon the rub mixture all over both sides. Using your fingertips, lightly press the rub so it adheres.

Grill the steak or broil 5 to 6 inches from the heat until the desired doneness, about 5 minutes on each side for medium-rare to 15 minutes on each side for well-done. Refrigerate one-fourth of the steak (6 ounces) in an airtight container for use in Flank Steak Burritos or Cook's-Choice Fried Rice. Cut the remaining steak diagonally across the grain into thin slices.

PER SERVING
calories 172
total fat 7.0 g
saturated 3.0 g
trans 0.0 g
polyunsaturated 0.5 g
monounsaturated 3.0 g
cholesterol 48 mg
sodium 189 mg
carbohydrates 2 g
fiber 1 g
sugars 1 g
protein 24 g
dietary exchanges
3 lean meat

COOK'S TIP ON GRILLING OR BROILING

Timing your grilling or broiling can be tricky. Different grills and broilers give off different amounts of heat, and the distance from the heat affects how quickly the meat cooks, as does whether the meat is chilled. Of course, the thickness of the cut also makes a difference. Watch your meat, and cut into the center to check for doneness.

COOK'S TIP ON CUTTING MEAT

As a rule of thumb, you'll have tenderer meat if you cut it across the grain. Look at the lines that run in one direction (the grain), and cut diagonally across those lines.

flank steak burritos

SERVES 4 · 1 burrito per serving
PREPARATION TIME · 15 minutes
MICROWAVE TIME · 3 minutes
or
COOKING TIME · 5 minutes

These "pass arounds" will be a family favorite. You'll like them because they utilize planned-overs from Taco-Rubbed Flank Steak (page 184), making it easy to get dinner on the table in next to no time. Your kids will like choosing their own combination of condiments and creating their own burritos. And everyone will like the taste.

2 cups shredded romaine or other lettuce

2 medium tomatoes, cored and seeded if desired, diced

1/4 cup chopped green onions

1/4 cup fat-free sour cream

1/4 cup salsa (lowest sodium available)

Snipped fresh cilantro (optional)

6 ounces cooked steak from Taco-Rubbed Flank Steak, at room temperature or heated briefly, cut into slices 1/2 inch wide

1/2 cup canned no-salt-added beans, such as pinto or kidney, mashed if desired

4 6-inch fat-free multigrain tortillas (lowest fat and sodium available)

Put the lettuce, tomatoes, green onions, sour cream, salsa, and cilantro in separate bowls. Put the steak in a serving dish.

Put the beans in a small microwaveable bowl. Microwave, covered, on 100 percent power (high) for 1 minute, or until hot, stirring once. Or warm the beans in a small saucepan over medium-high heat for 1 to 2 minutes, stirring once.

PER SERVING
calories 241
total fat 4.5 g
saturated 1.5 g
trans 0.0 g
polyunsaturated 0.5 g
monounsaturated 2.0 g
cholesterol 27 mg
sodium 382 mg
carbohydrates 30 g
fiber 5 g
sugars 6 g
protein 18 g
dietary exchanges
1 1/2 starch
1 vegetable
2 lean meat

Using the package directions, heat the tortillas in the microwave or oven until soft and pliable.

Let each diner assemble his or her own burrito.

COOK'S TIP

For mashed beans with a slightly thinner consistency, warm them with several tablespoons of salsa (lowest sodium available) or water. Start with 2 tablespoons, adding more if you like a thinner consistency.

TIME-SAVER If your microwave is large enough, warm the steak, beans, and tortillas at the same time.

minute steaks with sherry-mushroom sauce

SERVES 4 · 3 ounces beef and ¼ cup sauce per serving
PREPARATION TIME · 6 minutes
COOKING TIME · 11 minutes

express

For dinner in a flash, start with the very thin slices of lean beef known as minute steaks. It does take more than a minute to cook them—but not much!

1 teaspoon salt-free steak grilling blend

½ teaspoon dried oregano, crumbled

½ teaspoon paprika

4 minute steaks (about 4 ounces each and ⅛ to ¼ inch thick), all visible fat discarded

1 teaspoon canola or corn oil, 1 teaspoon canola or corn oil, and 1 teaspoon canola or corn oil, divided use

8 ounces presliced fresh button mushrooms

1 teaspoon bottled minced garlic or 2 medium garlic cloves, minced

¼ cup dry sherry and 1 tablespoon dry sherry, divided use

3 tablespoons fat-free half-and-half

½ teaspoon salt

¼ cup snipped fresh parsley

Pepper to taste (coarsely ground preferred)

In a small bowl, stir together the grilling blend, oregano, and paprika. Sprinkle over both sides of the beef. Using your fingers, gently press to adhere.

In a large nonstick skillet, heat 1 teaspoon oil over medium-high heat, swirling to coat the bottom. Cook 2 of the steaks for 1 minute on each side, or until the desired doneness. Transfer to a platter. Repeat with the second 1 teaspoon oil and the 2 remaining steaks. Transfer to the platter.

PER SERVING
calories 195
total fat 6.0 g
saturated 1.0 g
trans 0.0 g
polyunsaturated 1.5 g
monounsaturated 3.5 g
cholesterol 54 mg
sodium 359 mg
carbohydrates 4 g
fiber 1 g
sugars 2 g
protein 28 g
dietary exchanges
1 vegetable
3 lean meat

Pour the remaining 1 teaspoon oil into the same skillet, swirling to coat the bottom. Scrape to dislodge any browned bits. Cook the mushrooms for 4 minutes, or until beginning to richly brown, stirring frequently.

Stir in the garlic. Cook for 15 seconds, stirring constantly.

Pour in ¼ cup sherry. Cook for 1 minute, or until slightly reduced. Remove from the heat.

Stir in the half-and-half, salt, and remaining 1 tablespoon sherry. Spoon over the steaks. Sprinkle with parsley and pepper.

COOK'S TIP

In some areas of the country, minute steaks may be called thin top round steak. Just be sure the meat is *really* thin. It will be very tender if you don't overcook it.

ultimate steak sandwich

SERVES 4 · 1 sandwich per serving
PREPARATION TIME · 5 minutes
COOKING TIME · 12 to 15 minutes

It takes only a few minutes to make this out-of-this-world steak sandwich. Smoked paprika is what adds the "ultimate" to this dish.

1 teaspoon smoked paprika

¼ teaspoon pepper

4 cube steaks (about 4 ounces each), all visible fat discarded

2 teaspoons olive oil

2 cups frozen bell pepper and onion blend, or 1 cup chopped green bell pepper and 1 cup chopped onion

2½ to 3 ounces presliced fresh button mushrooms (about 1 cup)

2 teaspoons Worcestershire sauce (lowest sodium available)

4 whole-grain hamburger buns (lowest sodium available)

1 tablespoon plus 1 teaspoon prepared horseradish sauce (not prepared horseradish)

Sprinkle the smoked paprika and pepper over both sides of the cube steaks.

In a large nonstick skillet, heat the oil over medium-high heat, swirling to coat the bottom. Add the steaks and cook for 4 to 5 minutes on each side, or until browned. Transfer the steaks to a large plate. Cover with aluminum foil to keep warm.

In the same skillet, stir together the pepper and onion blend, mushrooms, and Worcestershire sauce. Cook, still over medium-high heat, for 3 to 5 minutes, or until tender, stirring frequently.

To assemble the sandwiches, place one bun bottom on each plate. Spread each bun bottom with the horseradish sauce. Top with the steaks and bell pepper mixture. Place the remaining bun pieces on top.

PER SERVING
calories 301
total fat 8.0 g
saturated 1.5 g
trans 0.0 g
polyunsaturated 1.5 g
monounsaturated 3.0 g
cholesterol 59 mg
sodium 280 mg
carbohydrates 28 g
fiber 4 g
sugars 8 g
protein 29 g
dietary exchanges
2 starch
3 lean meat

COOK'S TIP ON SMOKED PAPRIKA

Made from ground smoked sweet peppers, smoked paprika adds a wonderful wood-smoked flavor to food. Try sprinkling the paprika on soups, salads, and fish for a new flavor sensation. It's a handy no-sodium enhancer and definitely one spice worth adding to your collection.

COOK'S TIP ON HORSERADISH SAUCE

Horseradish sauce combines a mayonnaise-like base with ground fresh horseradish. Check the condiment section of the supermarket for bottles of this creamy hot and tangy sauce.

no-chop stew

SERVES 6 · 1½ cups per serving
PREPARATION TIME · 10 minutes
COOKING TIME · 34 to 35 minutes

This hearty dinner in a bowl is a great comfort after a hectic day, especially since you don't need to chop anything to prepare it.

1 pound extra-lean ground beef

2 14.5-ounce cans no-salt-added diced or stewed tomatoes, undrained

6 ounces shredded coleslaw mix (about 3 cups)

2 cups water

1 10-ounce package frozen mixed vegetables, thawed

1 cup frozen chopped green bell pepper

¼ cup cider vinegar or dry red wine (regular or nonalcoholic)

1 tablespoon very low sodium beef bouillon granules

1 tablespoon dried oregano, crumbled

½ teaspoon sugar

¼ cup finely snipped fresh parsley

1 teaspoon salt

Pepper to taste

Heat a Dutch oven over high heat. Cook the beef until browned, 3 to 4 minutes, stirring frequently to turn and crumble the beef. Drain and discard any liquid.

Stir in the tomatoes with liquid, coleslaw, water, mixed vegetables, bell pepper, vinegar, bouillon granules, oregano, and sugar. Reduce the heat and simmer, covered, for 30 minutes. Remove from the heat.

Stir in the parsley, salt, and pepper.

PER SERVING
calories 181
total fat 4.0 g
saturated 1.5 g
trans 0.0 g
polyunsaturated 0.5 g
monounsaturated 1.5 g
cholesterol 42 mg
sodium 526 mg
carbohydrates 18 g
fiber 5 g
sugars 9 g
protein 19 g
dietary exchanges
½ starch
2 vegetable
2 lean meat

COOK'S TIP
This is a great make-ahead dish, and it freezes well, too.

cranberry-topped meat loaf

SERVES 4 · 3 ounces per serving
PREPARATION TIME · 12 minutes
COOKING TIME · 1 hour to 1 hour 10 minutes
STANDING TIME · 5 to 10 minutes

Shredded potatoes serve as a tasty alternative to the bread crumbs that traditionally hold meat loaf ingredients together.

Cooking spray

1½ cups refrigerated fat-free shredded hash brown potatoes (lowest sodium available) (do not use frozen)

¼ cup dehydrated minced onions

¼ cup egg substitute

2 teaspoons dried oregano, crumbled

1 teaspoon bottled minced garlic or 2 medium garlic cloves, minced

¼ teaspoon salt

¼ teaspoon pepper

¾ cup jellied cranberry sauce (½ of 16-ounce can)

¼ cup no-salt-added ketchup

1 pound extra-lean ground beef

Preheat the oven to 350°F. Line a roasting pan with aluminum foil. Lightly spray the foil with cooking spray.

In a large bowl, stir together the potatoes, onions, egg substitute, oregano, garlic, salt, and pepper.

In a small bowl, stir together the cranberry sauce and ketchup. Measure ¼ cup cranberry mixture and stir into the potato mixture. Set aside the remaining cranberry mixture for the meat loaf topping.

Using your hands, work the ground beef into the potato mixture, just until blended. Transfer to the roasting pan. Lightly pat into an 8 x 4 x 2-inch loaf.

Bake for 1 hour to 1 hour 10 minutes, or until the meat loaf reaches an internal temperature of 160°F. Let stand for 5 to 10 minutes before slicing.

PER SERVING
calories 314
total fat 6.0 g
saturated 2.5 g
trans 0.5 g
polyunsaturated 0.5 g
monounsaturated 2.5 g
cholesterol 62 mg
sodium 315 mg
carbohydrates 39 g
fiber 2 g
sugars 18 g
protein 28 g
dietary exchanges
1 starch
1½ carbohydrate
3 lean meat

middle eastern spiced beef

SERVES 4 · 1 cup beef mixture and ½ cup couscous per serving
PREPARATION TIME · 12 minutes
COOKING TIME · 13 minutes

Don't be scared off by the use of sugar in this highly aromatic one-dish meal. It just heightens the flavors of the spices, onions, and pecans.

1 teaspoon canola or corn oil

12 ounces extra-lean ground beef

1 medium yellow summer squash, chopped

1 medium red bell pepper, diced

½ cup diced onion

¾ cup water and ¼ cup water, divided use

½ cup uncooked whole-wheat couscous

½ cup (about 2 ounces) finely chopped pecans or whole pine nuts

2½ teaspoons sugar

1 teaspoon ground cinnamon

½ teaspoon ground cumin

¼ teaspoon ground allspice

¼ teaspoon salt

In a large nonstick skillet, heat the oil over medium-high heat, swirling to coat the bottom. Cook the beef for 2 minutes, stirring constantly and turning and crumbling the beef. Drain and discard any liquid.

Stir in the squash, bell pepper, and onion. Cook for 8 minutes, or until the onion is soft, stirring frequently. Remove from the heat.

Meanwhile, in a small saucepan over high heat, heat ¾ cup water to boiling. Remove from the heat and stir in the couscous. Cover tightly and let stand for 5 minutes, or until the liquid is absorbed. Fluff with a fork.

PER SERVING

calories 368
total fat 17.0 g
  saturated 3.0 g
  trans 0.5 g
  polyunsaturated 4.0 g
  monounsaturated 8.5 g
cholesterol 47 mg
sodium 215 mg
carbohydrates 33 g
  fiber 7 g
  sugars 6 g
protein 25 g
dietary exchanges
  2 starch
  1 vegetable
  2½ lean meat
  2 fat

In a small skillet, dry-roast the pecans over medium heat for about 4 minutes, or until just fragrant, stirring frequently. Remove from the skillet so they don't burn. (For pine nuts, dry-roast over medium-high heat for 1 to 2 minutes, or until they are fragrant and turning golden, stirring frequently.) Stir the pecans, sugar, cinnamon, cumin, allspice, salt, and remaining 1/4 cup water into the beef mixture. Serve over the couscous.

COOK'S TIP

Whole-wheat couscous is available in major supermarkets, usually near the rice, and in health food stores. Couscous doesn't have a lot of flavor, so it lends itself well to the addition of many different herbs and spices.

mediterranean beef and rice

SERVES 6 · 1¼ cups per serving
PREPARATION TIME · 5 minutes
COOKING TIME · 17 to 18 minutes
STANDING TIME · 5 minutes

When you need a satisfying meal that uses ground beef, try this recipe. It's as easy as 1-2-3. Just brown the beef, heat the sauce, and add the rice. Then ring the dinner bell!

1 pound extra-lean ground beef

1 14.5-ounce can no-salt-added stewed tomatoes, undrained

1 cup water

1 teaspoon dried oregano, crumbled

1 teaspoon garlic powder

½ teaspoon paprika

½ teaspoon salt-free lemon pepper

½ teaspoon salt

1 15-ounce can no-salt-added navy beans, rinsed and drained

1 14.5-ounce can no-salt-added French-style green beans, drained

1 cup uncooked instant brown rice

In a large skillet, cook the beef over medium-high heat for 7 to 8 minutes, or until browned, stirring occasionally to turn and crumble the beef. Drain and discard any liquid.

Stir in the tomatoes with liquid, water, oregano, garlic powder, paprika, lemon pepper, and salt. Reduce the heat to medium. Cook for 5 minutes, stirring occasionally.

Stir in the beans and rice. Reduce the heat to medium low. Cook, covered, for 5 minutes. Turn off the heat. Let stand for 5 minutes, or until the rice is tender.

PER SERVING
calories 250
total fat 4.5 g
saturated 1.5 g
trans 0.0 g
polyunsaturated 0.5 g
monounsaturated 1.5 g
cholesterol 42 mg
sodium 273 mg
carbohydrates 29 g
fiber 6 g
sugars 6 g
protein 23 g
dietary exchanges
1½ starch
1 vegetable
2½ very lean meat

cheddar jack chili mac

SERVES 4 · 1½ cups per serving
PREPARATION TIME · 5 minutes
COOKING TIME · 19 to 24 minutes

A classic dish gets a quick makeover. Some flavor combinations never go out of style!

12 ounces extra-lean ground beef

3 cups water

1 14.5-ounce can no-salt-added stewed tomatoes, undrained

1 8-ounce can no-salt-added tomato sauce

1 teaspoon bottled minced garlic or 2 medium garlic cloves, minced

1 teaspoon dried oregano, crumbled

½ teaspoon sugar

¼ teaspoon salt

⅛ teaspoon pepper

1 cup dried whole-grain macaroni or other small whole-grain pasta

½ cup shredded low-fat Cheddar cheese, low-fat Monterey Jack, or a combination (about 2 ounces)

In a Dutch oven, cook the beef over medium-high heat for 8 to 10 minutes, or until no longer pink, stirring occasionally to turn and crumble the beef. Drain and discard any liquid.

Stir in the water, tomatoes with liquid, tomato sauce, garlic, oregano, sugar, salt, and pepper. Increase the heat to high and bring to a boil, covered, 1 to 2 minutes.

Stir in the pasta. Reduce the heat and simmer for 10 to 12 minutes, or until tender. Ladle the mixture into soup bowls. Sprinkle with the cheese.

COOK'S TIP

Instead of oregano, substitute 1 teaspoon of your favorite spice or dried herb. Here are some suggestions: chili powder, rosemary, ground cumin, thyme, basil, or fennel seeds.

PER SERVING

calories 263
total fat 5.0 g
  saturated 1.5 g
  trans 0.5 g
  polyunsaturated 1.0 g
  monounsaturated 1.5 g
cholesterol 49 mg
sodium 385 mg
carbohydrates 27 g
  fiber 4 g
  sugars 8 g
protein 28 g
dietary exchanges
  1 starch
  2 vegetable
  3 lean meat

asian beef and brown rice stir-fry

SERVES 4 · 1½ cups beef and vegetable mixture and ½ cup rice per serving
PREPARATION TIME · 16 to 18 minutes
COOKING TIME · 21 to 24 minutes

all-
in-
one

Lean ground beef and lots of vegetables, seasoned with peppers, garlic, gingerroot, and green onions, make a flavorful one-dish meal the whole family will enjoy.

1½ cups uncooked instant brown rice

1 pound extra-lean ground beef

2 teaspoons grated peeled gingerroot

1 teaspoon bottled minced garlic or 2 medium garlic cloves, minced

Cooking spray

3 medium carrots, thinly sliced crosswise

2 medium ribs of celery, thinly sliced crosswise

1 small red bell pepper, cut into 1-inch squares

1 tablespoon water

2 teaspoons sesame seeds

8 ounces fresh bean sprouts

3 medium green onions (green and white parts), sliced crosswise into ¼-inch pieces

1 cup fat-free, no-salt-added beef broth

1 tablespoon soy sauce (lowest sodium available)

2 teaspoons cornstarch

¼ teaspoon crushed red pepper flakes

¼ teaspoon pepper

Prepare the rice using the package directions, omitting the salt and oil.

Meanwhile, in a large skillet, cook the ground beef, gingerroot, and garlic over medium-high heat for about 5 minutes, or until the beef is browned, stirring frequently to turn and crumble the beef. Drain and discard any liquid. Transfer the beef to a plate. Set aside.

PER SERVING
calories 355
total fat 8.0 g
saturated 2.5 g
trans 0.5 g
polyunsaturated 1.5 g
monounsaturated 3.0 g
cholesterol 62 mg
sodium 284 mg
carbohydrates 40 g
fiber 6 g
sugars 7 g
protein 31 g
dietary exchanges
2 starch
2 vegetable
3 lean meat

Before returning the skillet to the heat, wipe it with a paper towel and lightly spray with cooking spray. With the skillet over medium-high heat, cook the carrots, celery, and bell pepper for 2 minutes, stirring frequently. Stir in the water. Cook, covered, for 2 minutes.

While the vegetables cook, dry-roast the sesame seeds in a small skillet over low heat for about 2 minutes, or just until fragrant and golden, stirring frequently. Watch carefully so they do not get too brown. Pour onto a small plate.

Stir the bean sprouts and green onions into the carrot mixture. Cook, covered, for 2 minutes. Stir in the beef.

In a small bowl, whisk together the remaining ingredients until the cornstarch is dissolved. Pour over the beef. Cook for about 2 minutes, or until bubbly and slightly thickened, stirring constantly. Serve over the rice. Sprinkle with the sesame seeds.

cajun skillet supper

SERVES 4 · 1¾ cups per serving
PREPARATION TIME · 5 minutes
COOKING TIME · 13 to 16 minutes

If you like gumbo, you will like this one-dish beef meal. This recipe lends itself well to experimentation, so try different vegetables and beans for variety. To stretch the number of servings, ladle the mixture over steamed brown rice.

12 ounces extra-lean ground beef

2 cups frozen cut okra (about 16 ounces)

1 15-ounce can no-salt-added corn, drained

1 15-ounce can no-salt-added kidney beans, rinsed and drained

1 14.25-ounce can no-salt-added stewed tomatoes, undrained

1 cup fat-free, no-salt-added beef broth

1 teaspoon ground cumin

1 teaspoon chili powder

1 teaspoon dried thyme, crumbled

1 teaspoon garlic powder

1 teaspoon onion powder

⅛ teaspoon pepper

In a large nonstick skillet over medium-high heat, cook the beef for 5 to 6 minutes, or until no longer pink, stirring occasionally to turn and crumble it. Drain and discard any liquid.

Stir in the remaining ingredients. Bring to a simmer. Reduce the heat and simmer for 8 to 10 minutes, or until the flavors have blended, stirring occasionally.

PER SERVING
calories 327
total fat 5.0 g
saturated 2.0 g
trans 0.5 g
polyunsaturated 1.0 g
monounsaturated 2.0 g
cholesterol 47 mg
sodium 133 mg
carbohydrates 45 g
fiber 9 g
sugars 11 g
protein 30 g
dietary exchanges
2½ starch
1 vegetable
3 very lean meat

blue cheese beef and fries

SERVES 4 · 1¼ cups per serving
PREPARATION TIME · 10 minutes
COOKING TIME · 31 to 32 minutes

Top oven fries with the works—tender beef, broccoli, brown gravy, and a bit of blue cheese. You can use leftover roast beef, such as part of the extra Tuscan Braised Beef (page 172), or buy the lowest-fat, lowest-sodium cooked beef you can find.

Olive oil spray

4 medium red potatoes (about 1⅓ pounds), cut into ⅛- to ¼-inch strips

½ teaspoon garlic powder

½ teaspoon paprika

⅛ teaspoon pepper

2 cups thinly sliced cooked beef from Tuscan Braised Beef or other low-sodium cooked roast beef (about 8 ounces), all visible fat discarded

2 cups frozen broccoli florets, thawed

1 cup bottled fat-free brown gravy

1½ tablespoons crumbled blue cheese

Preheat the oven to 400°F. Lightly spray a rimmed baking sheet with olive oil spray. Arrange the potatoes in a single layer on the baking sheet.

In a cup, stir together the garlic powder, paprika, and pepper. Sprinkle over the potatoes.

Bake for 25 minutes, or until the potatoes are tender. Arrange the beef and broccoli on the potatoes. Pour the gravy on top. Bake for 6 to 7 minutes, or until the mixture is warmed through. Sprinkle with the blue cheese.

PER SERVING

calories 231
total fat 2.5 g
  saturated 1.5 g
  trans 0.0 g
  polyunsaturated 0.0 g
  monounsaturated 1.0 g
cholesterol 35 mg
sodium 442 mg
carbohydrates 30 g
  fiber 4 g
  sugars 2 g
protein 22 g
dietary exchanges
  2 starch
  2½ very lean meat

TIME-SAVER Make fast work of slicing the potatoes for this dish by using the very fine julienne blade of a mandoline or the french-fry blade of a food processor.

beef and caramelized onion on hot french bread

SERVES 4 · 1 open-face sandwich per serving
PREPARATION TIME · 10 minutes
COOKING TIME · 8 minutes

Now you can have sweet caramelized onion without a lot of time and effort. Cook the onion over high heat, add a bit of sugar, then reduce the heat to finish the process. If you planned ahead and have some Grilled Sirloin with Honey-Mustard Marinade (page 176), it would be wonderful in this dish.

¼ long, wide French bread (about 4 ounces)

1 teaspoon canola or corn oil

1 large onion (yellow preferred) (about 8 ounces), thinly sliced

1 teaspoon sugar

⅓ cup water

2 tablespoons fat-free plain yogurt

2 teaspoons yellow mustard

12 ounces cooked beef from Grilled Sirloin with Honey-Mustard Marinade or other cooked lean, low-sodium beef, thinly sliced

Preheat the oven to 300°F. Wrap the bread in aluminum foil and put in the oven.

In a large nonstick skillet, heat the oil over high heat, swirling to coat the bottom. Cook the onion for 3 minutes, stirring constantly (using two utensils works well). Reduce the heat to medium high.

Stir in the sugar. Cook for 3 minutes, or until the onion is richly browned, stirring constantly. Stir in the water. Remove from the heat.

In a small bowl, whisk together the yogurt and mustard until completely blended.

Cut the bread in half lengthwise, then cut each piece in half crosswise. Spread the yogurt mixture on the cut side. Top with the beef, and then the onion.

PER SERVING
calories 296
total fat 7.5 g
saturated 2.5 g
trans 0.0 g
polyunsaturated 1.0 g
monounsaturated 4.0 g
cholesterol 62 mg
sodium 387 mg
carbohydrates 27 g
fiber 2 g
sugars 9 g
protein 29 g
dietary exchanges
1½ starch
1 vegetable
3 lean meat

blackberry pork with mixed rice and broccoli

SERVES 4 · 3 ounces pork and 1 cup rice mixture per serving
PREPARATION TIME · 15 minutes
COOKING TIME · 22 minutes

Sweet, pungent balsamic vinegar provides a subtle kick to this richly glazed dish.

½ 6- to 7-ounce box quick-cooking white and wild rice or oriental fried rice, with ½ seasoning packet discarded

2 cups frozen broccoli florets (8 ounces), thawed

½ cup all-fruit seedless blackberry spread

3 tablespoons balsamic vinegar

Cooking spray

4 boneless center-cut pork chops (about 4 ounces each and about ½ inch thick), all visible fat discarded

¼ teaspoon dried rosemary, crushed

In a medium saucepan, prepare the rice using the package directions, omitting the salt, margarine, and half the seasoning packet and cooking for 8 minutes. Stir in the broccoli. Cook, covered, for 3 minutes. Remove from the heat. Set aside, still covered.

Meanwhile, in a small bowl, whisk together the blackberry spread and vinegar. Set aside.

Lightly spray a large skillet with cooking spray. Cook the pork over medium-high heat for 3 minutes. Turn over. Sprinkle with the rosemary. Cook for 3 minutes, or until lightly browned (the pork won't be quite done). Remove from the skillet.

Add the blackberry spread mixture to the skillet. Increase the heat to high and bring to a boil. Boil for 1 minute.

Return the pork and any accumulated juices to the skillet. Cook for 1 minute. Turn the pork over. Cook for 45 seconds, or until slightly pink in the center. Serve the pork and glaze over the rice mixture.

PER SERVING
calories 349
total fat 6.0 g
saturated 2.0 g
trans 0.0 g
polyunsaturated 1.0 g
monounsaturated 2.5 g
cholesterol 64 mg
sodium 444 mg
carbohydrates 45 g
fiber 3 g
sugars 20 g
protein 29 g
dietary exchanges
1½ starch
1 vegetable
1 carbohydrate
3 lean meat

parmesan pork medallions

SERVES 4 · 3 ounces pork and ½ cup asparagus per serving
PREPARATION TIME · 13 to 15 minutes
COOKING TIME · 30 minutes

Combine this elegant dish with Savory Pecan Rice (page 280) for company-pleasing fare.

Olive oil spray

¼ cup all-purpose flour

¼ cup egg substitute

½ cup plain dry bread crumbs

½ teaspoon dried Italian seasoning, crumbled, and 1 teaspoon dried Italian seasoning, crumbled, divided use

1 pound pork tenderloin, all visible fat discarded, cut crosswise into 12 slices

12 ounces fresh asparagus (12 to 15 medium spears)

1 8-ounce can no-salt-added tomato sauce

2 tablespoons crumbled soft goat cheese

1½ tablespoons shredded or grated Parmesan cheese

Preheat the oven to 400°F. Lightly spray a large shallow baking pan with olive oil spray.

Put the flour and egg substitute in separate shallow bowls. In a third bowl, stir together the bread crumbs and ½ teaspoon Italian seasoning. Set the bowls and the baking pan in a row, assembly-line fashion. Dip 1 pork slice in the flour, turning to coat and gently shaking off any excess. Dip in the egg substitute mixture, turning to coat and letting any excess drip off. Dip in the bread crumb mixture. Using your fingertips, lightly press the mixture so it adheres to the pork. Repeat with the remaining pork. Put the pieces in a single layer in the baking pan. Lightly spray with olive oil spray.

Bake for 25 minutes.

PER SERVING
calories 267
total fat 4.5 g
saturated 2.0 g
trans 0.0 g
polyunsaturated 1.0 g
monounsaturated 1.5 g
cholesterol 77 mg
sodium 254 mg
carbohydrates 23 g
fiber 3 g
sugars 6 g
protein 31 g
dietary exchanges
1 starch
2 vegetable
3 very lean meat

Meanwhile, fill a large skillet with water to a depth of 1 inch. Bring to a boil over high heat.

While the water heats, trim and discard the bottom 1 inch of each asparagus spear. Add the asparagus to the boiling water. Reduce the heat to medium high. Cook for 2 to 3 minutes, or until tender-crisp. Drain well in a colander. Cover and set aside to keep warm.

In a small bowl, stir together the tomato sauce and remaining 1 teaspoon Italian seasoning. After the pork has baked for 25 minutes, spoon the tomato sauce mixture over it. Sprinkle with the goat cheese and Parmesan.

Bake for 5 minutes, or until the pork is slightly pink in the center and the cheeses are melted. Serve over the asparagus.

roasted lemon pork with cinnamon sweet potatoes

SERVES 4 · 3 ounces pork and ½ sweet potato per serving
PREPARATION TIME · 13 minutes
COOKING TIME · 55 minutes to 1 hour
STANDING TIME · 5 minutes

While this meat-and-potatoes combo cooks, prepare a green vegetable and one of our speedy desserts.

Cooking spray

1 1-pound pork tenderloin, all visible fat discarded

1 medium lemon, halved

¼ cup finely snipped fresh parsley

1½ teaspoons bottled minced roasted or plain garlic or 3 medium raw or roasted garlic cloves, minced

½ to 1 teaspoon salt-free lemon pepper

¼ teaspoon salt

2 large sweet potatoes, halved lengthwise

2 teaspoons light tub margarine

1½ teaspoons dark or light brown sugar

½ teaspoon ground cinnamon

Preheat the oven to 325°F. Lightly spray a broiler pan with cooking spray.

Put the pork in the pan, tucking any thin ends under to cook evenly. Squeeze the lemon over the pork. Sprinkle with the parsley, garlic, lemon pepper, and salt. Using your fingertips, lightly press the seasonings so they adhere to the pork.

Wrap each potato half individually in aluminum foil. Place around the pork.

Bake for 50 to 55 minutes, or until the pork registers 150°F on an instant-read thermometer or is slightly pink in the very center. Transfer the pork to a cutting board. (Continue baking the potatoes.) Let stand for about 10 minutes before slicing. The pork will continue to cook during the standing time, reaching about 160°F.

PER SERVING
calories 253
total fat 3.0 g
saturated 1.0 g
trans 0.0 g
polyunsaturated 0.5 g
monounsaturated 1.5 g
cholesterol 74 mg
sodium 300 mg
carbohydrates 29 g
fiber 5 g
sugars 10 g
protein 26 g
dietary exchanges
2 starch
3 very lean meat

Meanwhile, in a small bowl, stir together the margarine, brown sugar, and cinnamon until smooth.

Slice the pork and arrange on plates. Unwrap the potatoes and place beside the pork. Top the potatoes with the margarine mixture.

orange sesame pork

SERVES 4 · 3 ounces pork per serving (plus 12 ounces pork reserved)
PREPARATION TIME · 10 minutes
COOKING TIME · 20 to 25 minutes
STANDING TIME · 5 minutes

planned-
overs

Dry-roasted sesame seeds, often found in Chinese-inspired dishes like this one, add a rich nuttiness that teams well with pork. You'll be tempted to eat every bite, but save some to make Cook's-Choice Fried Rice (page 210).

Cooking spray

¼ cup plain rice vinegar, or ¼ cup plain or cider vinegar plus 1 teaspoon sugar

3 tablespoons soy sauce (lowest sodium available)

2 tablespoons frozen orange juice concentrate or ½ cup orange juice

2 teaspoons bottled chopped garlic or 4 medium garlic cloves, chopped

⅛ to ¼ teaspoon crushed red pepper flakes

2 1-pound pork tenderloins, all visible fat discarded

1 to 2 tablespoons water (as needed)

1 tablespoon sesame seeds

Preheat the oven to 425°F. Lightly spray a 13 x 9 x 2-inch baking pan with cooking spray.

In a small bowl, stir together the vinegar, soy sauce, orange juice concentrate, garlic, and red pepper flakes.

Tucking any thin ends under so they cook evenly, put the pork in the baking pan so the pieces do not touch. Pour the vinegar mixture over the pork.

Roast for 10 minutes. Turn over. Roast for 10 to 15 minutes, or until the internal temperature registers 150°F on an instant-read thermometer or is slightly pink in the very center. While the pork cooks, if the sauce appears to be burning (it may in corners or in dark pans), tilt the pan and loosen and stir the thicker sticky substances. Add the water if needed.

PER SERVING
calories 143
total fat 3.0 g
saturated 1.0 g
trans 0.0 g
polyunsaturated 0.5 g
monounsaturated 1.0 g
cholesterol 74 mg
sodium 208 mg
carbohydrates 3 g
fiber 0 g
sugars 2 g
protein 25 g
dietary exchanges
3 very lean meat

Meanwhile, in a small skillet, dry-roast the sesame seeds over low heat for about 2 minutes, or just until fragrant and golden, stirring frequently. Watch carefully so they don't get too brown. Pour onto a small plate.

Transfer the pork to a cutting board. Let stand for about 10 minutes. The pork will continue to cook during the standing time, reaching about 160°F. Cut diagonally, making long, thin slices. Refrigerate half the pork (12 ounces) in an airtight container for use in Cook's-Choice Fried Rice. Transfer the remaining pork to plates. Spoon the pan juices over the pork. Sprinkle with the sesame seeds.

cook's-choice fried rice

SERVES 4 · 1½ cups per serving
PREPARATION TIME · 15 minutes
COOKING TIME · 11 to 15 minutes

Although this dish calls for leftover Orange Sesame Pork (page 208), it's so versatile that you can use almost any leftover lean meat—from baked chicken to Taco-Rubbed Flank Steak (page 184). No frozen peas and fresh carrots on hand? No problem. Use what you have—bell pepper, broccoli florets, asparagus, or whatever vegetables you prefer. You'll need about 2½ cups in addition to the onion.

1 cup frozen green peas

12 ounces cooked pork from Orange Sesame Pork or other lean, low-sodium cooked meat, cut into ½-inch cubes (about 2 cups)

2 tablespoons soy sauce (lowest sodium available)

1 tablespoon vinegar (plain rice vinegar preferred)

1 tablespoon canola or corn oil

2 medium carrots, diced (about 1½ cups)

1 medium onion, sliced

¼ teaspoon crushed red pepper flakes

2 cups cooked brown rice (cold preferred)

¼ cup fat-free, low-sodium chicken broth or water (if using cold rice)

Put the peas in a colander to begin thawing.

In a medium bowl, stir together the pork, soy sauce, and vinegar.

In a nonstick wok or large nonstick skillet, heat the oil over high heat for about 1 minute, or until very hot, swirling to coat the bottom. Cook the carrots, onion, and red pepper flakes for 4 to 6 minutes, or until the vegetables begin to soften, stirring constantly.

PER SERVING
calories 342
total fat 8.0 g
saturated 1.5 g
trans 0.0 g
polyunsaturated 2.0 g
monounsaturated 3.5 g
cholesterol 74 mg
sodium 478 mg
carbohydrates 37 g
fiber 5 g
sugars 8 g
protein 30 g
dietary exchanges
2 starch
1 vegetable
3 lean meat

Stir in the peas and rice. If using cold rice, add the broth. (Hot, moist rice won't need liquid.) Cook for 2 minutes, stirring occasionally to break up the rice.

Stir in the pork mixture. Cook for 3 to 5 minutes, or until all the ingredients are heated through, stirring occasionally.

COOK'S TIP ON FRIED RICE

Fried rice is best when made with cold rice because the rice grains stay firm and separate.

red-hot pork stir-fry

SERVES 4 · 1¾ cups per serving
PREPARATION TIME · 12 minutes
COOKING TIME · 7 minutes

Here's proof that a home-cooked meal can take less time than making a run for fast food.

1 7-ounce box quick-cooking white and wild rice, seasoning packet discarded

2 tablespoons soy sauce (lowest sodium available)

2 tablespoons dry sherry

1 tablespoon sugar

½ teaspoon cornstarch

¼ to ½ teaspoon crushed red pepper flakes

1 pound pork tenderloin, all visible fat discarded, cut into strips about 2 inches long and ¼ inch wide

1 pound fresh prewashed spinach, large stems discarded

¼ cup water

Prepare the rice using the package directions, omitting the salt, margarine, and seasoning packet.

Meanwhile, in a small bowl, whisk together the soy sauce, sherry, sugar, cornstarch, and red pepper flakes until the cornstarch is completely dissolved. Set aside.

Heat a nonstick wok or large nonstick skillet over high heat for about 1 minute, or until very hot. Cook the pork for 3 minutes, stirring constantly.

Add the soy sauce mixture. Cook for about 1 minute, or until the pork is cooked through and the sauce is thickened, stirring constantly. Remove from the heat.

Arrange the rice on a platter, leaving room for the spinach on the outer edge. Spoon the pork and sauce over the rice. Cover the platter with aluminum foil to keep warm.

PER SERVING
calories 344
total fat 3.0 g
saturated 1.0 g
trans 0.0 g
polyunsaturated 0.5 g
monounsaturated 1.0 g
cholesterol 74 mg
sodium 347 mg
carbohydrates 46 g
fiber 3 g
sugars 4 g
protein 32 g
dietary exchanges
2½ starch
1 vegetable
3 very lean meat

Return the wok with any pan residue to high heat. Add about half the spinach and half the water. Cook for about 1 minute, or until the spinach is just limp, stirring constantly. Arrange around the outer edge of the rice. Re-cover the platter. Repeat with the remaining spinach and water.

Red-Hot Chicken Stir-Fry

Instead of the pork, use 1 pound thinly sliced chicken tenders or boneless, skinless chicken breasts, all visible fat discarded.

PER SERVING

calories 345
total fat 2.0 g
  saturated 0.5 g
  trans 0.0 g
  polyunsaturated 0.5 g
  monounsaturated 0.5 g
cholesterol 66 mg
sodium 361 mg
carbohydrates 46 g
  fiber 3 g
  sugars 4 g
protein 34 g
dietary exchanges
  2$^1/_2$ starch
  1 vegetable
  3 very lean meat

asian pork stir-fry

SERVES 4 · 1 cup per serving
PREPARATION TIME · 10 minutes
COOKING TIME · 11 minutes

Using prewashed spinach and presliced mushrooms makes preparation of an easy entrée even easier. Serve this stir-fry over hot brown rice to add a whole grain to your meal.

1 tablespoon minced peeled gingerroot

1 teaspoon bottled minced garlic or 2 medium garlic cloves, minced

2 tablespoons soy sauce (lowest sodium available)

1 tablespoon cornstarch

1 teaspoon toasted sesame oil

1/4 teaspoon crushed red pepper flakes

1 butterfly pork chop (about 6 ounces), all visible fat discarded, cut into 1 1/2 x 1/2-inch strips

1 tablespoon plus 1 teaspoon canola or corn oil

8 cups fresh prewashed spinach, large stems discarded

8 ounces presliced fresh button mushrooms

2 teaspoons vinegar

2 teaspoons sugar

In a small dish, stir together the gingerroot and garlic.

In a medium bowl, stir together the soy sauce, cornstarch, sesame oil, and red pepper flakes.

Stir the pork into the soy sauce mixture.

Heat a nonstick wok or large nonstick skillet over high heat for about 1 minute, or until very hot. Cook the pork mixture for about 2 minutes, or until the pork is cooked through, stirring constantly. Remove from the wok.

Pour the oil into the wok, swirling to coat the bottom. Heat for about 30 seconds. Cook the gingerroot mixture for about 30 seconds, stirring constantly.

PER SERVING
calories 159
total fat 8.5 g
saturated 1.5 g
trans 0.0 g
polyunsaturated 2.0 g
monounsaturated 4.5 g
cholesterol 24 mg
sodium 272 mg
carbohydrates 9 g
fiber 2 g
sugars 3 g
protein 13 g
dietary exchanges
2 vegetable
1 1/2 lean meat
1 fat

Stir in the spinach and mushrooms. Cook for about 5 minutes, or until the spinach is wilted, stirring occasionally.

Stir in the pork mixture, vinegar, and sugar. Cook for about 2 minutes, or until all the ingredients are heated through and well combined, stirring constantly.

COOK'S TIP

Like most other stir-fries, this one cooks quickly. That's why you need all the ingredients ready before you heat the wok.

rosemary braised pork chops

SERVES 4 · 3 ounces pork per serving
PREPARATION TIME · 5 minutes
COOKING TIME · 14 to 19 minutes

No more dry pork chops! Our tender chops are braised to keep them moist. Serve with your favorite green vegetable and Orange-Flavored Acorn Squash and Sweet Potato (page 286).

RUB

1 tablespoon chopped fresh rosemary or 1 teaspoon dried, crushed

1 teaspoon garlic powder

1 teaspoon onion powder

⅛ teaspoon pepper

• • •

2 butterfly pork chops (about 8 ounces each and ¾ inch thick), cut in half, or 4 boneless pork loin chops (about 4 ounces each and ¾ inch thick), all visible fat discarded

Olive oil spray

½ cup water

In a small bowl, stir together the rub ingredients. Sprinkle on both sides of the pork. Using your fingertips, press the rub into the pork.

Lightly spray a large skillet with olive oil spray. Cook the pork over medium-high heat for 2 minutes on each side, or until lightly browned.

Pour in the water. Reduce the heat to medium low. Cook for 10 to 15 minutes, or until the pork is no longer pink in the center. Using a slotted spoon or slotted spatula, transfer the pork to plates.

PER SERVING
calories 160
total fat 5.5 g
saturated 2.0 g
trans 0.0 g
polyunsaturated 0.5 g
monounsaturated 2.5 g
cholesterol 64 mg
sodium 69 mg
carbohydrates 1 g
fiber 0 g
sugars 0 g
protein 25 g
dietary exchanges
3 lean meat

Celery-Sage Pork Chops

Replace the rosemary rub with 1 tablespoon chopped fresh sage (about 10 leaves) or 1 teaspoon dried sage, $\frac{1}{2}$ teaspoon celery seeds, $\frac{1}{2}$ teaspoon onion powder, and $\frac{1}{8}$ teaspoon pepper.

COOK'S TIP

If you have the time or the rest of the meal isn't ready yet, you can simmer these chops for up to 1 hour. (Don't forget to add more water when needed.) Although they'll be fine to eat even after 10 to 15 minutes, the pork chops will become even tenderer if cooked longer.

sweet-and-sour black-eyed peas with ham

SERVES 4 · 1 cup per serving
PREPARATION TIME · 5 minutes
COOKING TIME · 5 minutes

If you've been on the lookout for new ways to use leftover ham, here's a main dish to try. Pineapple slices are a great complement as a side dish or for dessert. Replace the spicy brown mustard with a flavored mustard, such as orange, horseradish, or honey, if you wish.

2 15.5-ounce cans no-salt-added black-eyed peas, rinsed and drained

1 cup low-fat, lower-sodium ham, all visible fat discarded, cut into ³/₄-inch cubes (about 4 ounces)

3 tablespoons all-fruit black cherry spread

2 tablespoons light brown sugar

1¹/₂ tablespoons spicy brown mustard

1 tablespoon cider vinegar

¹/₈ teaspoon salt

¹/₈ teaspoon pepper

2 tablespoons snipped fresh parsley (optional)

In a medium saucepan, stir together all the ingredients except the parsley. Cook over medium heat for 5 minutes, or until warmed through, stirring occasionally. Sprinkle with the parsley.

PER SERVING
calories 279
total fat 1.0 g
saturated 0.5 g
trans 0.0 g
polyunsaturated 0.0 g
monounsaturated 0.5 g
cholesterol 12 mg
sodium 367 mg
carbohydrates 49 g
fiber 9 g
sugars 20 g
protein 17 g
dietary exchanges
2¹/₂ starch
1 carbohydrate
1¹/₂ very lean meat

ham and hash brown casserole

SERVES 4 · 4½-inch square per serving
PREPARATION TIME · 12 to 15 minutes
BAKING TIME · 55 minutes
or
MICROWAVE TIME · 16 minutes

Combine leftover ham with frozen hash browns and get an incredibly easy casserole to serve for brunch or dinner.

Cooking spray

12 ounces frozen fat-free, no-salt-added shredded hash brown potatoes

4 ounces lower-sodium, low-fat ham, thinly sliced and chopped (about 1 cup)

¾ cup chopped red bell pepper

½ cup chopped onion, thawed if frozen

½ cup chopped green onions (green and white parts) (about 9 medium)

½ cup fat-free sour cream

½ cup fat-free evaporated milk

1 finely chopped medium fresh jalapeño or ¼ teaspoon cayenne

⅛ teaspoon salt

3 ounces shredded low-fat sharp Cheddar cheese (about ¾ cup)

Preheat the oven to 350°F. Lightly spray a 9-inch square glass baking dish with cooking spray.

In a large bowl, stir together all the ingredients except the Cheddar. Spoon into the baking dish.

Bake for 50 minutes, or until the potatoes are tender. Stir in half the Cheddar. Sprinkle with the remaining Cheddar. Bake for 5 minutes, or until the Cheddar is melted.

TIME-SAVER You can save almost 40 minutes by using your microwave when preparing this dish. In a 9-inch square microwaveable baking dish, stir together all the ingredients except the Cheddar. Cook, covered, on 100 percent power (high) for 15 minutes, or until the potatoes are tender, stirring every 5 minutes. Sprinkle with all the Cheddar. Cook, uncovered, on 100 percent power (high) for 1 minute, or until the Cheddar is melted.

PER SERVING
calories 201
total fat 2.5 g
saturated 1.5 g
trans 0.0 g
polyunsaturated 0.0 g
monounsaturated 1.0 g
cholesterol 23 mg
sodium 445 mg
carbohydrates 28 g
fiber 2 g
sugars 9 g
protein 17 g
dietary exchanges
2 starch
1 very lean meat

smoked sausage skillet supper

SERVES 4 · 1 cup per serving
PREPARATION TIME · 5 minutes
COOKING TIME · 20 minutes

Today's low-fat sausages make it easy to enjoy heart-healthy versions of some Eastern European dishes, such as this one.

Cooking spray

1 tablespoon canola or corn oil

7½ ounces precooked low-fat smoked sausage ring, cut lengthwise into quarters, then crosswise into ¼- to ½-inch slices

4 cups shredded cabbage or coleslaw mix (about 8 ounces)

3 cups frozen fat-free, no-salt-added cubed hash brown potatoes or 4 medium potatoes, peeled and diced (about 1 pound)

1 14.5-ounce can no-salt-added stewed tomatoes, undrained

½ cup chopped onion

1 teaspoon bottled minced garlic or 2 medium garlic cloves, minced

⅛ to ¼ teaspoon crushed red pepper flakes

½ cup dry white wine (regular or nonalcoholic) or water

Lightly spray a Dutch oven with cooking spray. Pour in the oil, swirling to coat the bottom. Heat over medium-low heat. Add the remaining ingredients except the wine, stirring well. Cook, covered, for 10 minutes.

Stir in the wine. Cook for 10 minutes, or until the potatoes are tender, scraping several times to dislodge any browned bits.

PER SERVING
calories 277
total fat 5.0 g
saturated 0.5 g
trans 0.0 g
polyunsaturated 1.0 g
monounsaturated 3.0 g
cholesterol 11 mg
sodium 490 mg
carbohydrates 45 g
fiber 6 g
sugars 7 g
protein 9 g
dietary exchanges
2½ starch
2 vegetable
1 lean meat

vegetarian entrées

Herbed Edamame, Black Beans, and Quinoa

Avocado Veggie Wraps

Quinoa with Mixed Squash and Arugula

Portobello Sandwiches with Zesty Red Onions

Pita Pizzas

Portobello Pizzas with Peppery Greens

Pasta with Italian Vegetables
Italian Vegetable Stew
Italian Vegetable Stew with Pasta
Italian Vegetables

Oven-Roasted Vegetables and Pasta

Rosemary Peas and Pasta

Rigatoni with Cauliflower and Tomato Sauce

Pasta with Kale and Sun-Dried Tomatoes

Vegetables in Thai Sauce with Jasmine Rice

Tex-Mex Pilaf

Slow-Cooker Rajma

Adzuki Beans and Rice

Black Beans and Rice
Black Bean and Rice Salad

Green Chile, Black Bean, and Corn Stew

Bean and Vegetable Burgers

Vegetarian Chili

Vegetable, Bean and Barley Stew

Greek White Beans

Southwestern Posole Stew

Red Lentils with Vegetables and Brown Rice

Greek-Style Brown Rice Casserole

Crustless Mushroom and Spinach Pie

Pasta Frittata
Cajun Frittata with Pasta

Broccoli Potato Frittata

Mushroom Quesadillas

Mozzarella Polenta with Roasted Vegetable Salsa

Tofu and Vegetable Stir-Fry

Tofu Cacciatore

herbed edamame, black beans, and quinoa

SERVES 4 · 1½ cups per serving
PREPARATION TIME · 8 minutes
COOKING TIME · 13 to 14 minutes

The contrasting bright green edamame, shiny black beans, and snow-white feta cheese in this dish will please your eyes as well as your palate.

1⅓ cups water

⅔ cup uncooked quinoa

½ 15-ounce can no-salt-added black beans, rinsed and drained

1 cup frozen shelled edamame, thawed

2 cups loosely packed spring greens, coarsely chopped

2 teaspoons grated lemon zest

2 tablespoons lemon juice

1 tablespoon olive oil (extra-virgin preferred)

2 teaspoons chopped fresh oregano or ¾ teaspoon dried, crumbled

½ teaspoon finely chopped fresh rosemary or ⅛ teaspoon dried, crushed

½ teaspoon bottled minced garlic or 1 medium garlic clove, minced

¼ teaspoon salt

2 ounces feta cheese, crumbled (about ½ cup)

In a medium saucepan, bring the water to a boil over high heat, 3 to 4 minutes. Stir in the quinoa. Reduce the heat and simmer, covered, for 8 minutes.

Stir in the beans and edamame. Cook, covered, for 2 minutes, or until the water is evaporated.

Meanwhile, in a large bowl, stir together the remaining ingredients except the feta. Add the quinoa mixture and the feta, tossing until the spring greens are wilted.

PER SERVING
calories 275
total fat 10.0 g
saturated 3.0 g
trans 0.0 g
polyunsaturated 1.5 g
monounsaturated 3.5 g
cholesterol 13 mg
sodium 317 mg
carbohydrates 32 g
fiber 7 g
sugars 4 g
protein 14 g
dietary exchanges
2 starch
1 lean meat
1 fat

avocado veggie wraps

SERVES 4 · 1 wrap per serving
PREPARATION TIME · 15 minutes
WARMING TIME · 10 minutes
or
MICROWAVE TIME · 20 to 30 seconds

This pita wrap is bulging with vegetables combined with a lime and sour cream dressing.

4 6-inch whole-grain pita rounds	1 medium avocado, diced
1 cup canned no-salt-added chick-peas, rinsed and drained	1/4 cup finely chopped red onion
1 cup diced cucumber	1/2 cup fat-free sour cream
1 medium tomato, seeded and chopped	2 tablespoons fat-free milk
	1 1/2 tablespoons lime juice
	1/8 teaspoon salt

If using the oven to heat the pita rounds, preheat to 350°F. Wrap the pita rounds in aluminum foil and heat for 10 minutes, or until warmed through. If using the microwave oven, put the pita rounds on a microwaveable plate and cover with damp paper towels. Microwave on 100 percent power (high) for 20 to 30 seconds, or until warmed through.

Meanwhile, in a large bowl, stir together the chick-peas, cucumber, tomato, avocado, and onion.

In a small bowl, whisk together the remaining ingredients until smooth. Gently stir into the chick-pea mixture.

To assemble, spoon the mixture down the center of each pita. Fold a pita over the filling and secure by pushing two 6-inch bamboo skewers in an *X* through the pita. Repeat with the remaining pitas.

COOK'S TIP ON SEEDING TOMATOES
To seed tomatoes easily, cut the tomato crosswise and squeeze out the seeds and liquid.

PER SERVING

calories 353
total fat 9.5 g
  saturated 1.5 g
  trans 0.0 g
  polyunsaturated 1.5 g
  monounsaturated 5.0 g
cholesterol 5 mg
sodium 441 mg
carbohydrates 58 g
  fiber 11 g
  sugars 6 g
protein 13 g
dietary exchanges
  3 1/2 starch
  1 vegetable
  1/2 lean meat
  1 fat

quinoa with mixed squash and arugula

SERVES 4 · 1 cup per serving
PREPARATION TIME · 14 to 16 minutes
COOKING TIME · 12 to 17 minutes
MICROWAVE TIME · 30 seconds

all-in-one

Lemon-tinged cream cheese tempers peppery arugula in this nutrition-packed entrée.

2 cups low-sodium vegetable broth

1 cup uncooked quinoa

Cooking spray

1 small yellow summer squash, halved lengthwise, then sliced crosswise into 1/4-inch pieces

1 small zucchini, halved lengthwise, then sliced crosswise into 1/4-inch pieces

1/2 cup chopped onion

1 cup grape tomatoes, halved

2 cups lightly packed arugula

3 tablespoons light tub cream cheese

1 tablespoon lemon juice

1/4 cup shredded or grated Parmesan cheese

In a medium saucepan, stir together the broth and quinoa. Cook over medium-high heat until the mixture comes to a boil, about 2 minutes. Reduce the heat and simmer, covered, for 10 to 15 minutes, or until all the broth is absorbed.

Meanwhile, lightly spray a large skillet with cooking spray. Cook the yellow summer squash, zucchini, and onion over medium-high heat for about 5 minutes, or until softened, stirring occasionally.

Stir the tomatoes into the squash mixture. Cook for 1 to 2 minutes, stirring occasionally.

PER SERVING
calories 245
total fat 6.0 g
saturated 2.5 g
trans 0.0 g
polyunsaturated 1.5 g
monounsaturated 1.5 g
cholesterol 11 mg
sodium 175 mg
carbohydrates 36 g
fiber 5 g
sugars 5 g
protein 11 g
dietary exchanges
2 starch
1 vegetable
1 fat

Stir in the arugula. Cook for 1 to 2 minutes, or until it wilts, stirring occasionally. Remove from the heat.

In a small microwaveable bowl, microwave the cream cheese on 100 percent power (high) for about 30 seconds, or until melted. Whisk in the lemon juice. Pour over the squash mixture.

Stir the quinoa into the squash mixture. Sprinkle with the Parmesan.

COOK'S TIP ON QUINOA
Quinoa (KEEN-wah) can usually be found in the health food section of the grocery store. High in iron and protein, among other nutrients, it is delicately flavored, making it well-suited to substitute for rice and other grains.

portobello sandwiches with zesty red onions

SERVES 4 · 1 sandwich per serving
PREPARATION TIME · 15 minutes
COOKING TIME · 18 to 20 minutes

all-in-one

Layers of mushroom slices, red bell peppers, and cheese, all seasoned with a sweet-and-sour onion mixture, combine to create a unique sandwich.

Cooking spray

3 tablespoons low-sodium vegetable broth or water

1 teaspoon toasted sesame oil

1 to 2 cups sliced red onions (1/4 inch thick)

1 large or 2 medium red bell peppers, sliced

2 tablespoons light brown sugar

1 tablespoon vinegar

1 tablespoon lemon juice

1 teaspoon dried basil, crumbled, or 1 tablespoon snipped fresh basil

1/8 to 1/4 teaspoon crushed red pepper flakes

2 fresh portobello mushrooms (4 to 6 ounces each), stems discarded

2 ounces provolone cheese, sliced

1/2 long, wide loaf French or Italian bread (about 8 ounces)

Lightly spray a large skillet, roasting pan, and roasting rack with cooking spray.

Pour the broth and oil into the skillet, swirling to coat the bottom. Cook the onions and bell pepper over medium-high heat for about 2 minutes, stirring occasionally. Reduce the heat to medium and cook until the onions are quite limp and beginning to brown, about 10 minutes, stirring occasionally.

Meanwhile, preheat the broiler.

In a small bowl, whisk together the brown sugar, vinegar, lemon juice, basil, and red pepper flakes until the sugar dissolves. Lightly brush both sides of the mushrooms with part of the mixture, reserving the remaining mixture.

PER SERVING
calories 287
total fat 6.0 g
saturated 3.0 g
trans 0.0 g
polyunsaturated 1.0 g
monounsaturated 1.5 g
cholesterol 10 mg
sodium 501 mg
carbohydrates 47 g
fiber 3 g
sugars 12 g
protein 12 g
dietary exchanges
2 1/2 starch
2 vegetable
1/2 medium-fat meat

Broil the mushrooms on the roasting rack about 4 inches from the heat for 5 minutes on each side, or until they darken and begin to shrivel.

When the onions are beginning to brown, stir in the remaining brown sugar mixture. Bring to a boil over medium heat and boil until the onions are coated and no liquid remains.

Slice the bread in half lengthwise, then into quarters crosswise (8 pieces total). Cut the mushrooms into 3/4-inch slices. Spread the onion mixture over 4 pieces of the bread. Add the mushrooms, then the provolone. Top with the remaining bread and serve, or put the open sandwiches and remaining bread on the roasting rack used for the mushrooms and broil for 1 minute, or until the provolone melts and the bread is toasted.

COOK'S TIP

If you're watching your sodium intake, use half as much bread as the recipe calls for and serve this sandwich open-face. You'll need knives and forks.

pita pizzas

SERVES 4 · 1 pizza per serving
PREPARATION TIME · 10 minutes
COOKING TIME · 4 to 6 minutes

Pita bread is the perfect starter for a healthful thin-crust pizza. Then use the toppings listed here or substitute other vegetables, such as broccoli, artichokes, and spinach. It's as much fun to put the pizzas together as it is to eat them.

½ cup no-salt-added tomato sauce

½ teaspoon dried oregano, crumbled, and 1 teaspoon dried oregano, crumbled, divided use

⅛ teaspoon sugar

2 6-inch whole-wheat pita pockets, split open into rounds

1 cup grated low-fat mozzarella cheese (4 ounces)

½ cup thinly sliced green bell pepper

4 ounces presliced fresh button mushrooms

Preheat the broiler.

In a small bowl, stir together the tomato sauce, ½ teaspoon oregano, and sugar.

To assemble, place 2 pita halves in the center of a large baking sheet. Place the remaining 2 pita halves on another baking sheet. Spread 2 tablespoons sauce on each pita half. Sprinkle with the mozzarella, top with the bell pepper and mushrooms, and sprinkle with the remaining 1 teaspoon oregano.

Broil half the pizzas 3 to 4 inches from the heat for 2 to 3 minutes, or until the mozzarella melts and the edges begin to brown. Transfer to plates. Repeat with the remaining pizzas.

PER SERVING
calories 159
total fat 3.5 g
saturated 1.0 g
trans 0.0 g
polyunsaturated 0.5 g
monounsaturated 0.5 g
cholesterol 10 mg
sodium 365 mg
carbohydrates 22 g
fiber 4 g
sugars 3 g
protein 11 g
dietary exchanges
1 starch
1 vegetable
1 lean meat

portobello pizzas with peppery greens

SERVES 4 · 1 pizza per serving
PREPARATION TIME · 10 minutes
COOKING TIME · 15 minutes

No kneading or rising time is required for this mushroom-based pizza. Place it on a bed of arugula and watercress flavored with a feta dressing, and serve as they do in Europe—with a knife and fork.

Olive oil spray

4 fresh portobello mushrooms, stems discarded

2 medium Italian plum (Roma) tomatoes

¼ cup bottled roasted red bell peppers, drained

1 cup shredded low-fat mozzarella cheese (about 4 ounces)

2 tablespoons sliced black olives, drained

½ teaspoon dried oregano, crumbled

2 tablespoons crumbled feta cheese

2 tablespoons white wine vinegar

2½ teaspoons olive oil

½ to 1 teaspoon sugar

2 cups arugula leaves

2 cups watercress leaves

Preheat the oven to 400°F.

Lightly spray both sides of the mushrooms with olive oil spray. Place with the smooth side down on a nonstick baking sheet.

Bake for 10 minutes, or until tender.

Meanwhile, thinly slice the tomatoes and roasted peppers. When the mushrooms are ready, top with the tomato slices. Sprinkle with the roasted peppers, mozzarella, olives, and oregano.

Bake for 5 minutes, or until the mozzarella is melted.

Meanwhile, in a large bowl, whisk together the feta, vinegar, oil, and sugar. Add the arugula and watercress, tossing to coat. Arrange on plates. Top with the portobellos.

PER SERVING
calories 129
total fat 7.0 g
saturated 2.0 g
trans 0.0 g
polyunsaturated 0.5 g
monounsaturated 3.0 g
cholesterol 14 mg
sodium 310 mg
carbohydrates 8 g
fiber 2 g
sugars 3 g
protein 10 g
dietary exchanges
1 vegetable
1 very lean meat
1 fat

pasta with italian vegetables

SERVES 4 · heaping 1¾ cups per serving
PREPARATION TIME · 15 minutes
COOKING TIME · 30 minutes

all-in-one

With its Old World flavors and tempting aroma, this versatile dish is a big hit at potluck suppers. Depending on whether you use the main recipe or one of the variations, you can create an entrée, a one-dish meal, or a side dish from the same basic ingredients.

2 14.5-ounce cans no-salt-added diced tomatoes, undrained

8 ounces zucchini, cut into ⅛-inch slices

8 ounces eggplant, diced

8 ounces presliced fresh button mushrooms

1 cup diced green bell pepper

1 tablespoon dried oregano, crumbled

1 teaspoon sugar

¼ teaspoon salt and ¼ teaspoon salt, divided use

6 ounces dried whole-grain penne pasta

1 tablespoon olive oil (extra-virgin preferred)

In a Dutch oven, stir together the tomatoes with liquid, zucchini, eggplant, mushrooms, bell pepper, oregano, sugar, and ¼ teaspoon salt. Bring to a boil over high heat. Reduce the heat and simmer, covered, for 25 minutes, or until the vegetables are tender. Remove from the heat.

Meanwhile, prepare the pasta using the package directions, omitting the salt and oil. Drain well in a colander.

Spoon the pasta onto plates. Stir the remaining ¼ teaspoon salt into the tomato mixture. Spoon over the pasta. Drizzle with the oil.

PER SERVING
calories 266
total fat 5.0 g
saturated 0.5 g
trans 0.0 g
polyunsaturated 1.5 g
monounsaturated 2.5 g
cholesterol 0 mg
sodium 407 mg
carbohydrates 49 g
fiber 10 g
sugars 13 g
protein 12 g
dietary exchanges
2 starch
3 vegetable
½ fat

Italian Vegetable Stew

SERVES 4 · 1½ cups per serving

Omit the pasta and oil. Reduce the salt to ¼ teaspoon total. After the vegetables are cooked and the salt is added, top each portion with ¼ cup shredded fat-free mozzarella cheese (4 ounces total).

Italian Vegetable Stew with Pasta

SERVES 4 · 1½ cups per serving

Replace the zucchini with one 16-ounce can no-salt-added green beans, drained. Omit the oil. Prepare the pasta as directed on page 230. Drain well in a colander. Pour into a 12 x 8 x 2-inch broilerproof baking dish. Spoon the cooked vegetable mixture over the pasta, and top with 6 ounces shredded low-fat mozzarella cheese. In a preheated broiler, broil at least 5 inches from the heat for 2 to 3 minutes, or until the mozzarella is bubbly and beginning to lightly brown.

Italian Vegetables

SERVES 12 · ½ cup per serving

Omit the pasta and increase the oil to 2 tablespoons. After cooking the vegetables, remove from the heat. Stir in the oil and ¼ teaspoon salt.

oven-roasted vegetables and pasta

SERVES 4 · scant 2 cups per serving
PREPARATION TIME · 20 minutes
COOKING TIME · 15 minutes

Roasting vegetables usually takes 45 minutes or longer. The technique we use here takes only 15 minutes, yet provides excellent slow-roasted flavor. For a change, omit the pasta and serve the vegetables as a side dish.

6 ounces dried whole-grain pasta, such as rotini

Cooking spray

1 pound yellow summer squash, or 8 ounces yellow summer squash and 8 ounces zucchini, cut into matchstick-size strips

2 medium onions (yellow preferred), cut into eighths, then halved crosswise

1 medium green bell pepper, cut into 1-inch squares

8 ounces cherry tomatoes, halved

1/4 cup finely chopped fresh basil (about 2/3 ounce before removing stems) or 1 1/2 tablespoons dried basil, crumbled

1 1/2 tablespoons cider vinegar or balsamic vinegar

1 tablespoon olive oil (extra-virgin preferred)

2 teaspoons bottled minced garlic or 4 medium garlic cloves, minced

2 1/2 ounces low-fat feta cheese, crumbled (heaping 1/2 cup)

1/4 teaspoon salt

1/8 to 1/4 teaspoon crushed red pepper flakes

Prepare the pasta using the package directions, omitting the salt and oil. Drain well in a colander.

Meanwhile, preheat the broiler. Line a large broiler pan or two baking sheets with aluminum foil. Lightly spray the foil with cooking spray.

Arrange the squash, onions, bell pepper, and tomatoes in a single layer on the foil.

PER SERVING
calories 283
total fat 9.0 g
saturated 3.0 g
trans 0.0 g
polyunsaturated 1.5 g
monounsaturated 3.5 g
cholesterol 16 mg
sodium 378 mg
carbohydrates 44 g
fiber 7 g
sugars 11 g
protein 12 g
dietary exchanges
2 starch
3 vegetable
1 1/2 fat

Broil about 5 inches from the heat for 15 minutes, or until the edges are browned and the bell pepper is just tender, stirring every 5 minutes.

In a small bowl, whisk together the basil, vinegar, oil, and garlic.

In a large bowl, stir together all the ingredients except the basil mixture. Pour in the basil mixture, tossing well.

rosemary peas and pasta

SERVES 8 · 1½ cups per serving
PREPARATION TIME · 5 minutes
COOKING TIME · 15 minutes

Rosemary and two kinds of pepper ramp up the flavor of this tempting, inexpensive entrée.

12 ounces dried medium whole-grain pasta shells

1 tablespoon olive oil

1 20-ounce package frozen green peas (4 cups)

¾ cup coarsely chopped onion (sweet preferred, such as Vidalia, OsoSweet, or Maui)

2 tablespoons bottled minced garlic or 12 medium garlic cloves, minced

1 teaspoon dried rosemary, crushed

¼ teaspoon crushed red pepper flakes

½ teaspoon pepper

¼ cup shredded or grated Parmesan cheese

Prepare the pasta using the package directions, omitting the salt and oil. Reserve 2 cups cooking liquid. Drain the pasta well in a colander.

Meanwhile, in a large skillet, heat the oil over medium heat, swirling to coat the bottom. Stir in the peas, onion, garlic, rosemary, and red pepper flakes. Cook, covered, for 7 to 10 minutes, stirring occasionally.

Stir in the reserved cooking liquid and pepper. Cook, covered, for 3 minutes, stirring occasionally.

In a large bowl, stir together the pasta and pea mixture. Sprinkle with the Parmesan.

PER SERVING
calories 231
total fat 4.0 g
saturated 0.5 g
trans 0.0 g
polyunsaturated 1.0 g
monounsaturated 1.5 g
cholesterol 2 mg
sodium 146 mg
carbohydrates 40 g
fiber 6 g
sugars 5 g
protein 12 g
dietary exchanges 2½ starch

rigatoni with cauliflower and tomato sauce

SERVES 8 · 2 cups per serving
PREPARATION TIME · 10 minutes
COOKING TIME · 29 to 34 minutes

To vary this flavorful dish, serve the sauce over another kind of pasta or brown rice.

16 ounces dried rigatoni

SAUCE

2 tablespoons olive oil

1 20-ounce package frozen cauliflower florets (4 cups)

1 cup coarsely snipped fresh parsley (Italian, or flat-leaf, preferred)

3/4 cup coarsely chopped onion

1/4 cup coarsely chopped fresh basil (about 2/3 ounce before removing stems)

2 to 3 tablespoons bottled minced garlic or 12 to 18 medium garlic cloves, finely chopped

32 ounces marinara sauce (lowest sodium available)

2 cups water

1/4 cup dry red wine (regular or nonalcoholic)

1/8 teaspoon cayenne

Pepper to taste

• • •

3 tablespoons shredded or grated Parmesan cheese

Prepare the pasta using the package directions, omitting the salt and oil. Drain well in a colander. Set aside.

Meanwhile, in a Dutch oven, heat the oil over medium heat, swirling to coat the bottom. Stir in the cauliflower, parsley, onion, basil, and garlic. Cook, covered, for 10 minutes, or until the vegetables release some liquids, stirring occasionally.

Stir in the remaining sauce ingredients. Increase the heat to medium high and bring to a boil, covered. Cook at a medium boil for 12 to 15 minutes, or until the cauliflower is tender, stirring occasionally.

Pour the pasta into a large bowl. Spoon half the sauce over the pasta. Using two spoons, toss to coat. Spoon the remaining sauce over the pasta. Sprinkle with the Parmesan.

PER SERVING
calories 388
total fat 7.5 g
saturated 1.5 g
trans 0.0 g
polyunsaturated 1.5 g
monounsaturated 3.5 g
cholesterol 1 mg
sodium 472 mg
carbohydrates 64 g
fiber 7 g
sugars 13 g
protein 12 g
dietary exchanges
4 starch
1 vegetable
1 fat

pasta with kale and sun-dried tomatoes

all-in-one

SERVES 5 · 1½ cups per serving
PREPARATION TIME · 5 minutes
COOKING TIME · 22 minutes

Feta cheese lends a little pungent punch and complements the sweetness of the sun-dried tomatoes in this colorful entrée for five or side dish for a crowd.

1 ounce dry-packed sun-dried tomatoes (about ⅓ cup)

½ cup boiling water

16 ounces dried medium whole-grain pasta shells

2 teaspoons olive oil

2 teaspoons minced garlic or 4 medium garlic cloves, minced

¼ teaspoon crushed red pepper flakes

8 ounces packaged chopped fresh kale

3 ounces crumbled low-fat feta cheese (about ¾ cup)

Put the tomatoes in a small shallow bowl. Pour in the water. Stir. Set aside.

Prepare the pasta using the package directions, omitting the salt and oil and cooking until still firm when you bite into it (start tasting 3 minutes before the package says it will be done). Drain well in a colander. Return to the pot. Cover and set aside.

Meanwhile, in a large skillet, heat the oil over medium heat, swirling to coat the bottom. Cook the garlic and red pepper flakes for 30 to 60 seconds, or until the garlic becomes aromatic and begins to brown. Stir in the kale.

PER SERVING
calories 417
total fat 8.5 g
saturated 3.0 g
trans 0.0 g
polyunsaturated 2.0 g
monounsaturated 2.0 g
cholesterol 15 mg
sodium 266 mg
carbohydrates 72 g
fiber 8 g
sugars 3 g
protein 20 g
dietary exchanges
4 starch
2 vegetable
½ lean meat
½ fat

Drain the tomatoes, combining the soaking liquid with enough water to equal ¾ cup. Pour the liquid into the kale mixture. Chop the tomatoes. Stir into the kale mixture. Increase the heat to medium high and bring to a boil. Reduce the heat and simmer, covered, for 5 to 10 minutes, or until the kale has wilted and is slightly tender. Stir into the pasta. Before serving, sprinkle with the feta.

COOK'S TIP
Vary the flavor of this dish by replacing the feta cheese with ¼ cup minced green olives or black olives, such as kalamata or niçoise.

vegetables in thai sauce with jasmine rice

SERVES 5 · 1 cup vegetables and ½ cup rice per serving
PREPARATION TIME · 5 minutes
COOKING TIME · 28 to 38 minutes

Bottled peanut satay sauce is a convenient way to add the traditional Thai flavor combination of basil, peanut, and coconut to your cooking.

1 cup uncooked jasmine rice

1 teaspoon canola or corn oil

2 16-ounce packages frozen mixed stir-fry vegetables

½ cup coarsely chopped fresh basil (about 1⅓ ounces before removing stems)

2 tablespoons bottled minced garlic or 12 medium garlic cloves, minced

¼ teaspoon crushed red pepper flakes

2 cups fat-free milk

1 7-ounce bottle peanut satay sauce

2 tablespoons lime juice

¼ cup unsalted dry-roasted peanuts

Prepare the rice using the package directions, omitting the salt and margarine.

Meanwhile, in a large saucepan, heat the oil over medium heat. Stir in the vegetables, basil, garlic, and red pepper flakes. Cook, covered, for 12 to 15 minutes, or until heated through, stirring occasionally.

Stir in the milk, satay sauce, and lime juice. Cook for 3 to 5 minutes, or until heated through, stirring occasionally. Serve over the rice. Sprinkle with the peanuts.

PER SERVING
calories 315
total fat 11.5 g
saturated 1.5 g
trans 0.0 g
polyunsaturated 4.0 g
monounsaturated 5.0 g
cholesterol 2 mg
sodium 247 mg
carbohydrates 43 g
fiber 6 g
sugars 15 g
protein 14 g
dietary exchanges
1 starch
3 vegetable
1 carbohydrate
1 lean meat
1½ fat

tex-mex pilaf

SERVES 4 · 1³/₄ cups per serving
PREPARATION TIME · 5 minutes
COOKING TIME · 50 minutes

all-
in-
one

This eclectic pilaf is a real time-saver. You need to spend only about five minutes to get it going, then you can leave it alone to cook while you do other things—and you'll have just one pan to wash.

2 teaspoons olive oil

¹/₂ cup chopped onion

1 15-ounce can no-salt-added kidney beans, rinsed and drained

1¹/₄ cups low-sodium vegetable broth or water

1 cup uncooked brown rice

1 cup fresh or frozen whole-kernel corn

1 cup chunky salsa (lowest sodium available)

¹/₄ cup uncooked lentils, sorted for stones and shriveled lentils and rinsed

¹/₄ cup chopped red bell pepper

¹/₂ teaspoon chili powder, or to taste

¹/₄ teaspoon crushed red pepper flakes, or to taste

Dash of garlic powder

In a medium saucepan, heat the oil over medium-high heat, swirling to coat the bottom. Cook the onion for 2 minutes, or until soft, stirring occasionally.

Stir in the remaining ingredients. Increase the heat to high and bring to a boil. Reduce the heat and simmer, covered, for 40 minutes, or until the lentils and rice are cooked through.

COOK'S TIP

If you want a nonvegetarian version of this dish, substitute fat-free, low-sodium chicken broth for the vegetable broth and add a little chopped skinless chicken or lower-sodium, low-fat ham with the other ingredients.

PER SERVING
calories 391
total fat 4.0 g
saturated 0.5 g
trans 0.0 g
polyunsaturated 1.0 g
monounsaturated 2.5 g
cholesterol 0 mg
sodium 263 mg
carbohydrates 75 g
fiber 9 g
sugars 7 g
protein 16 g
dietary exchanges
4¹/₂ starch
1 vegetable
1 very lean meat

slow-cooker rajma

SERVES 4 · 1½ cups per serving

PREPARATION TIME · 12 to 14 minutes

SOAKING TIME · 6 to 12 hours

COOKING TIME · 14 minutes

SLOW-COOKER TIME · 3 hours 15 minutes to 4 hours 15 minutes on high
or 8 to 10 hours on low plus 15 minutes on high

Rajma, red beans slowly simmered in a rich blend of spices, is a favorite in India and other parts of Asia. Don't be daunted by the long ingredients list—your slow cooker does the work for you. Just remember to soak the beans the night before you plan to prepare the rajma.

1 cup dried red beans, sorted for stones and shriveled beans, rinsed, and drained

6 cups cold water, 6 cups cold water, and 2 cups water, divided use

1½ cups chopped onion

1 tablespoon grated peeled gingerroot

2 medium fresh jalapeños, seeds and ribs discarded, minced

2 teaspoons ground cumin

2 teaspoons garam masala or curry powder

4 medium garlic cloves, minced, or 2 teaspoons bottled minced garlic

½ teaspoon ground cinnamon

½ teaspoon ground cardamom

½ teaspoon ground cloves

1 large tomato, seeded and chopped

2 tablespoons snipped fresh cilantro

¼ teaspoon salt

Put the dried beans in a medium saucepan of nonreactive material, such as stainless steel. Pour 6 cups cold water over the beans and allow them to soak for 6 to 12 hours.

Drain the beans in a colander, return to the same saucepan, and pour in the second 6 cups cold water. Heat over high heat until the water comes to a boil, about 4 minutes. Boil for 10 minutes. Drain in a colander. Pour the beans into a 3½- to 4-quart slow cooker.

PER SERVING
calories 199
total fat 1.0 g
saturated 0.0 g
trans 0.0 g
polyunsaturated 0.0 g
monounsaturated 0.0 g
cholesterol 0 mg
sodium 179 mg
carbohydrates 38 g
fiber 5 g
sugars 4 g
protein 13 g
dietary exchanges
2 starch
1 vegetable
½ very lean meat

Stir in the onion, gingerroot, jalapeños, cumin, garam masala, garlic, cinnamon, cardamom, and cloves. Pour in the remaining 2 cups water. Cook, covered, on low for 8 to 10 hours or on high for 3 to 4 hours, or until the beans are tender.

Stir in the tomato, cilantro, and salt. Cook, covered, on high for 15 minutes.

COOK'S TIP ON DRIED SPICES AND HERBS

Dried spices and herbs should always be fresh for the best flavor, but this is especially true when using a slow cooker. If they are old, are stale, or have lost their aroma, they may not provide the rich flavor you are seeking or, worse, can produce a somewhat bitter flavor in a slow cooker. Ideally, spices should be replaced about every 6 to 12 months. (Put the date on the container when you open it.) If you are trying a new seasoning or are choosing one that you may not use often, consider sharing it with a friend or neighbor and perhaps splitting the cost.

COOK'S TIP ON GARAM MASALA

Garam masala is an Indian blend of spices usually including pepper, cinnamon, cloves, cumin, and chiles. The name means "warm" or "hot," indicating that dishes containing this blend are spicy.

TIME-SAVER Instead of soaking the beans overnight, put them in a saucepan and add 3 cups of hot water. Bring to a boil over high heat, then reduce the heat to medium and cook for 2 minutes. Cover the saucepan and remove it from the heat. Let the beans stand for 1 hour. Drain the beans in a colander, rinse them, and return them to the pan. Cover the beans with fresh water and boil for at least 10 minutes. Drain them, put them in the slow cooker, and proceed with the recipe.

adzuki beans and rice

SERVES 4 · ¾ cup rice and ⅓ cup beans per serving
PREPARATION TIME · 10 minutes
COOKING TIME · 12 to 13 minutes
STANDING TIME · 5 minutes

all-in-one

Asian adzuki beans and fresh mushrooms contrast nicely with aromatic vegetables, thyme, and cumin in this updated version of a classic dish.

RICE

1 teaspoon olive oil

1 medium rib of celery, diced

⅓ cup chopped onion

¼ cup chopped green bell pepper

1 teaspoon bottled minced garlic or 2 medium garlic cloves, minced

1 cup fresh mushrooms (shiitake preferred), stems discarded, sliced

1½ cups uncooked instant brown rice

1¼ cups low-sodium vegetable broth

1 teaspoon dried thyme, crumbled

⅛ teaspoon crushed red pepper flakes or cayenne

BEANS

1 15-ounce can no-salt-added adzuki beans or kidney beans, rinsed and drained

½ teaspoon ground cumin

¼ teaspoon salt

● ● ●

2 tablespoons snipped fresh parsley or cilantro (optional)

In a medium saucepan, heat the oil over medium-high heat, swirling to coat the bottom. Stir in the celery, onion, bell pepper, and garlic. Cook for about 3 minutes, or until tender, stirring occasionally.

Stir in the mushrooms. Cook for 1 to 2 minutes, stirring occasionally.

Stir in the remaining rice ingredients. Increase the heat to high and bring to a boil. Reduce the heat and simmer, covered, for 5 minutes. Fluff with a fork. Remove from the heat. Let stand, covered, for 5 minutes.

PER SERVING
calories 246
total fat 2.5 g
saturated 0.0 g
trans 0.0 g
polyunsaturated 0.5 g
monounsaturated 1.5 g
cholesterol 0 mg
sodium 187 mg
carbohydrates 44 g
fiber 6 g
sugars 1 g
protein 10 g
dietary exchanges
3 starch
½ very lean meat

Meanwhile, in a small saucepan, stir together beans, cumin, and salt. Cook over medium-low heat for 3 to 4 minutes, or until warmed through, stirring occasionally. Keep warm over low heat.

Spoon the rice mixture into bowls. Top with the beans. Sprinkle with the parsley.

COOK'S TIP ON ADZUKI BEANS

Red bean paste, a popular ingredient in Chinese and Japanese cooking, is made from lightly sweetened adzuki beans (also spelled *aduki* and *azuki*). Whole adzuki beans have a delicate texture, mild flavor, and deep red color. Use them in soups, salads, and casseroles. If your supermarket doesn't carry these beans, check health food stores or Asian grocery stores.

black beans and rice

SERVES 4 · 1½ cups per serving
PREPARATION TIME · 5 minutes
COOKING TIME · 15 minutes

To jazz up black beans and rice, add the exciting flavors of rich olive oil, tangy lime juice, and assertive garlic.

2 cups uncooked instant brown rice

¼ cup lime juice

2 tablespoons plus 2 teaspoons olive oil (extra-virgin preferred)

1 teaspoon bottled minced garlic or 2 medium garlic cloves, minced

½ teaspoon salt

1 15-ounce can no-salt-added black beans, rinsed and drained

2 tablespoons finely snipped fresh cilantro (optional)

In a medium saucepan, prepare the rice using the package directions, omitting the salt and margarine.

Meanwhile, in a small bowl, whisk together the lime juice, oil, garlic, and salt.

Stir the beans into the cooked rice. Drizzle with the lime juice mixture. Stir in the cilantro.

PER SERVING

calories 346
total fat 10.5 g
  saturated 1.0 g
  trans 0.0 g
  polyunsaturated 1.5 g
  monounsaturated 7.0 g
cholesterol 0 mg
sodium 301 mg
carbohydrates 52 g
  fiber 6 g
  sugars 4 g
protein 10 g
dietary exchanges
  3½ starch
  1½ fat

Black Bean and Rice Salad

SERVES 4 · 1 ¾ cups per serving

Prepare the rice as directed above. Spread in a thin layer on a baking sheet. Let cool for 5 to 8 minutes, stirring occasionally. Increase the lime juice to ¼ cup plus 2 tablespoons. Increase the salt to ½ plus ⅛ teaspoon. Add 1 cup chopped red or green bell pepper when stirring in the beans.

PER SERVING

calories 355
total fat 10.5 g
  saturated 1.5 g
  trans 0.0 g
  polyunsaturated 1.5 g
  monounsaturated 7.0 g
cholesterol 0 mg
sodium 375 mg
carbohydrates 55 g
  fiber 7 g
  sugars 5 g
protein 10 g
dietary exchanges
  3½ starch
  1½ fat

green chile, black bean, and corn stew

SERVES 4 · 1¼ cups per serving
PREPARATION TIME · 5 minutes
COOKING TIME · 28 minutes
STANDING TIME · 5 to 10 minutes

all-in-one

If you want to, you can stretch this hearty southwestern stew by serving it over brown rice. Put about a half-cup of cooked rice in each bowl, then top with the stew.

1 teaspoon olive oil

6 to 8 ounces Anaheim peppers, poblano peppers, or green bell pepper, chopped

2 cups frozen or canned no-salt-added whole-kernel corn, drained if canned

1 15-ounce can no-salt-added black beans, rinsed and drained

1 14.5-ounce can no-salt-added diced tomatoes or no-salt-added stewed tomatoes, undrained

1 cup water

1 tablespoon chili powder

1 teaspoon ground cumin

½ teaspoon salt

In a Dutch oven, heat the oil over medium-high heat, swirling to coat the bottom. Cook the peppers for 6 minutes, or until tender-crisp, stirring frequently.

Stir in the remaining ingredients except the salt. Bring to a boil. Reduce the heat and simmer, covered, for 20 minutes. Remove from the heat.

Stir in the salt. Let stand, uncovered, for 5 to 10 minutes so the flavors blend and the stew thickens slightly.

PER SERVING

calories 219
total fat 2.5 g
  saturated 0.5 g
  trans 0.0 g
  polyunsaturated 0.5 g
  monounsaturated 1.0 g
cholesterol 0 mg
sodium 359 mg
carbohydrates 44 g
  fiber 10 g
  sugars 11 g
protein 10 g
dietary exchanges
  2½ starch
  2 vegetable

bean and vegetable burgers

SERVES 6 · 1 burger and ½ pita bread per serving
PREPARATION TIME · 20 minutes
COOKING TIME · 6 to 8 minutes

You may want to prepare a double batch of these burgers so you'll have enough to serve without the pita bread at another meal. Try them with roasted sweet potato wedges and fresh fruit.

BURGERS

1 15-ounce can no-salt-added kidney beans, rinsed and drained

1 15-ounce can no-salt-added black beans, rinsed and drained

½ cup preshredded carrots

4 medium green onions, thinly sliced

¼ cup plain dry bread crumbs

1 teaspoon chili powder

1 teaspoon garlic powder

¼ teaspoon salt

• • •

1 tablespoon olive oil

Olive oil spray

6 lettuce leaves, any variety

3 6-inch whole-wheat pita breads, halved into pockets

¾ cup salsa (lowest sodium available)

In a food processor or blender, pulse the beans for 20 to 30 seconds, or until the mixture is slightly chunky. Transfer to a medium bowl. Stir in the remaining burger ingredients. Shape into 6 flat patties.

In a large skillet, heat the oil over medium-high heat, swirling to coat the bottom. Cook the patties on one side for 3 to 4 minutes, or until browned. Remove the skillet from the heat. Lightly spray the tops of the patties with olive oil spray. Turn over. Cook for 3 to 4 minutes, or until browned.

Put the burgers and lettuce in the pita pockets. Serve with the salsa.

PER SERVING
calories 262
total fat 3.5 g
saturated 0.5 g
trans 0.0 g
polyunsaturated 0.5 g
monounsaturated 2.0 g
cholesterol 0 mg
sodium 422 mg
carbohydrates 47 g
fiber 9 g
sugars 6 g
protein 12 g
dietary exchanges
3 starch
1 very lean meat

vegetarian chili

SERVES 4 · 1½ cups per serving
PREPARATION TIME · 10 minutes
COOKING TIME · 23 to 33 minutes

all-in-one

When your meat-loving guests taste this chili, they'll be amazed that a meatless dish can be so hearty.

1 cup low-sodium mixed-vegetable juice

½ cup uncooked bulgur

Cooking spray

2 tablespoons olive oil

½ cup chopped onion

2 teaspoons bottled minced garlic or 4 medium garlic cloves, minced

2 16-ounce cans no-salt-added pinto or kidney beans, undrained

1 14.5-ounce can no-salt-added diced tomatoes, undrained

1 4-ounce can chopped green chiles, drained

2 tablespoons chili powder

1 teaspoon ground cumin

1 teaspoon dried oregano, crumbled

¼ teaspoon cayenne

In a medium saucepan, bring the juice to a boil over high heat. Add the bulgur, stirring several times. Remove from the stovetop. Set aside.

Lightly spray a Dutch oven with cooking spray. Heat the oil over medium-high heat, swirling to coat the bottom. Cook the onion and garlic for about 3 minutes, or until the onion is soft and the garlic is aromatic, stirring occasionally.

Stir in the remaining ingredients. Increase the heat to high and bring to a boil. Stir in the bulgur mixture. Return to a boil. Reduce the heat and simmer for 10 to 20 minutes (the longer simmering time lets the flavors blend more).

COOK'S TIP ON BULGUR

Bulgur is made of wheat berries that have been cooked and drained. It makes a good substitute for ground beef in many recipes. Bulgur soaks up liquid, so add more water for a soupier chili or when reheating leftovers.

PER SERVING
calories 367
total fat 8.0 g
saturated 1.0 g
trans 0.0 g
polyunsaturated 1.0 g
monounsaturated 5.0 g
cholesterol 0 mg
sodium 229 mg
carbohydrates 59 g
fiber 19 g
sugars 7 g
protein 16 g
dietary exchanges
3½ starch
2 vegetable
1 lean meat

vegetable, bean, and barley stew

SERVES 4 · 1 ¾ cups per serving
PREPARATION TIME · 12 to 14 minutes
COOKING TIME · 36 minutes

or

SLOW-COOKER TIME · 3 ½ to 4 hours on high or
7 to 9 hours on low and 30 minutes on high

Rich-tasting, thick, and so flavorful—no one will miss the meat in this stew.

Cooking spray

2 medium carrots, cut crosswise into 1-inch pieces

1 medium onion, coarsely chopped

1 medium rib of celery, cut crosswise into ½-inch pieces

1 small zucchini, halved lengthwise and sliced crosswise into ¼-inch pieces

1 14.5-ounce can no-salt-added tomatoes, undrained

2 cups low-sodium mixed-vegetable juice

1 cup water

¾ cup frozen whole-kernel corn

2½ teaspoons dried Italian seasoning, crumbled

½ teaspoon garlic powder

¼ teaspoon pepper

⅛ teaspoon salt

1 15-ounce can low-sodium Great Northern beans, rinsed and drained

½ cup uncooked quick-cooking barley

Lightly spray a Dutch oven with cooking spray. Cook the carrots, onion, celery, and zucchini over medium-high heat for 3 minutes, stirring occasionally.

Stir in the tomatoes with liquid, vegetable juice, water, corn, Italian seasoning, garlic powder, pepper, and salt. Cook, covered, until the mixture comes to a boil, about 3 minutes. Reduce the heat to low and cook, covered, for 20 minutes, or until the vegetables are tender, stirring occasionally and breaking up the tomatoes.

Stir in the beans and barley. Cook, covered, for 10 minutes, or until the barley is tender, stirring occasionally.

PER SERVING
calories 244
total fat 1.0 g
saturated 0.0 g
trans 0.0 g
polyunsaturated 0.5 g
monounsaturated 0.0 g
cholesterol 0 mg
sodium 382 mg
carbohydrates 51 g
fiber 10 g
sugars 16 g
protein 11 g
dietary exchanges
2½ starch
3 vegetable

Slow-Cooker Method

Combine the carrots, onion, celery, zucchini, tomatoes with liquid, vegetable juice, water, corn, Italian seasoning, garlic powder, pepper, and salt in a $3\frac{1}{2}$- to 4-quart slow cooker. Cook, covered, on low for 7 to 9 hours or on high for 3 to $3\frac{1}{2}$ hours. Stir in the beans and barley. Cook, covered, on high for about 30 minutes, or until the barley is tender.

greek white beans

SERVES 4 · 1½ cups per serving
PREPARATION TIME · 10 minutes
COOKING TIME · 16 to 21 minutes

Greeks often serve white beans on days of fasting as a filling alternative to meat. Good alone or served over orzo or brown rice, these beans have even more flavor the second day.

2 tablespoons olive oil

1 medium rib of celery, chopped

1 medium carrot, chopped

½ cup chopped onion

2 15-ounce cans no-salt-added navy or Great Northern beans, undrained

½ cup snipped fresh parsley

2 tablespoons no-salt-added tomato paste

1 tablespoon chopped fresh oregano or 1 teaspoon dried oregano, crumbled

1 teaspoon pepper

½ teaspoon crushed red pepper flakes

½ teaspoon salt

In a large saucepan, heat the oil over medium-high heat, swirling to coat the bottom. Cook the celery, carrot, and onion for 8 to 10 minutes, or until softened, stirring frequently.

Stir in the remaining ingredients. Bring to a boil. Reduce the heat and simmer for 5 to 8 minutes, or until heated through.

COOK'S TIP ON FREEZING TOMATO PASTE
Measure 1-tablespoon portions of leftover tomato paste, freeze them on a baking sheet, then store them in an airtight plastic bag in the freezer so they'll be ready whenever you need them. Remove just the amount the recipe calls for. If the dish requires cooking, you don't even need to thaw the tomato paste first.

PER SERVING

calories 276
total fat 7.0 g
  saturated 1.0 g
  trans 0.0 g
  polyunsaturated 1.0 g
  monounsaturated 5.0 g
cholesterol 0 mg
sodium 329 mg
carbohydrates 40 g
  fiber 10 g
  sugars 10 g
protein 13 g
dietary exchanges
  2½ starch
  1 vegetable
  1 very lean meat
  1 fat

southwestern posole stew

SERVES 4 · 1¼ cups per serving
PREPARATION TIME · 10 minutes
COOKING TIME · 12 minutes

express

Golden hominy, which has the aroma and flavor of corn tortillas, is one of the highlights of this zesty stew.

1 tablespoon olive oil

2 medium ribs of celery, finely chopped

½ cup chopped onion

1 teaspoon bottled minced garlic or 2 medium garlic cloves, minced

1 15-ounce can no-salt-added pinto beans, undrained

1 15-ounce can golden hominy, rinsed and drained

1 cup water

1 8-ounce can no-salt-added tomato sauce

2 teaspoons chili powder

1 teaspoon ground cumin

⅛ teaspoon pepper

⅛ teaspoon salt

¼ cup shredded low-fat Cheddar cheese (about 1 ounce)

In a large saucepan, heat the oil over medium-high heat, swirling to coat the bottom. Cook the celery, onion, and garlic for about 3 minutes, or until tender, stirring occasionally.

Stir in the beans, hominy, water, tomato sauce, chili powder, cumin, and pepper. Increase the heat to high and bring to a boil. Reduce the heat and simmer for 5 minutes, or until warmed through. Stir in the salt. Sprinkle with the Cheddar.

PER SERVING
calories 227
total fat 4.5 g
saturated 1.0 g
trans 0.0 g
polyunsaturated 0.5 g
monounsaturated 2.5 g
cholesterol 2 mg
sodium 584 mg
carbohydrates 40 g
fiber 9 g
sugars 4 g
protein 10 g
dietary exchanges
2 starch
2 vegetable
1 lean meat

COOK'S TIP ON HOMINY

Look for canned hominy, yellow or white, near the canned corn in the supermarket.

red lentils with vegetables and brown rice

SERVES 8 · scant 1½ cups per serving
PREPARATION TIME · 10 minutes
COOKING TIME · 48 to 52 minutes

This recipe makes a lot, but the dish tastes even better the second day and lends itself well to variations. For instance, you can warm the leftovers and serve them in whole-grain pita pockets or add 1 tablespoon fat-free Italian or balsamic vinaigrette and ½ cup chopped raw vegetables to every ½ cup cooked and chilled red lentils.

1 tablespoon olive oil

2 medium carrots, chopped

1 teaspoon bottled minced garlic
or 2 medium garlic cloves,
minced

4 cups water

3 cups low-sodium vegetable broth

1 14.5-ounce can no-salt-added
stewed tomatoes, undrained

1 cup uncooked red lentils, sorted
for stones or shriveled lentils
and rinsed

1 teaspoon fennel seeds; dried basil
or thyme, crumbled; or dried
rosemary, crushed

1 teaspoon dried oregano,
crumbled

¾ teaspoon salt

⅛ teaspoon pepper

2 cups uncooked instant brown
rice

In a stockpot, heat the oil over medium-high heat, swirling to coat the bottom. Cook the carrots and garlic for 2 to 3 minutes, or until the carrots are slightly tender, stirring frequently.

Stir in the remaining ingredients except the brown rice. Increase the heat to high and bring to a boil. Reduce the heat and simmer, covered, for 30 minutes, or until the lentils are tender. Using the stirring spoon, break up any large pieces of tomato.

PER SERVING
calories 216
total fat 3.0 g
saturated 0.0 g
trans 0.0 g
polyunsaturated 0.5 g
monounsaturated 1.5 g
cholesterol 0 mg
sodium 266 mg
carbohydrates 37 g
fiber 6 g
sugars 4 g
protein 10 g
dietary exchanges
2 starch
1 vegetable
½ lean meat

Stir in the rice. Cook, covered, for 12 to 15 minutes, or until the rice is tender.

COOK'S TIP ON RED LENTILS
Red lentils are colorful (more orange than red), are versatile, and take less time to cook than other varieties. You may need to go to a grocery or health food store that sells items in bulk to find them.

greek-style brown rice casserole

SERVES 4 · 1¾ cups per serving
PREPARATION TIME · 7 to 9 minutes
COOKING TIME · 52 minutes

all-
in-
one

Capture some of the best flavors of Greece—spinach, tomatoes, oregano, garlic, and feta—in this family-pleasing vegetarian casserole.

Cooking spray

1½ cups uncooked instant brown rice

½ cup chopped onion

1 teaspoon bottled minced garlic or 2 medium garlic cloves, minced

2 14.5-ounce cans no-salt-added diced tomatoes, undrained

1 10-ounce package frozen chopped spinach, thawed, drained well, and squeezed dry

8 ounces frozen soy crumbles (2 cups)

1 teaspoon dried Italian seasoning, crumbled

1 teaspoon dried oregano, crumbled

¼ teaspoon pepper

3 tablespoons crumbled low-fat feta

Preheat the oven to 350°F. Lightly spray an 11 x 7 x 1½-inch glass baking dish and a medium saucepan with cooking spray.

Prepare the rice using the package directions, omitting the salt and margarine.

Meanwhile, in the prepared medium saucepan, cook the onion and garlic over medium-high heat for about 3 minutes, or until the onion is soft, stirring frequently.

Stir in the remaining ingredients except the feta. Cook, covered, until the mixture comes to a boil, about 2 minutes. Reduce the heat to low and cook, covered, for 5 minutes.

PER SERVING
calories 268
total fat 2.0 g
saturated 0.5 g
trans 0.0 g
polyunsaturated 0.5 g
monounsaturated 0.5 g
cholesterol 3 mg
sodium 431 mg
carbohydrates 45 g
fiber 10 g
sugars 8 g
protein 21 g
dietary exchanges
2 starch
3 vegetable
1½ very lean meat

Spread the rice in the baking dish. Spread the spinach mixture over the rice.

Bake, covered, for 30 minutes, or until heated through. Sprinkle with the feta. Bake, uncovered, for 5 minutes, or until the cheese is warm.

COOK'S TIP

No-salt-added diced tomatoes may be a little more difficult to find than no-salt-added whole tomatoes. If so, purchase the whole ones and pour them into a small bowl. Using kitchen shears, snip the tomatoes into bite-size pieces, then use them, and any collected liquid, as you would diced tomatoes. Alternatively, wait until the whole tomatoes are softened from cooking, then break them into small pieces with the stirring spoon.

TIME-SAVER The night before you will be making this casserole, place the package of frozen spinach on a plate and refrigerate it. It will be thawed and ready to drain the next day.

crustless mushroom and spinach pie

SERVES 4 · 1 wedge per serving
PREPARATION TIME · 15 minutes
COOKING TIME · 36 to 42 minutes

all-in-one

Nutritious brown rice enhances the flavor and texture of this scrumptious two-cheese pie. Try it for dinner or brunch.

Cooking spray

1 teaspoon olive oil

4 ounces presliced fresh button mushrooms

1/2 cup chopped onion

1/2 teaspoon bottled minced garlic or 1 medium garlic clove, minced

1 1/2 cups fat-free milk

1 10-ounce package frozen chopped spinach, thawed, drained well, and squeezed dry

1 cup uncooked instant brown rice

1/2 cup egg substitute

3 slices (3/4 ounce each) low-fat Jarlsberg cheese, cut into 1-inch strips

1/4 cup shredded or grated Parmesan cheese

1/4 teaspoon ground nutmeg

1/4 teaspoon red hot-pepper sauce, plus more for sprinkling if desired

Preheat the oven to 350°F. Lightly spray a deep 9-inch pie pan with cooking spray.

In a large nonstick skillet, heat the oil over medium-high heat, swirling to coat the bottom. Cook the mushrooms and onion for 3 minutes, or until tender, stirring frequently.

Stir in the garlic. Cook for 30 seconds, stirring frequently.

Pour in the milk. Heat for 1 1/2 to 2 minutes, or until hot but not boiling. Remove from the heat.

PER SERVING
calories 236
total fat 6.0 g
saturated 2.5 g
trans 0.0 g
polyunsaturated 0.5 g
monounsaturated 2.0 g
cholesterol 13 mg
sodium 323 mg
carbohydrates 28 g
fiber 4 g
sugars 7 g
protein 19 g
dietary exchanges
1 1/2 starch
1 vegetable
2 lean meat

Stir in the spinach, rice, egg substitute, Jarlsberg, Parmesan, nutmeg, and ¼ teaspoon hot-pepper sauce, breaking up any large clumps of spinach. Carefully pour into the pie pan.

Bake for 30 to 35 minutes, or until a knife inserted into the center of the pie comes out clean. Sprinkle with additional hot sauce.

COOK'S TIP ON DRAINING SPINACH

A potato ricer, a gadget that resembles a very large garlic press, is ideal for making creamy mashed potatoes. As a bonus, it is handy for easily pressing water out of cooked or thawed spinach.

COOK'S TIP ON JARLSBERG CHEESE

A mild Swiss-style cheese with large irregular holes, Jarlsberg is smooth and melts readily. Check the gourmet cheese section of the supermarket for the low-fat variety of this delicious cheese. If you can't find it, you can substitute low-fat Swiss, but the total fat, saturated fat, and sodium of the Swiss will be higher.

pasta frittata

SERVES 6 · 1 wedge per serving
PREPARATION TIME · 15 minutes
COOKING TIME · 16 minutes
STANDING TIME · 5 minutes

This mildly seasoned frittata—basically an omelet without the work—is a different way to use leftover pasta.

Cooking spray

8 ounces presliced fresh button mushrooms

1 medium zucchini, thinly sliced (about 1 cup)

1 cup chopped onion (yellow preferred)

1 cup egg substitute

1/4 cup fat-free milk

2 tablespoons finely snipped fresh parsley

1 1/2 teaspoons dried oregano, crumbled

1/4 teaspoon salt

2 cups cooked whole-grain spaghetti or no-yolk noodles (4 ounces dried)

3/4 cup shredded low-fat mozzarella cheese (about 3 ounces)

2 tablespoons shredded or grated Parmesan cheese

Lightly spray a large skillet with cooking spray. Cook the mushrooms, zucchini, and onion over medium-high heat for 8 minutes, or until the zucchini is tender, stirring frequently.

Meanwhile, in a medium bowl, whisk together the egg substitute, milk, parsley, oregano, and salt.

Stir the pasta into the mushroom mixture. Pour the egg substitute mixture over all. Reduce the heat to medium low and cook, covered, for 8 minutes.

Sprinkle with the mozzarella. Remove from the heat. Let stand, covered, for 5 minutes to continue cooking and melt the mozzarella. Serve sprinkled with the Parmesan.

PER SERVING
calories 140
total fat 2.5 g
saturated 1.0 g
trans 0.0 g
polyunsaturated 0.5 g
monounsaturated 0.5 g
cholesterol 6 mg
sodium 330 mg
carbohydrates 18 g
fiber 3 g
sugars 4 g
protein 13 g
dietary exchanges
1 starch
1 lean meat

Cajun Frittata with Pasta

Substitute chopped green or red bell pepper for the zucchini, salt-free Cajun seasoning for the salt, and 3 ounces shredded low-fat sharp Cheddar cheese for the mozzarella and Parmesan.

PER SERVING

calories 131
total fat 1.5 g
  saturated 0.5 g
  trans 0.0 g
  polyunsaturated 0.5 g
  monounsaturated 0.5 g
cholesterol 3 mg
sodium 190 mg
carbohydrates 18 g
  fiber 3 g
  sugars 3 g
protein 12 g
dietary exchanges
  1 starch
  1 very lean meat

COOK'S TIP

If you don't have any leftover pasta, cook 4 ounces of dried angel hair (without salt or oil) to use instead of the spaghetti or noodles. The angel hair will cook in about the same amount of time it takes you to cook the mushrooms, zucchini, and onion. Don't use fresh or refrigerated pasta in this recipe. It will break down and become a solid mass.

broccoli potato frittata

SERVES 4 · 1 wedge per serving
PREPARATION TIME · 10 minutes
COOKING TIME · 15 to 17 minutes

Choose fresh fruit salad or cold soup, such as Chilled Strawberry-Orange Soup (page 51), to complement this quichelike dish.

3 cups frozen fat-free, no-salt-added shredded hash brown potatoes

1 teaspoon olive oil

¼ cup chopped onion

1 teaspoon bottled minced garlic or 2 medium garlic cloves, minced

2 cups broccoli florets, cut into ¾-inch pieces (about 8 ounces)

⅛ teaspoon pepper

1 cup egg substitute

¼ cup low-fat grated Cheddar cheese (about 1 ounce)

1½ tablespoons shredded or grated Parmesan cheese

2 medium Italian plum (Roma) tomatoes, sliced (optional)

Put the potatoes in a colander. Rinse with warm water for 1 to 2 minutes to partially thaw. Set aside to drain well.

In a large nonstick skillet, heat the oil over medium-high heat, swirling to coat the bottom. Cook the onion and garlic for 2 minutes, stirring occasionally.

Stir in the broccoli. Cook for 1 minute, stirring occasionally.

Stir in the potatoes. Sprinkle with the pepper. Pour the egg substitute over all. Sprinkle with the Cheddar and the Parmesan. Reduce the heat to medium low and cook, covered, for 10 to 12 minutes, or until the egg substitute is set. Cut into wedges. Garnish with the tomato slices.

PER SERVING
calories 200
total fat 2.5 g
saturated 1.0 g
trans 0.0 g
polyunsaturated 0.0 g
monounsaturated 1.0 g
cholesterol 3 mg
sodium 251 mg
carbohydrates 33 g
fiber 4 g
sugars 2 g
protein 13 g
dietary exchanges
2 starch
1 vegetable
1 very lean meat

mushroom quesadillas

SERVES 4 · 3 pieces per serving
PREPARATION TIME · 10 minutes
COOKING TIME · 4 to 6 minutes
MICROWAVE TIME · 3 minutes

Mushrooms and chiles are covered with cheese that's been fired with jalapeño, then wrapped in a warm tortilla to make a rich and creamy— and slightly messy—Tex-Mex treat.

1 teaspoon canola or corn oil

16 ounces presliced fresh button mushrooms

1/2 cup low-fat condensed cream of mushroom soup (lowest sodium available)

2 tablespoons chopped canned green chiles, drained

4 6-inch corn tortillas

1 cup grated low-fat jalapeño Jack or low-fat Monterey Jack cheese (about 4 ounces)

1/4 cup spicy salsa (lowest sodium available)

In a medium skillet, heat the oil over medium heat, swirling to coat the bottom. Cook the mushrooms for 2 to 4 minutes, stirring occasionally. Drain the liquid, if any.

Stir in the soup and chiles. Cook for 2 minutes, or until heated through, stirring frequently.

Meanwhile, using the package directions, warm the tortillas in a microwave oven.

Place the warm tortillas on a microwaveable tray. Spread the mushroom mixture on one half of each tortilla, leaving 1/2 inch around the edge. Sprinkle the jalapeño Jack over the filling. Fold each tortilla in half over the filling. Press the edges together. Microwave on 100 percent power (high) for 1 minute. Cut each tortilla into 3 pieces. Put a dab of salsa on each piece.

PER SERVING
calories 139
total fat 4.5 g
saturated 1.5 g
trans 0.0 g
polyunsaturated 0.5 g
monounsaturated 1.5 g
cholesterol 8 mg
sodium 406 mg
carbohydrates 14 g
fiber 2 g
sugars 3 g
protein 12 g
dietary exchanges
1/2 starch
1 vegetable
1 lean meat

mozzarella polenta with roasted vegetable salsa

SERVES 4 · 2 polenta rounds and ½ cup salsa per serving
PREPARATION TIME · 15 minutes
COOKING TIME · 14 minutes

This vegetable-rich entrée is a breeze to make with prepared polenta.

Cooking spray

SALSA

2 medium tomatoes

1 large green bell pepper

1 large zucchini (about 8 ounces)

1 large yellow summer squash (about 7 ounces)

1 tablespoon cider vinegar

2 teaspoons extra-virgin olive oil

1 teaspoon dried oregano, crumbled

½ teaspoon bottled minced garlic or 1 medium garlic clove, minced

⅛ teaspoon salt

¼ cup finely snipped fresh parsley or fresh cilantro

• • •

1 16-ounce package prepared fat-free polenta

¾ cup shredded low-fat mozzarella cheese (about 3 ounces)

Preheat the broiler. Line two baking sheets with aluminum foil. Lightly spray the foil with cooking spray.

Cut the tomatoes in half crosswise. Cut the bell pepper in half lengthwise. Discard the ribs, seeds, and stem of the pepper. Flatten each half with your palm, pulling out any parts of the pepper that curve under. Set on one baking sheet. Cut the zucchini and summer squash in half lengthwise. Put all with the cut side up on the same baking sheet. Lightly spray all the vegetables with cooking spray.

PER SERVING
calories 182
total fat 4.5 g
saturated 1.0 g
trans 0.0 g
polyunsaturated 0.5 g
monounsaturated 2.0 g
cholesterol 8 mg
sodium 537 mg
carbohydrates 25 g
fiber 4 g
sugars 7 g
protein 10 g
dietary exchanges
1 starch
2 vegetable
1 lean meat

Broil about 4 inches from the heat for 5 minutes. Turn over. Broil for 3 minutes, or until lightly charred.

Meanwhile, in a small bowl, stir together the remaining salsa ingredients except the parsley.

Gently rinse the polenta under running water. Pat dry. Cut the polenta into 8 rounds and put on the second baking sheet. Set aside.

Using a knife and fork, coarsely chop the broiled vegetables. Transfer to a medium bowl. Stir in the vinegar mixture and parsley. Cover with aluminum foil to keep warm.

Broil the polenta for 3 minutes. Turn over. Broil for 2 minutes. Sprinkle with the mozzarella and broil for 1 minute, or until beginning to lightly brown. Arrange the polenta rounds on plates, spooning the salsa on and around each serving.

COOK'S TIP

The salsa is also delicious served at room temperature. For peak flavor, wait until serving time to toss the vegetables with the vinegar mixture.

COOK'S TIP ON POLENTA

Look for prepared polenta (basically cornmeal cooked with water) in plastic-wrapped cylinders in the produce department or with the pastas. In addition to plain polenta, you'll also discover everything from Mexican-inspired combinations to polenta flavored with exotic mushrooms.

tofu and vegetable stir-fry

SERVES 4 · 1²/₃ cups per serving
PREPARATION TIME · 16 to 18 minutes
COOKING TIME · 31 to 32 minutes

This recipe will eliminate all doubt that good-for-you tofu can be tasty, too!

Cooking spray

24 ounces light extra-firm tofu, cut into ½-inch cubes

1 tablespoon soy sauce and 1 tablespoon soy sauce (lowest sodium available), divided use

1 tablespoon low-sodium vegetable broth and ²/₃ cup low-sodium vegetable broth, divided use

1 tablespoon sesame seeds

1 tablespoon cornstarch

2 teaspoons grated peeled gingerroot

¼ teaspoon crushed red pepper flakes

8 to 10 ounces fresh asparagus, trimmed and cut into 1-inch pieces

1 medium red bell pepper, cut into thin strips

½ medium onion, thinly sliced

1½ teaspoons bottled minced garlic or 3 medium garlic cloves, minced

4 ounces fresh bean sprouts

Preheat the oven to 400°F. Lightly spray a rimmed baking sheet with cooking spray.

Put the tofu in a medium bowl. Sprinkle with 1 tablespoon soy sauce and 1 tablespoon broth, stirring well. Place the tofu in a single layer on the baking sheet.

Bake for 30 minutes.

Meanwhile, in a small skillet over low heat, dry-roast the sesame seeds for about 2 minutes, or just until fragrant and golden, stirring frequently. Watch carefully so they do not get too brown. Pour onto a small plate. Set aside.

PER SERVING
calories 200
total fat 6.0 g
saturated 0.5 g
trans 0.0 g
polyunsaturated 1.5 g
monounsaturated 3.5 g
cholesterol 0 mg
sodium 275 mg
carbohydrates 18 g
fiber 5 g
sugars 5 g
protein 19 g
dietary exchanges
½ starch
1 vegetable
2 lean meat

In a small bowl, stir together the cornstarch, gingerroot, red pepper flakes, remaining 1 tablespoon soy sauce, and remaining ⅔ cup broth. Set aside.

When the tofu has about 20 minutes of baking time remaining, lightly spray a large skillet with cooking spray. Cook the asparagus, bell pepper, onion, and garlic over medium-high heat for 4 minutes, stirring frequently.

Stir in the bean sprouts. Cook for 2 minutes, stirring frequently.

Stir the cornstarch mixture. Stir into the asparagus mixture. Cook for 1 to 2 minutes, or until thickened and bubbly, stirring constantly.

Gently stir in the tofu. Cook for 1 to 2 minutes, or until heated through. Sprinkle with the sesame seeds.

tofu cacciatore

SERVES 4 · 1³/₄ cups per serving
PREPARATION TIME · 15 minutes
COOKING TIME · 25 to 29 minutes

For a delicious Italian dinner, serve this flavorful combination of porto-bello mushrooms, bell peppers, and plum tomatoes with brown rice or on your favorite whole-grain pasta.

2 medium bell peppers (red, yellow, green, or a combination), cut into ¹/₂-inch strips

4 to 6 ounces presliced fresh portobello mushrooms

1 large onion (sweet preferred), cut vertically into thick slices

1 large carrot, finely chopped

2 teaspoons bottled minced garlic or 4 medium garlic cloves, minced

1 tablespoon plus 1 teaspoon olive oil (extra-virgin preferred)

1 28-ounce can no-salt-added whole peeled Italian plum (Roma) tomatoes, undrained

¹/₄ cup dry red wine (regular or nonalcoholic)

1 teaspoon dried oregano, crumbled

1 teaspoon dried thyme, crumbled

¹/₄ teaspoon pepper

1 12- to 14-ounce package light extra-firm tofu, cut into small cubes

Heat a large skillet or Dutch oven over medium-high heat. Add the bell peppers, mushrooms, onion, carrot, garlic, and oil, stirring well to coat. Cook, covered, for 5 to 7 minutes, or until the bell peppers soften and release some of their liquid, stirring occasionally.

Stir in the remaining ingredients except the tofu. Using a spoon, break the tomatoes into large pieces. Increase the heat to high and bring to a medium-high boil, covered. Reduce the heat to medium high. Cook for 10 to 12 minutes, or until the bell peppers are soft, stirring occasionally.

Stir in the tofu. Cook for 5 minutes, or until hot, stirring occasionally.

PER SERVING
calories 174
total fat 6.0 g
saturated 1.0 g
trans 0.0 g
polyunsaturated 1.0 g
monounsaturated 3.5 g
cholesterol 0 mg
sodium 129 mg
carbohydrates 21 g
fiber 5 g
sugars 11 g
protein 10 g
dietary exchanges
4 vegetable
1 lean meat
¹/₂ fat

vegetables and side dishes

asparagus with sesame oil

SERVES 4 · 4 to 5 spears per serving
PREPARATION TIME · 10 minutes
COOKING TIME · 4 minutes

Broiling the asparagus intensifies its natural flavor and sweetness, and the toasted sesame oil adds a subtle nuttiness. You can serve this dish warm or at room temperature, making it a natural for a buffet.

Cooking spray

1 pound fresh asparagus (16 to 20 medium spears), trimmed and patted completely dry

2 teaspoons toasted sesame oil

⅛ teaspoon salt

Preheat the broiler. Line a baking sheet with aluminum foil. Lightly spray the foil with cooking spray.

Place the asparagus in a single layer on the baking sheet. Lightly spray the asparagus with cooking spray.

Broil about 4 inches from the heat for 4 minutes, or just until the asparagus is tender-crisp and a few brown spots appear. Remove from the broiler.

Using a pastry brush, brush the sesame oil over the asparagus. Sprinkle with the salt.

COOK'S TIP ON ASPARAGUS

To trim asparagus, hold the cut end of a spear. Bend the spear gently until you feel where the tough part begins, often about 1 inch from the bottom. Snap the spear at that point, discarding the woody end. A rule of thumb is that the thinner the asparagus, the tenderer it will be. If you peel the thicker stalks, they'll also be tender. Be sure to pat the asparagus completely dry after you clean it so it will roast properly.

PER SERVING

calories 41
total fat 2.5 g
  saturated 0.5 g
  trans 0.0 g
  polyunsaturated 1.0 g
  monounsaturated 1.0 g
cholesterol 0 mg
sodium 73 mg
carbohydrates 4 g
  fiber 2 g
  sugars 2 g
protein 2 g
dietary exchanges
  1 vegetable
  ½ fat

bell peppers with nuts and olives

SERVES 8 · ²/₃ cup per serving
PREPARATION TIME · 10 minutes
COOKING TIME · 12 to 18 minutes

Nuts and olives make this an extra-fancy side dish to serve with baked chicken or on a vegetable plate.

2 tablespoons pine nuts

1 tablespoon olive oil

3 medium bell peppers (various colors), sliced

1 medium onion, sliced

1 teaspoon bottled minced garlic or 2 medium garlic cloves, minced

⅛ to ¼ teaspoon pepper, or to taste

⅛ teaspoon salt

2 tablespoons chopped kalamata olives

In a large skillet, dry-roast the pine nuts over medium-high heat for 1 to 2 minutes, or until they're just fragrant, stirring frequently. Remove from the skillet so they don't burn.

Pour the oil into the same skillet, swirling to coat the bottom. Increase the heat to high. Cook the bell peppers, onion, and garlic for 10 to 15 minutes, or until the desired texture, stirring occasionally. Stir in the pepper and salt. Serve sprinkled with the olives and pine nuts.

COOK'S TIP

If you prefer, you can use chopped pecans instead of the pine nuts and/or substitute other good-quality black olives or stuffed green olives for the kalamata olives.

COOK'S TIP ON SKILLETS

A heavy skillet heats more evenly and cooks food more quickly than thinner skillets, which tend to burn in some areas while undercooking in others.

PER SERVING

calories 45
total fat 3.0 g
  saturated 0.5 g
  trans 0.0 g
  polyunsaturated 0.5 g
  monounsaturated 2.0 g
cholesterol 0 mg
sodium 67 mg
carbohydrates 4 g
  fiber 1 g
  sugars 2 g
protein 1 g
dietary exchanges
  1 vegetable
  ½ fat

broccoli with sweet-and-sour tangerine sauce

SERVES 4 · $1/2$ cup broccoli and 1 tablespoon sauce per serving
PREPARATION TIME · 10 minutes
COOKING TIME · 8 to 11 minutes

This sweet-and-sour side dish pairs nicely with Asian recipes, as well as with ham or turkey. On its own, the sauce enhances almost any cooked vegetable or meat and is good as a dipping sauce for potstickers.

2 cups broccoli florets (about 8 ounces)

SAUCE
$1/4$ cup tangerine or orange marmalade

1 to 2 tablespoons plain rice vinegar

$1/2$ teaspoon grated peeled gingerroot or $1/8$ teaspoon ground ginger

2 or 3 drops hot-pepper oil

In a medium saucepan, steam the broccoli for 6 to 8 minutes, or until tender.

Meanwhile, in a small saucepan, stir together the sauce ingredients. Cook over low heat for 2 to 3 minutes, or until the marmalade is melted, stirring occasionally. Spoon over the cooked broccoli.

PER SERVING

calories 66
total fat 0.0 g
  saturated 0.0 g
  trans 0.0 g
  polyunsaturated 0.0 g
  monounsaturated 0.0 g
cholesterol 0 mg
sodium 15 mg
carbohydrates 16 g
  fiber 1 g
  sugars 13 g
protein 1 g
dietary exchanges
  1 carbohydrate

sesame broccoli

SERVES 4 · heaping ½ cup per serving
PREPARATION TIME · 10 minutes
COOKING TIME · 10 minutes

The rich-tasting sesame seeds add lots of flavor to this dish. If you use the broccoli stems as well as the florets, you can serve more people.

1 teaspoon olive or canola oil

1 tablespoon sesame seeds

1½ pounds broccoli, cut into small florets, stems peeled and diced, if desired

2 tablespoons water

1 tablespoon soy sauce (lowest sodium available)

1½ teaspoons lemon juice

⅛ to ¼ teaspoon crushed red pepper flakes

In a large skillet, heat the oil over medium-high heat. Cook the sesame seeds for 1 minute, or until beginning to brown, stirring constantly with a long-handled spoon (be careful—sesame seeds will "spit").

Add the broccoli. Increase the heat to high. Cook for about 3 minutes, or until the broccoli turns bright green, stirring constantly.

Stir in the remaining ingredients. Reduce the heat to medium. Cook, covered, for 5 minutes, or until the broccoli is the desired tenderness.

PER SERVING
calories 95
total fat 3.0 g
saturated 0.5 g
trans 0.0 g
polyunsaturated 1.0 g
monounsaturated 1.5 g
cholesterol 0 mg
sodium 165 mg
carbohydrates 14 g
fiber 5 g
sugars 3 g
protein 6 g
dietary exchanges
3 vegetable
½ fat

roasted brussels sprouts

SERVES 4 · $\frac{1}{2}$ cup per serving
PREPARATION TIME · 5 minutes
COOKING TIME · 17 to 19 minutes

Combined with the tang of balsamic vinegar and the crunch of pecans, these roasted brussels sprouts will win over even the most sprout-phobic.

Cooking spray
1 10-ounce package frozen brussels
   sprouts
2 teaspoons olive oil

$\frac{1}{4}$ teaspoon salt
$\frac{1}{8}$ teaspoon pepper
2 tablespoons chopped pecans
1 tablespoon balsamic vinegar

Preheat the oven to 450°F. Lightly spray a rimmed baking sheet with cooking spray.

Put the brussels sprouts in a single layer on the baking sheet. Drizzle with the olive oil. Sprinkle with the salt and pepper.

Bake for 17 to 19 minutes, stirring occasionally.

Meanwhile, put the pecans in a single layer in a small skillet over medium heat. Dry-roast for about 4 minutes, or until just fragrant, stirring frequently. Remove from the skillet so they don't burn.

PER SERVING
calories 78
total fat 5.0 g
saturated 0.5 g
trans 0.0 g
polyunsaturated 1.0 g
monounsaturated 3.0 g
cholesterol 0 mg
sodium 153 mg
carbohydrates 7 g
fiber 3 g
sugars 4 g
protein 3 g
dietary exchanges
1 vegetable
1 fat

Transfer the brussels sprouts to a medium bowl. Add the vinegar, tossing to coat. Sprinkle with the pecans.

TIME-SAVER When time allows, dry-roast extra nuts. Freeze what you don't need right away in an airtight freezer bag for up to three months, and the nuts will be ready whenever you need them.

apricot carrots

SERVES 4 · ½ cup per serving
PREPARATION TIME · 5 minutes
COOKING TIME · 8 to 10 minutes

The light, sweet glaze on these carrots is sure to please.

¼ cup water (plus 1 to
   2 tablespoons more if needed)
12 ounces carrots, sliced crosswise
   ½ inch thick (about 2 cups)

⅛ teaspoon salt
2 tablespoons all-fruit apricot
   spread

In a medium saucepan, bring ¼ cup water to a boil over medium-high heat. Add the carrots and salt. Reduce the heat to medium. Cook, covered, for 7 to 9 minutes, or until tender-crisp, adding the remaining 1 to 2 tablespoons water if needed to keep the pan from boiling dry. Drain if necessary.

Add the apricot spread, stirring until melted.

PER SERVING
calories 55
total fat 0.0 g
saturated 0.0 g
trans 0.0 g
polyunsaturated 0.0 g
monounsaturated 0.0 g
cholesterol 0 mg
sodium 132 mg
carbohydrates 13 g
fiber 2 g
sugars 8 g
protein 1 g
dietary exchanges
1 vegetable
½ carbohydrate

greek green beans

SERVES 8 · ¹/₂ cup per serving
PREPARATION TIME · 10 minutes
COOKING TIME · 15 to 23 minutes

The dillweed provides a pleasant aroma, the red pepper flakes give a bit of a kick, and the feta cheese adds tanginess to this attractive green bean and tomato pairing.

2 teaspoons olive oil

¹/₂ cup chopped onion

¹/₈ teaspoon crushed red pepper flakes, or to taste

1 pound fresh or frozen green beans, trimmed if fresh

¹/₄ cup water (plus more as needed)

¹/₂ teaspoon dried dillweed, crumbled

¹/₄ teaspoon salt

¹/₄ teaspoon pepper, or to taste

1 14.5-ounce can no-salt-added diced tomatoes, undrained, or 3 medium tomatoes, minced

2 ounces low-fat feta cheese, crumbled (about ¹/₂ cup)

In a wide, deep skillet, heat the oil over medium-high heat, swirling to coat the bottom. Cook the onion and red pepper flakes for 2 minutes, or until the onion is soft, stirring occasionally.

Stir in the green beans, ¹/₄ cup water, dillweed, salt, and pepper. Cook for 10 minutes for fresh beans or 15 minutes for frozen, or until they are almost cooked to taste, adding water if necessary.

Stir in the tomatoes with liquid. Cook for 2 to 5 minutes, or until the beans are cooked to the desired tenderness. Sprinkle with the feta.

PER SERVING
calories 59
total fat 2.5 g
saturated 1.0 g
trans 0.0 g
polyunsaturated 0.0 g
monounsaturated 1.0 g
cholesterol 6 mg
sodium 177 mg
carbohydrates 7 g
fiber 3 g
sugars 3 g
protein 3 g
dietary exchanges
1 vegetable
¹/₂ fat

garlic kale

SERVES 6 · ½ cup per serving
PREPARATION TIME · 5 minutes
COOKING TIME · 14 to 15 minutes

Antioxidant-rich kale is sure to become a staple in your kitchen after you taste it paired with onion-and-garlic bread crumbs.

2 teaspoons olive oil

1 cup chopped onion

1 tablespoon bottled minced garlic or 6 medium garlic cloves, minced

½ cup plain dry bread crumbs

8 ounces packaged chopped fresh kale (about 5 cups)

½ cup fat-free, low-sodium chicken broth

Red hot-pepper sauce to taste (optional)

In a large nonstick skillet, heat the oil over medium-high heat, swirling to coat the bottom. Cook the onion for 3 minutes, or until soft, stirring frequently.

Stir in the garlic. Cook for 30 seconds, stirring frequently.

Stir in the bread crumbs. Cook for 2 to 3 minutes, or until lightly brown, stirring frequently. Transfer to a small bowl.

In the same skillet, stir together the kale and broth. Reduce the heat to medium and cook, covered, for 6 minutes, or until the liquid is absorbed and the kale is tender and wilted, stirring occasionally.

Stir in the bread crumb mixture. Sprinkle with the hot-pepper sauce.

PER SERVING
calories 81
total fat 2.5 g
saturated 0.5 g
trans 0.0 g
polyunsaturated 0.5 g
monounsaturated 1.0 g
cholesterol 0 mg
sodium 89 mg
carbohydrates 13 g
fiber 2 g
sugars 2 g
protein 3 g
dietary exchanges
½ starch
1 vegetable
½ fat

mixed mushrooms and spinach

SERVES 4 · ½ cup per serving
PREPARATION TIME · 12 minutes
SOAKING TIME · 10 minutes
COOKING TIME · 8 minutes

For a light entrée, serve this richly flavored mixture over brown rice.

3 tablespoons dried mushrooms

¼ cup hot water

8 ounces prewashed fresh spinach

¼ cup fat-free, low-sodium chicken broth

10 ounces presliced fresh button mushrooms

2 tablespoons dry sherry

¼ teaspoon salt

Pepper to taste

¼ teaspoon ground nutmeg

⅛ teaspoon crushed red pepper flakes (optional)

In a small shallow bowl, stir together the dried mushrooms and water. Let stand for 10 minutes.

Meanwhile, discard any large spinach stems. Coarsely chop the leaves. Set aside.

In a large skillet, bring the broth to a simmer over medium-high heat. Cook the fresh mushrooms for 2 minutes, or until they begin to release their liquid, stirring frequently.

Stir in the sherry, salt, and pepper. Cook for 3 minutes, or until the liquid is slightly reduced.

Using a slotted spoon, remove the dried mushrooms from the liquid. Rinse. Transfer to a cutting board and chop the mushrooms. Pour the reserved liquid through a strainer lined with a paper coffee filter or paper towel (to trap any grit). Stir the chopped mushrooms, reserved liquid, and spinach into the fresh mushroom mixture in the skillet. Reduce the heat to medium and cook for about 1 minute, or until the spinach is just wilted, stirring constantly.

Stir in the nutmeg and red pepper flakes.

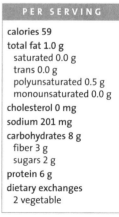

PER SERVING

calories 59
total fat 1.0 g
  saturated 0.0 g
  trans 0.0 g
  polyunsaturated 0.5 g
  monounsaturated 0.0 g
cholesterol 0 mg
sodium 201 mg
carbohydrates 8 g
  fiber 3 g
  sugars 2 g
protein 6 g
dietary exchanges
  2 vegetable

herbed peas and mushrooms

SERVES 6 · ³/₄ cup per serving
PREPARATION TIME · 5 minutes
COOKING TIME · 10 to 13 minutes

As an accompaniment for anything from roasted turkey at a holiday feast to grilled burgers on the patio, this side dish is hard to beat.

1 teaspoon olive oil

10 ounces presliced fresh mushrooms (button, cremini, portobello, or a combination)

³/₄ cup coarsely chopped onion

1 16-ounce package frozen tiny or regular-size green peas (about 3 cups)

¼ cup orange juice

½ teaspoon dried mint, crumbled

¼ to ½ teaspoon dried oregano, crumbled

⅛ to ¼ teaspoon pepper

In a large skillet, heat the oil over medium heat, swirling to coat the bottom. Cook the mushrooms and onion, covered, for 7 to 9 minutes, or until the mushrooms are tender, stirring occasionally.

Stir in the remaining ingredients. Cook, covered, for 2 to 3 minutes, or until heated through, stirring occasionally.

PER SERVING
calories 94
total fat 1.0 g
saturated 0.0 g
trans 0.0 g
polyunsaturated 0.5 g
monounsaturated 0.5 g
cholesterol 0 mg
sodium 89 mg
carbohydrates 16 g
fiber 4 g
sugars 8 g
protein 6 g
dietary exchanges
1 starch
1 vegetable

roasted red and white potatoes

SERVES 6 · ½ cup per serving (plus 3 cups potatoes reserved)
PREPARATION TIME · 10 minutes
COOKING TIME · 40 minutes

One kind of roasted potato is good, and two kinds are doubly delicious. This recipe is twice as good in another way, too: You get roasted potatoes for today and a start on German or Mexican Potato Salad (pages 80, 81) for later.

Olive oil spray

2½ pounds small potatoes, red and white

1 tablespoon chopped fresh rosemary or 1 teaspoon dried rosemary, crushed

2 teaspoons olive oil

¾ teaspoon salt

Pepper to taste

1 large onion (sweet preferred)

Preheat the oven to 425°F. Lightly spray a rimmed baking sheet with olive oil spray.

Cut the potatoes into 1-inch cubes. Pat dry. Put in a large bowl.

Stir in the remaining ingredients except the onion. Spread in a single layer on the baking sheet.

Roast for 20 minutes, stirring once halfway through.

Meanwhile, cut the onion into 1-inch cubes. After the potatoes have cooked for 20 minutes, add the onion, stirring well. Roast for 20 minutes, or until the potatoes are lightly browned and tender when pierced with a fork, stirring once halfway through. If the onion seems to be browning too quickly, stir more frequently. Refrigerate half the potatoes (3 cups) in an airtight container for use in German or Mexican Potato Salad. Serve the remaining potatoes.

PER SERVING
calories 80
total fat 1.0 g
saturated 0.0 g
trans 0.0 g
polyunsaturated 0.0 g
monounsaturated 0.5 g
cholesterol 0 mg
sodium 152 mg
carbohydrates 17 g
fiber 2 g
sugars 2 g
protein 2 g
dietary exchanges
1 starch

coconut-scented rice with almonds

SERVES 8 · ½ cup per serving
PREPARATION TIME · 5 minutes
COOKING TIME · 18 to 19 minutes

Using a small amount of crushed dry-roasted almonds lets you distribute their nutty flavor throughout this dish without adding much fat.

2 cups fat-free milk
¼ teaspoon salt
2 cups uncooked instant white rice

¼ cup sliced almonds (about 1 ounce)
½ teaspoon coconut extract

In a medium saucepan, bring the milk and salt to a boil over medium-high heat, about 12 minutes.

Stir in the rice. Return to a boil, about 1 minute. Reduce the heat and simmer, covered, for 5 to 6 minutes, or until the liquid is absorbed.

Meanwhile, in a small skillet, dry-roast the almonds over medium heat for about 4 minutes, or until just fragrant, stirring frequently. Remove from the skillet so they don't burn. Let cool for 1 minute. Using the back of a spoon or fork, finely crush the almonds, or wrap them loosely in plastic wrap and crush with a rolling pin or the side of a glass.

Add the coconut extract to the rice, fluffing with a fork. Stir in the almonds.

PER SERVING
calories 127
total fat 2.0 g
saturated 0.0 g
trans 0.0 g
polyunsaturated 0.5 g
monounsaturated 1.0 g
cholesterol 1 mg
sodium 101 mg
carbohydrates 22 g
fiber 0 g
sugars 3 g
protein 5 g
dietary exchanges
1½ starch

savory pecan rice

SERVES 6 · ³/₄ cup per serving
PREPARATION TIME · 5 minutes
COOKING TIME · 23 to 25 minutes

With their assertive flavors, the dried cherries, pecans, and mushrooms in this dish pair well with poultry or game. You can also use this recipe to make a vegetarian stuffing for baked winter squash, such as butternut.

2 cups water

1 7-ounce package pecan rice or
    1 cup other uncooked aromatic
    rice

¼ cup dried cherries (about
    1 ounce)

¼ teaspoon salt

1 teaspoon olive oil

8 ounces presliced fresh button
    mushrooms

½ cup chopped red bell pepper

½ teaspoon fennel seeds or
    1 teaspoon dried thyme,
    crumbled

¼ cup chopped pecans (about
    1 ounce)

In a large saucepan, stir together the water, rice, cherries, and salt. Bring to a boil over high heat, 3 to 5 minutes. Reduce the heat and simmer, covered, for 20 minutes, or until the rice is tender.

Meanwhile, in a large nonstick skillet, heat the oil over high heat, swirling to coat the bottom. Cook the mushrooms, bell pepper, and fennel seeds for about 7 minutes, or until the bell pepper is soft, stirring occasionally.

In a medium bowl, stir together the rice, mushroom mixture, and pecans.

PER SERVING
calories 191
total fat 4.5 g
saturated 0.5 g
trans 0.0 g
polyunsaturated 1.0 g
monounsaturated 2.5 g
cholesterol 0 mg
sodium 102 mg
carbohydrates 34 g
fiber 2 g
sugars 4 g
protein 4 g
dietary exchanges
2 starch
½ fat

spinach and mushroom sauté

SERVES 4 · 1/2 cup per serving

PREPARATION TIME · 5 minutes

COOKING TIME · 5 to 6 minutes

Crunchy pine nuts enhance this side dish with their distinctive flavor.

1 teaspoon olive oil

1 1/2 cups presliced fresh button mushrooms (about 4 ounces)

1/2 cup chopped onion

1 teaspoon bottled minced garlic or 2 medium garlic cloves, minced

6 ounces fresh baby spinach

1/2 cup grape tomatoes, halved

3 tablespoons shredded or grated Parmesan cheese

1 tablespoon plus 1 teaspoon pine nuts, dry-roasted if desired

In a large nonstick skillet, heat the oil over medium-high heat, swirling to coat the bottom. Cook the mushrooms and onion for 3 minutes, or until soft, stirring frequently.

Stir in the garlic. Cook for 30 seconds, stirring frequently.

Stir in the spinach. Cook for 1 1/2 to 2 minutes, or until just wilted, stirring frequently. Remove the skillet from the heat.

Gently stir in the tomatoes. Sprinkle with the Parmesan and pine nuts.

PER SERVING

calories 69

total fat 4.0 g
  saturated 1.0 g
  trans 0.0 g
  polyunsaturated 1.0 g
  monounsaturated 1.5 g

cholesterol 3 mg

sodium 102 mg

carbohydrates 6 g
  fiber 2 g
  sugars 3 g

protein 5 g

dietary exchanges
  1 vegetable
  1 fat

bulgur-stuffed
yellow summer squash

SERVES 8 · 1 piece per serving
PREPARATION TIME · 10 minutes
COOKING TIME · 20 to 22 minutes

An attractive dish for entertaining, this recipe has a Middle-Eastern flavor. If you are really in a hurry, try the alternate cooking method.

4 medium yellow summer squash (1¼ to 1½ pounds)

2 tablespoons water

½ cup whole fresh mushrooms, stems discarded

1 teaspoon olive oil

¼ cup chopped onion

½ cup fat-free, low-sodium chicken broth

½ cup frozen peas

¼ cup uncooked bulgur

¼ cup bottled roasted red bell peppers, drained and chopped (optional)

½ teaspoon dried dillweed, crumbled

⅛ teaspoon pepper

1 tablespoon plus 1 teaspoon shredded or grated Parmesan cheese

1 tablespoon plus 1 teaspoon pine nuts

Preheat the oven to 350°F.

Cut the squash in half lengthwise. Using a spoon or melon baller, scoop out the pulp, leaving 8 shells (reserve the pulp).

Put the squash with the cut side down in a 13 x 9 x 2-inch nonstick baking pan. Pour the water into the pan.

Bake for 8 to 10 minutes, or until the squash is tender. Drain the liquid. Turn the squash over. Leave the oven on.

Meanwhile, in a food processor or blender, process the reserved squash pulp and mushrooms for 10 to 15 seconds, or until coarsely chopped.

PER SERVING
calories 53
total fat 1.5 g
saturated 0.5 g
trans 0.0 g
polyunsaturated 0.5 g
monounsaturated 0.5 g
cholesterol 1 mg
sodium 34 mg
carbohydrates 8 g
fiber 2 g
sugars 3 g
protein 3 g
dietary exchanges
½ starch
½ fat

In a large skillet, heat the oil over medium-high heat, swirling to coat the bottom. Cook the squash mixture and onion for about 3 minutes, or until the onion is soft, stirring occasionally.

Stir in the broth, peas, bulgur, roasted bell peppers, dillweed, and pepper. Bring to a simmer. Reduce the heat to medium low. Cook, covered, for 10 minutes, or until the bulgur is tender. Spoon into the squash shells. Sprinkle with the Parmesan and pine nuts.

Bake for 6 to 8 minutes, or until warmed through.

TIME-SAVER To skip the baking and processing steps, thinly slice the squash and mushrooms, then cook with the onion as directed above. Simmer with the broth, peas, bulgur, roasted bell peppers, dillweed, and pepper, also as directed in the recipe. Serve sprinkled with the Parmesan and pine nuts.

oven-fried zucchini with salsa dip

SERVES 4 · 6 wedges per serving
PREPARATION TIME · 20 minutes
COOKING TIME · 22 to 24 minutes

A seasoned cornmeal crust makes the zucchini so crisp that you could easily mistake it for deep-fried. Try the zucchini and dip for a party appetizer as well as for a side dish.

Cooking spray

2 small zucchini (about 6 ounces each)

1/4 cup all-purpose flour

Whites of 2 large eggs

1/3 cup yellow cornmeal

2 tablespoons shredded or grated Parmesan cheese

1 teaspoon dried parsley, crumbled

3/4 teaspoon dried oregano, crumbled

1/2 teaspoon dried basil, crumbled

1/2 teaspoon garlic powder

SALSA DIP

1/4 cup fat-free sour cream

1/4 cup salsa (lowest sodium available)

Preheat the oven to 450°F. Lightly spray a large baking sheet with cooking spray.

Cut each zucchini lengthwise into quarters. Cut each quarter crosswise into 3 pieces. (You should have 24 pieces.)

Put three small shallow bowls in a row, assembly-line style. Put the flour in the first, lightly whisk the egg whites in the second, and stir together the cornmeal, Parmesan, parsley, oregano, basil, and garlic powder in the third. Put the baking sheet next to the third bowl.

PER SERVING
calories 121
total fat 1.0 g
saturated 0.5 g
trans 0.0 g
polyunsaturated 0.0 g
monounsaturated 0.5 g
cholesterol 4 mg
sodium 147 mg
carbohydrates 22 g
fiber 2 g
sugars 3 g
protein 6 g
dietary exchanges 1 1/2 starch

Dip 1 wedge of the zucchini into the flour, then into the egg whites, and finally into the cornmeal mixture, turning to coat and gently shaking off the excess, or letting it drip off, at each step. Place the zucchini on the baking sheet. Repeat with the remaining zucchini. Lightly spray the zucchini with cooking spray.

Bake for 22 to 24 minutes, or until lightly browned and crisp.

Meanwhile, in a small bowl, stir together the sour cream and salsa. Serve the zucchini wedges with the salsa dip on the side.

COOK'S TIP

Fresh salsa often is lower in sodium than bottled salsa, so don't forget to compare label information.

---

orange-flavored acorn squash and sweet potato

SERVES 6 · 2 slices squash and 8 to 10 slices sweet potato per serving
PREPARATION TIME · 20 minutes
COOKING TIME · 30 minutes

Serve this attractive side dish with your holiday meal or with roast beef for Sunday dinner. Baking at a high temperature slightly caramelizes the bottom of the squash for a delightful taste.

Cooking spray
1 teaspoon grated orange zest
2 tablespoons orange juice
2 teaspoons light tub margarine, melted

1 medium acorn squash (about 1½ pounds)
1 6- to 7½-inch sweet potato
2 tablespoons light brown sugar
¼ teaspoon ground nutmeg

Preheat the oven to 400°F. Lightly spray one extra-large or two large baking pans with cooking spray. Set aside.

In a small bowl, stir together the orange zest, orange juice, and margarine. Set aside.

Discard the ends of the squash. Cut the squash crosswise into ¼-inch slices (about 12). Using a spoon, discard the seeds and strings. Put the squash slices in a single layer on the baking sheet(s). Peel the sweet potato and cut into ⅛-inch slices (48 to 60). Place 4 or 5 overlapping slices of sweet potato in the center of each squash ring.

Pour the orange juice mixture over the stacks. Sprinkle with the brown sugar and nutmeg. Lightly spray with cooking spray.

Bake for 30 minutes, or until tender when pierced with a fork. Use a large, flat spatula to transfer the stacks to plates.

PER SERVING
calories 80
total fat 0.5 g
saturated 0.0 g
trans 0.0 g
polyunsaturated 0.0 g
monounsaturated 0.5 g
cholesterol 0 mg
sodium 27 mg
carbohydrates 19 g
fiber 2 g
sugars 8 g
protein 1 g
dietary exchanges
1½ starch

breads and breakfast dishes

tropical sunrise smoothie

SERVES 4 · 1 cup per serving
PREPARATION TIME · 10 minutes

Does your morning routine need a wake-up call? This smoothie will energize you—and might even make you look forward to getting out of bed!

1 cup orange juice

16 ounces fat-free vanilla, raspberry, or strawberry yogurt

2 cups coarsely chopped mango pieces (about 2 large)

2 cups coarsely chopped papaya pieces without seeds (about 22 ounces before peeling and seeding)

In a food processor or blender, process all the ingredients until smooth.

> **COOK'S TIP**
> You may substitute 2 cups halved strawberries for the mango or papaya if either is not readily available or is too expensive.

PER SERVING

calories 239
total fat 0.5 g
  saturated 0.0 g
  trans 0.0 g
  polyunsaturated 0.0 g
  monounsaturated 0.0 g
cholesterol 2 mg
sodium 84 mg
carbohydrates 54 g
  fiber 4 g
  sugars 47 g
protein 7 g
dietary exchanges
  2½ fruit
  1 fat-free milk

morning energy drink

SERVES 4 · 1 cup per serving
PREPARATION TIME · 5 minutes

Get up and go with this satisfying breakfast drink. For a frosty presentation, put empty glasses in the freezer for just a few minutes while you are preparing the drink.

1½ cups fat-free plain soy milk

1 cup frozen unsweetened sliced peaches

1 cup strawberries, hulled

1 cup carrot juice

1 small banana

2 tablespoons wheat germ or oat bran (optional)

2 tablespoons honey

In a food processor or blender, process all the ingredients until smooth.

PER SERVING
calories 125
total fat 0.5 g
saturated 0.0 g
trans 0.0 g
polyunsaturated 0.0 g
monounsaturated 0.0 g
cholesterol 0 mg
sodium 71 mg
carbohydrates 28 g
fiber 3 g
sugars 20 g
protein 4 g
dietary exchanges
1 fruit
½ fat-free milk
½ carbohydrate

Morning Energy "Soup"

For a change, serve this dish as a cold breakfast "soup." Pour 1 cup into a bowl and top with about ¼ cup of your favorite fat-free or low-fat cereal, such as wheat biscuits.

PER SERVING
calories 173
total fat 1.0 g
saturated 0.0 g
trans 0.0 g
polyunsaturated 0.5 g
monounsaturated 0.0 g
cholesterol 0 mg
sodium 72 mg
carbohydrates 39 g
fiber 4 g
sugars 21 g
protein 5 g
dietary exchanges
1 fruit
1 starch
½ fat-free milk

mini cinnamon stack ups

SERVES 4 · 1 waffle and ½ cup yogurt per serving
PREPARATION TIME · 5 minutes
COOKING TIME · 10 minutes

Have fun at breakfast with this terrific taste combination of mini waffles, cinnamon-sugared fruits, and yogurt. Or serve later in the day with frozen yogurt as a different way to enjoy an old-fashioned ice cream "cone."

4 4-piece frozen low-fat whole-wheat waffles

1 tablespoon sugar

¼ teaspoon ground cinnamon

2 cups fat-free vanilla yogurt

2 green kiwifruit, peeled, each cut crosswise into 6 pieces

1 star fruit, or carambola, cut crosswise into 8 pieces (optional)

½ cup fresh blueberries

1 cup fresh raspberries or strawberries, hulled

Toast the waffles. Separate each into 4 pieces and arrange on plates.

Meanwhile, in a small bowl, stir together the sugar and cinnamon.

To assemble, sprinkle half the cinnamon sugar over the waffles. Spoon the yogurt onto each serving. Arrange 3 slices kiwifruit, 2 slices star fruit, blueberries, and raspberries on each. Sprinkle the remaining cinnamon sugar over all.

PER SERVING
calories 245
total fat 2.0 g
saturated 0.5 g
trans 0.0 g
polyunsaturated 0.5 g
monounsaturated 0.5 g
cholesterol 2 mg
sodium 300 mg
carbohydrates 51 g
fiber 5 g
sugars 33 g
protein 9 g
dietary exchanges
1 starch
1½ fruit
1 fat-free milk

ricotta and blackberry breakfast sandwiches

SERVES 4 · 2 English muffin halves, 1/4 cup ricotta cheese, and 1/2 cup blackberries per serving
PREPARATION TIME · 5 minutes
COOKING TIME · 1 to 2 minutes

These delicious, good-for-you breakfast sandwiches are reminiscent of traditional Danish pastries straight from the bakery.

4 light multigrain English muffins, toasted

1 cup low-fat ricotta cheese

1/4 cup all-fruit apricot or seedless blackberry spread

1/2 teaspoon ground cinnamon

2 cups fresh blackberries

Preheat the broiler.

Place the 8 English muffin halves in a single layer on a small baking sheet.

In a small bowl, whisk together the ricotta cheese, apricot spread, and cinnamon. Spoon over the English muffins.

Broil about 4 inches from the heat for 1 to 2 minutes, or until warm. Top with the blackberries. Serve immediately.

PER SERVING

calories 232
total fat 4.0 g
  saturated 1.5 g
  trans 0.0 g
  polyunsaturated 1.0 g
  monounsaturated 0.5 g
cholesterol 15 mg
sodium 246 mg
carbohydrates 44 g
  fiber 12 g
  sugars 14 g
protein 11 g
dietary exchanges
  2 starch
  1 fruit
  1 lean meat

COOK'S TIP ON ENGLISH MUFFINS

Use the tines of a fork instead of a knife to split English muffins in half. This helps preserve the muffin's holey texture.

oatmeal pancakes with bananas

SERVES 4 · 2 pancakes per serving
PREPARATION TIME · 12 minutes
COOKING TIME · 6 to 10 minutes

Have a nutritious start to your morning when you add oatmeal and whole-wheat flour to your pancakes. Topped with granola, bananas, and maple syrup, they're amazing!

½ cup quick-cooking rolled oats

¼ cup all-purpose flour

¼ cup whole-wheat flour

3 tablespoons firmly packed light brown sugar

1½ teaspoons baking powder

½ teaspoon ground cinnamon

½ cup fat-free milk

½ cup unsweetened applesauce

¼ cup egg substitute

1 tablespoon canola or corn oil

2 medium bananas, sliced

¼ cup low-fat granola

¼ cup maple syrup

In a medium bowl, stir together the oats, flours, brown sugar, baking powder, and cinnamon.

In a small bowl, whisk together the milk, applesauce, egg substitute, and oil. Stir into the flour mixture just until combined. (Do not overmix or the pancakes will be tough.)

Heat a nonstick griddle over medium heat. Test the griddle by sprinkling a few drops of water on it. If the water evaporates quickly, the griddle is ready. Pour about ¼ cup batter per pancake onto the griddle (probably about 4 pancakes per batch, depending on the size of your griddle). Cook for 2 to 3 minutes, or until bubbles appear all over the surface.

PER SERVING
calories 316
total fat 4.5 g
saturated 0.5 g
trans 0.0 g
polyunsaturated 1.5 g
monounsaturated 2.5 g
cholesterol 1 mg
sodium 209 mg
carbohydrates 65 g
fiber 5 g
sugars 35 g
protein 7 g
dietary exchanges
2 starch
1 fruit
1½ carbohydrate
½ fat

Flip the pancakes. Cook for 1 to 2 minutes, or until cooked through and golden brown. Repeat until all the batter has been used. (You should have 8 pancakes total.) Serve topped with the bananas, granola, and maple syrup.

COOK'S TIP

If you aren't serving the first batch as soon as you remove the pancakes from the griddle, put them on a plate and cover loosely with aluminum foil. If you cover them tightly, they will steam and become soggy. Leftover pancakes will taste fresher and have a drier texture if you reheat them in a toaster oven rather than in a microwave oven.

yogurt brûlée with blueberries

SERVES 4 · 1 cup per serving
PREPARATION TIME · 5 minutes
COOKING TIME · 2 to 4 minutes

This breakfast treat looks so elegant, your family will think it took hours instead of minutes to prepare. You can also serve this as dessert, but caution is advised: You may be tempted to eat dessert first!

2 cups fresh or frozen blueberries, thawed if frozen, patted dry
½ teaspoon ground cinnamon
½ teaspoon vanilla extract

2 cups fat-free vanilla yogurt
2 tablespoons plus 2 teaspoons light brown sugar

Preheat the broiler. Put four 1-cup custard cups or ramekins on a broilerproof baking sheet.

In a medium bowl, stir together the blueberries, cinnamon, and vanilla. Spoon ½ cup mixture into each custard cup. Top each with about ½ cup yogurt and 2 teaspoons brown sugar.

Broil about 4 inches from the heat for 2 to 4 minutes, or until the sugar is melted and bubbly. Watch carefully to keep the sugar from burning.

PER SERVING
calories 191
total fat 0.5 g
saturated 0.0 g
trans 0.0 g
polyunsaturated 0.0 g
monounsaturated 0.0 g
cholesterol 2 mg
sodium 87 mg
carbohydrates 42 g
fiber 2 g
sugars 38 g
protein 7 g
dietary exchanges
1 fruit
1 fat-free milk
1 carbohydrate

fruitful brown rice cereal

SERVES 4 · $^2/_3$ cup per serving
PREPARATION TIME · 5 minutes
COOKING TIME · 15 minutes

This sweet, fragrant breakfast dish is even more delicious and healthful when topped with slices of banana or strawberries and additional fat-free milk.

Cooking spray
1¼ cups fat-free milk
1 cup unsweetened apple juice
1 teaspoon vanilla extract
2 cups uncooked instant brown rice

¼ cup dried fruit, such as currants, cherries, blueberries, or raisins, or a combination
1 teaspoon ground cinnamon

Lightly spray a medium saucepan with cooking spray. Pour in the milk, apple juice, and vanilla. Bring to a boil over high heat, about 4 minutes.

Stir in the rice, dried fruit, and cinnamon. Reduce the heat and simmer, covered, for 10 minutes, or until the liquids are absorbed and the rice is tender.

PER SERVING
calories 255
total fat 1.5 g
saturated 0.0 g
trans 0.0 g
polyunsaturated 0.5 g
monounsaturated 0.5 g
cholesterol 2 mg
sodium 45 mg
carbohydrates 52 g
fiber 3 g
sugars 17 g
protein 7 g
dietary exchanges
2½ starch
1 fruit

huevos rancheros casserole

SERVES 4 · 1 cup per serving
PREPARATION TIME · 15 minutes
COOKING TIME · 49 to 50 minutes

Capture the traditional flavors of huevos rancheros with this any-time-of-day casserole. You can make it and bake it right away or prepare it ahead of time and bake it the next day.

Cooking spray

2 ounces turkey breakfast sausage (2 links), casings discarded

1 Anaheim pepper, seeded and diced

6 6-inch corn tortillas, diced

1 15-ounce can no-salt-added black beans, rinsed and drained

1 cup cherry tomatoes, halved

2 cups fat-free milk

1½ cups egg substitute

2 tablespoons sliced black olives, drained

Preheat the oven to 350°F. Lightly spray a 9-inch square baking pan with cooking spray. Set aside.

In a small nonstick skillet, cook the sausage over medium-high heat for 3 minutes, stirring to break up the pieces. Stir in the pepper. Cook for 1 to 2 minutes, or until the pepper is tender and the sausage is no longer pink. Spoon into the baking pan.

Top, in order, with the tortillas, beans, and tomatoes.

In a medium bowl, whisk together the milk and egg substitute. Pour over the casserole.

Bake for 45 minutes, or until the center is set (doesn't jiggle when the casserole is gently shaken). Sprinkle with the olives.

COOK'S TIP
To make the casserole ahead of time, assemble as directed, then cover and refrigerate, unbaked, for up to 12 hours. Remove from the refrigerator 15 minutes before baking.

PER SERVING

calories 275
total fat 4.0 g
  saturated 0.5 g
  trans 0.0 g
  polyunsaturated 1.0 g
  monounsaturated 1.0 g
cholesterol 14 mg
sodium 416 mg
carbohydrates 38 g
  fiber 6 g
  sugars 13 g
protein 23 g
dietary exchanges
  2 starch
  1 vegetable
  2 very lean meat

desserts

Lemon Cake with Apricot Glaze
Lemon Cake with Apricot Topping
Lemon Cupcakes with Apricot Glaze

Chocolate Pudding Cake

Spice Cake

Double-Decker Pumpkin Cupcakes

Devil's Food Cupcakes with
Caramel Drizzles

Cinnamon Apple Bars

Ginger Snacks
Ginger Banana Snacks

Chocolate Zucchini Brownies

Nectarine and Raspberry Pie with
Phyllo Crust

Coffee-Flavored Sweet Cherry
Frozen Yogurt Pie

Pear Crisp
Apple Crisp

Lemon Mini Tarts
Lemon-Blueberry Parfaits

Bread Pudding with Peaches and
Bourbon Sauce

Ambrosia Parfait

Cranberry Cinnamon Baked Apples

Two-Way Strawberry Freeze
Two-Way Mixed-Fruit Freeze

Cheesecake-Sauced Fruit

lemon cake with apricot glaze

SERVES 16 · 1 slice per serving
PREPARATION TIME · 10 minutes
COOKING TIME · 26 to 32 minutes

Lemon juice and zest give this cake a refreshing taste. The sweetness of the apricot preserves balances the tartness of the lemon.

Cooking spray

1 18.25-ounce package lemon cake mix

6 large egg whites

½ cup water

1½ tablespoons grated lemon zest

¼ cup plus 2 tablespoons lemon juice

¾ cup all-fruit apricot preserves

1 cup frozen fat-free whipped topping, thawed in refrigerator

Preheat the oven to 325°F. Lightly spray a 13 x 9 x 2-inch metal baking pan with cooking spray.

Put the cake mix, egg whites, water, lemon zest, and lemon juice in a large mixing bowl. Mix using the package directions. Pour the batter into the pan.

Bake for 25 to 30 minutes, or until a cake tester or wooden toothpick inserted in the center comes out clean. Transfer to a cooling rack.

In a small saucepan, heat the apricot preserves over medium-high heat for 1 to 2 minutes, or until melted, stirring constantly. Brush evenly over the cake (a basting brush works well). Serve warm or at room temperature. Garnish each serving with a dollop of the whipped topping.

PER SERVING
calories 162
total fat 2.5 g
saturated 1.0 g
trans 0.0 g
polyunsaturated 0.0 g
monounsaturated 1.0 g
cholesterol 0 mg
sodium 236 mg
carbohydrates 33 g
fiber 1 g
sugars 20 g
protein 2 g
dietary exchanges
2 carbohydrate
½ fat

Lemon Cake with Apricot Topping

Beat the unheated apricot preserves with a fork. Fold into 3 cups frozen fat-free whipped topping, thawed in the refrigerator. Spread over the completely cooled cake. Refrigerate any leftovers.

Lemon Cupcakes with Apricot Glaze

SERVES 12 · 1 cupcake per serving

Pour the batter into two 12-cup muffin pans. Follow the baking times on the package. Brush with the warmed apricot preserves. Increase the amount of whipped topping to 1$\frac{1}{2}$ cups.

COOK'S TIP ON CITRUS ZEST

An implement called a zester makes quick work of removing the peel, or zest, of citrus fruit. Use rather firm downward strokes, being careful to avoid cutting into any of the pith, the white bitter covering just beneath the peel. Measuring and cleanup will be easy if you work over a sheet of wax paper.

chocolate pudding cake

SERVES 24 · 1 square per serving
PREPARATION TIME · 20 minutes
COOKING TIME · 35 to 40 minutes
STANDING TIME · 15 minutes

A rich pool of fudge sauce works its way to the bottom of this decadent-tasting cake as it bakes. This dessert is best when served warm but is excellent even at room temperature.

Cooking spray

CAKE

2 cups all-purpose flour

1½ cups sugar

½ cup unsweetened cocoa powder

1 tablespoon plus 1 teaspoon baking powder

¼ teaspoon salt

1 cup fat-free milk

½ cup unsweetened applesauce

2 teaspoons vanilla extract

PUDDING

2 cups boiling water

1½ cups firmly packed light brown sugar

½ cup unsweetened cocoa powder

Preheat the oven to 350°F. Lightly spray a 13 x 9 x 2-inch metal baking pan with cooking spray. Set aside.

In a large bowl, whisk together the flour, sugar, cocoa powder, baking powder, and salt. Whisk in the milk, applesauce, and vanilla, blending thoroughly. Pour into the baking pan, spreading evenly.

In a large bowl, whisk together the pudding ingredients until the brown sugar and cocoa powder are dissolved. Pour carefully over the batter. (The pudding layer will be thin and runny.)

Bake for 35 to 40 minutes, or until the top is firm to the touch. (A toothpick inserted in the center of the cake won't be an accurate test for doneness.) Let the cake stand for 15 minutes before cutting. Serve the cake topped with the sauce, or pool the sauce on plates and top with the cake. Cover and refrigerate any leftovers for up to seven days, or wrap tightly and freeze for up to two months.

PER SERVING
calories 160
total fat 0.5 g
saturated 0.0 g
trans 0.0 g
polyunsaturated 0.0 g
monounsaturated 0.0 g
cholesterol 0 mg
sodium 100 mg
carbohydrates 37 g
fiber 1 g
sugars 27 g
protein 2 g
dietary exchanges
2½ carbohydrate

spice cake

SERVES 20 · 1 slice per serving
PREPARATION TIME · 5 minutes
COOKING TIME · 28 minutes

Carrots and fruit juice add a healthful twist to this very easy cake.

Cooking spray

1 18.25-ounce box spice cake mix

6 large egg whites

2 4-ounce jars baby food pureed
carrots

1 cup unsweetened apple juice or
orange juice

1/2 cup sifted confectioners' sugar

Preheat the oven to 350°F. Lightly spray a 15 x 10 x 1-inch rimmed baking sheet with cooking spray.

Put the cake mix, egg whites, carrots, and juice in a large mixing bowl. Mix using the package directions. Pour the batter into the pan.

Bake using the package directions.

Just before serving, dust with the confectioners' sugar.

PER SERVING
calories 128
total fat 2.0 g
saturated 1.0 g
trans 0.0 g
polyunsaturated 0.0 g
monounsaturated 0.5 g
cholesterol 0 mg
sodium 190 mg
carbohydrates 26 g
fiber 0 g
sugars 17 g
protein 2 g
dietary exchanges
1 1/2 carbohydrate
1/2 fat

double-decker pumpkin cupcakes

SERVES 24 · 1 cupcake per serving
PREPARATION TIME · 11 minutes
COOKING TIME · 15 minutes
COOLING TIME · 30 minutes

Cover a cakelike layer on the bottom with a custardlike layer on top to get cupcakes that seem almost like pumpkin pie.

1 18-ounce package carrot cake mix

1/2 cup canned solid-pack pumpkin and 1/4 cup canned solid-pack pumpkin (not pie filling), divided use

1 cup water

5 large egg whites

2 tablespoons canola or corn oil

1 1/2 teaspoons ground cinnamon

1/2 cup fat-free frozen whipped topping and 1 1/2 cups fat-free frozen whipped topping, thawed in refrigerator, divided use

2 tablespoons sugar

1 teaspoon vanilla extract

1/4 teaspoon ground nutmeg or ground cinnamon

Preheat the oven to 325°F. Put cupcake liners in two 12-cup muffin pans.

Put the cake mix, 1/2 cup pumpkin, water, egg whites, oil, and 1 1/2 teaspoons cinnamon in a large mixing bowl. Mix using the package directions. Spoon the batter into the muffin cups to fill about three-fourths full.

Bake for 15 minutes, or until a cake tester or wooden toothpick inserted in the center of a cupcake comes out clean. Transfer the pans to cooling racks and let cool for 5 minutes. Remove the cupcakes from the pans and let them cool completely on the racks, about 25 minutes.

PER SERVING
calories 115
total fat 2.5 g
saturated 0.5 g
trans 0.0 g
polyunsaturated 0.5 g
monounsaturated 1.0 g
cholesterol 0 mg
sodium 166 mg
carbohydrates 21 g
fiber 0 g
sugars 13 g
protein 2 g
dietary exchanges
1 1/2 carbohydrate
1/2 fat

In a medium bowl, stir together $\frac{1}{2}$ cup whipped topping, sugar, vanilla, nutmeg, and remaining $\frac{1}{4}$ cup pumpkin. Fold in the remaining $1\frac{1}{2}$ cups whipped topping.

At serving time, spoon a rounded tablespoon of the topping onto each cupcake you are serving, spreading to cover the top. Refrigerate or freeze any leftover muffins, with the topping in a separate container.

devil's food cupcakes with caramel drizzles

SERVES 24 · 1 cupcake per serving
PREPARATION TIME · 10 minutes
COOKING TIME · 17 to 22 minutes
COOLING TIME · 10 minutes

Ultramoist and deliciously gooey, these dark chocolate cupcakes will disappear quickly.

Cooking spray
1 18.25-ounce box devil's food
   cake mix
6 large egg whites

2 4-ounce jars baby food pureed
   prunes
1 cup cold coffee or water
$\frac{1}{2}$ cup fat-free caramel topping

Preheat the oven to 325°F. Lightly spray two 12-cup muffin pans with cooking spray.

Put the cake mix, egg whites, prunes, and coffee in a large mixing bowl. Mix using the package directions. Spoon the batter into the muffin cups.

Bake and cool using the package directions.

Just before serving, drizzle each cupcake with about 1 teaspoon caramel topping. (It will soak into the cupcakes if added sooner.) Serve warm or at room temperature.

PER SERVING
calories 140
total fat 2.0 g
saturated 1.0 g
trans 0.0 g
polyunsaturated 0.5 g
monounsaturated 0.5 g
cholesterol 0 mg
sodium 220 mg
carbohydrates 29 g
fiber 1 g
sugars 17 g
protein 2 g
dietary exchanges
2 carbohydrate
$\frac{1}{2}$ fat

cinnamon apple bars

SERVES 18 · 2 bars per serving
PREPARATION TIME · 10 minutes
COOKING TIME · 20 minutes
COOLING TIME · 10 minutes

The exquisite aroma of cinnamon, apples, and brown sugar baking will make it hard to wait for this treat to come out of the oven.

Cooking spray

2 cups all-purpose flour

1½ teaspoons baking powder

1 teaspoon ground cinnamon

¼ teaspoon baking soda

1 cup canned unsweetened apple slices or canned pears in fruit juice, drained, cut into ½-inch pieces

¾ cup firmly packed light brown sugar

½ cup cranberry applesauce or unsweetened applesauce

½ cup egg substitute

¼ cup sugar

2 tablespoons canola or corn oil

1 teaspoon vanilla extract

Preheat the oven to 350°F. Lightly spray a 13 x 9 x 2-inch metal baking pan with cooking spray.

In a medium bowl, stir together the flour, baking powder, cinnamon, and baking soda.

In another medium bowl, stir together the remaining ingredients. Add the flour mixture, stirring until just moistened. Pour the batter into the baking pan.

Bake for 20 minutes, or until a knife inserted in the center comes out clean. Let cool on a cooling rack for 10 minutes. Cut into 36 bars.

PER SERVING
calories 123
total fat 1.5 g
saturated 0.0 g
trans 0.0 g
polyunsaturated 0.5 g
monounsaturated 1.0 g
cholesterol 0 mg
sodium 68 mg
carbohydrates 25 g
fiber 1 g
sugars 14 g
protein 2 g
dietary exchanges
1½ carbohydrate
½ fat

ginger snacks

MAKES 16 · 1 muffin per serving
PREPARATION TIME · 15 minutes
COOKING TIME · 25 minutes

Baked with pumpkin for added flavor, moisture, and body, these ginger-bread muffins are perfect for brown-bagging or after-school snacks.

Cooking spray

1 14.5- or 15-ounce box
   gingerbread mix

1¼ cups orange juice or water

2 large egg whites

1 cup canned solid-pack pumpkin
   (not pie filling) (about
   ½ 15-ounce can)

¾ teaspoon ground cinnamon and
   ¼ teaspoon ground cinnamon,
   divided use

1½ tablespoons sugar

Preheat the oven to 350°F. Lightly spray 16 muffin cups of two 12-cup muffin pans with cooking spray. Pour several tablespoons of water into each of the 8 remaining cups to keep the pan from warping or burning.

In a large mixing bowl, stir together the gingerbread mix, orange juice, and egg whites. Beat using the package directions. Stir in the pumpkin and ¾ teaspoon cinnamon. Spoon the batter into the muffin cups.

Bake for 25 minutes, or until a muffin springs back slightly when you press gently on the center.

Meanwhile, stir together the sugar and remaining ¼ teaspoon cinnamon.

When the muffins are done, transfer the pans to cooling racks. Sprinkle the muffins with the sugar mixture.

PER SERVING
calories 135
total fat 3.5 g
saturated 1.0 g
trans 0.0 g
polyunsaturated 0.5 g
monounsaturated 2.0 g
cholesterol 0 mg
sodium 179 mg
carbohydrates 24 g
fiber 1 g
sugars 16 g
protein 2 g
dietary exchanges
1½ carbohydrate
1 fat

Ginger Banana Snacks

Substitute 1 cup mashed ripe banana for the pumpkin, unsweetened apple juice for the orange juice, and ground nutmeg for the ground cinnamon.

calories 143
total fat 3.5 g
  saturated 1.0 g
  trans 0.0 g
  polyunsaturated 0.5 g
  monounsaturated 2.0 g
cholesterol 0 mg
sodium 179 mg
carbohydrates 26 g
  fiber 1 g
  sugars 17 g
protein 2 g
dietary exchanges
  1 1/2 carbohydrate
  1 fat

chocolate zucchini brownies

SERVES 16 · 1 brownie, 1 tablespoon whipped topping, ½ teaspoon chocolate syrup, and ½ teaspoon chopped pecans per serving

PREPARATION TIME · 20 minutes

COOKING TIME · 20 to 25 minutes

COOLING TIME · 1 hour

You'll be happy to eat veggies for dessert when you taste these cakelike brownies. Zucchini is the surprise ingredient.

Cooking spray

BROWNIES

¾ cup sugar

½ cup firmly packed light brown sugar

¼ cup unsweetened applesauce

¼ cup canola or corn oil

1 tablespoon vanilla extract

2 cups shredded unpeeled zucchini (about 11 ounces)

2 cups all-purpose flour

½ cup unsweetened cocoa powder

1 teaspoon baking powder

½ teaspoon baking soda

¼ teaspoon salt

TOPPING

2 cups frozen fat-free whipped topping, thawed in refrigerator

2 tablespoons plus 2 teaspoons chocolate syrup

2 tablespoons plus 2 teaspoons chopped pecans

Preheat the oven to 350°F. Lightly spray a 13 x 9 x 2-inch metal baking pan with cooking spray.

In a large bowl, stir together the sugars, applesauce, oil, and vanilla until well blended. Fold in the zucchini.

In a medium bowl, stir together the remaining brownie ingredients. Stir into the sugar mixture until thoroughly combined. The batter will be very thick. Spoon into the baking pan, spreading with a rubber scraper.

PER SERVING
calories 200
total fat 5.0 g
saturated 0.5 g
trans 0.0 g
polyunsaturated 1.5 g
monounsaturated 3.0 g
cholesterol 0 mg
sodium 111 mg
carbohydrates 36 g
fiber 2 g
sugars 20 g
protein 3 g
dietary exchanges
2½ carbohydrate
1 fat

Bake for 20 to 25 minutes, or until a cake tester or wooden toothpick inserted in the center comes out almost clean. Transfer to a cooling rack and let cool for about 1 hour before cutting. Top each brownie with a heaping tablespoon whipped topping, $1/2$ teaspoon chocolate syrup, and $1/2$ teaspoon pecans.

COOK'S TIP ON ZUCCHINI
If you have a bountiful supply of fresh zucchini in the summer, shred and freeze 2-cup portions for later use, such as in this recipe. Discard the seeds first if a zucchini is extremely large.

nectarine and raspberry pie with phyllo crust

SERVES 8 · 1 slice per serving

PREPARATION TIME · 20 minutes

COOKING TIME · 30 minutes

Phyllo dough makes a feathery crust for this vibrantly colored pie.

Butter-flavor cooking spray

FILLING

1/4 cup honey

2 tablespoons light tub margarine

1 teaspoon grated lemon zest

1 tablespoon lemon juice

1/4 teaspoon ground nutmeg

6 medium nectarines, sliced (about 2 pounds), or 4 cups frozen unsweetened sliced peaches, thawed

1 1/4 cups fresh or frozen unsweetened raspberries, thawed (about 3/4 pint fresh or 12 ounces frozen)

CRUST

2 tablespoons sugar

1/2 teaspoon ground cinnamon

6 sheets frozen phyllo dough, thawed in refrigerator

Preheat the oven to 375°F. Lightly spray a 9-inch metal pie pan with cooking spray.

In a large bowl, stir together the honey, margarine, lemon zest, lemon juice, and nutmeg. Gently stir in the nectarines and raspberries.

In a small bowl, stir together the sugar and cinnamon.

Stack the phyllo sheets on a cutting board. Cut the sheets all at once into a 12-inch square, keeping the leftover strips. Working quickly, place 1 sheet of phyllo in the pie pan. Keep the other sheets of phyllo and the leftover strips covered with a damp cloth or damp paper towels to prevent drying. Lightly spray the phyllo in the pie pan with cooking

PER SERVING
calories 166
total fat 2.0 g
saturated 0.0 g
trans 0.0 g
polyunsaturated 0.5 g
monounsaturated 1.0 g
cholesterol 0 mg
sodium 92 mg
carbohydrates 37 g
fiber 4 g
sugars 21 g
protein 3 g
dietary exchanges
1 starch
1 fruit
1/2 carbohydrate

spray. Sprinkle with 1 teaspoon sugar mixture. Repeat with the remaining phyllo sheets and sugar mixture. Either layer the leftover strips over the phyllo sheets or save for making a lattice crust. Spoon the filling into the crust. Crisscross the strips for a lattice crust, if desired.

Bake for 30 minutes, or until the fruit is tender and the phyllo is golden brown.

COOK'S TIP ON PHYLLO

Phyllo (FEE-loh), available frozen in most large supermarkets and specialty groceries, is a tissue-thin pastry dough. To thaw, put the frozen phyllo dough in the refrigerator for about 6 hours. Thawed phyllo sheets quickly become dry and brittle, so use a damp dish towel to cover the dough you aren't using. Unopened thawed dough will keep in the refrigerator for about a month. If refrozen, phyllo dough can become brittle and crumbly.

coffee-flavored sweet cherry frozen yogurt pie

SERVES 8 · 1 pie wedge plus 1 tablespoon sauce and
1 tablespoon almonds per serving
PREPARATION TIME · 10 minutes
COOKING TIME · 7 minutes
FREEZING TIME · 4 hours (up to 48 hours)

The layers of coffee, dark cherry, and chocolate flavor make this dessert interesting, and the addition of the quick raspberry sauce at the end makes it pop!

3 cups frozen vanilla yogurt and
1 cup frozen vanilla yogurt,
slightly softened, divided use
1 tablespoon instant coffee
granules
8 ounces frozen dark sweet
cherries, coarsely chopped

2½ ounces chocolate graham
crackers, crushed (about ⅔ cup)
½ cup slivered or sliced almonds
(about 2 ounces)
½ cup all-fruit seedless raspberry
spread

In a 9-inch deep pie pan (glass preferred), spread 3 cups frozen yogurt.

In a medium bowl, stir together the remaining 1 cup frozen yogurt and coffee granules. Spoon dollops of the mixture over the vanilla yogurt in the pie pan. Using the back of a spoon, spread the coffee-flavored yogurt over the vanilla yogurt. Sprinkle with the cherries and cookie crumbs. Cover with plastic wrap. Freeze until firm, at least 4 hours.

Meanwhile, in a small skillet, dry-roast the almonds over medium heat for about 4 minutes, or until just fragrant, stirring frequently. Remove from the skillet so they don't burn.

PER SERVING
calories 231
total fat 4.5 g
saturated 0.5 g
trans 0.0 g
polyunsaturated 1.0 g
monounsaturated 2.5 g
cholesterol 2 mg
sodium 119 mg
carbohydrates 42 g
fiber 2 g
sugars 33 g
protein 7 g
dietary exchanges
3 carbohydrate
1 fat

At serving time, in the same skillet or a small saucepan, heat the raspberry spread over medium heat for 3 minutes, or until slightly melted. If you prefer, put the raspberry spread in a small microwaveable dish and microwave on 100 percent power (high) for about 20 seconds. Spoon about 1 tablespoon over each serving of pie. Sprinkle with the almonds.

COOK'S TIP

If you prefer, assemble the "pie" in eight 6-ounce ramekins instead of the pie pan. This is an easy way to control portion size.

pear crisp

SERVES 6 · ½ cup per serving
PREPARATION TIME · 10 minutes
COOKING TIME · 30 minutes
COOLING TIME · 20 minutes

Keep a big can of pears in the pantry, and you can enjoy this simple, spicy crisp any time.

¼ cup chopped pecans (about 1 ounce)

1 29-ounce can pears, sliced, or sliced peaches in fruit juice

¼ cup dry white wine (regular or nonalcoholic) and ½ cup juice from the pears or peaches, or ¾ cup juice from the pears or peaches

2 tablespoons sugar

¼ teaspoon ground ginger

¼ teaspoon ground cloves or ground cinnamon

½ cup uncooked rolled oats

½ cup firmly packed light brown sugar

2 tablespoons whole-wheat pastry flour or all-purpose flour

¼ teaspoon ground nutmeg

2 teaspoons canola or corn oil

Preheat the oven to 350°F.

In a small ovenproof skillet, dry-roast the pecans in a single layer in the preheating oven for about 10 minutes, or until golden brown, stirring several times. Remove from the skillet so they don't burn.

Put the pears in a 1-quart casserole dish or 9-inch glass pie pan.

In a medium saucepan, stir together the wine and juice, sugar, ginger, and cloves. Bring to a boil over medium-high heat. Cook for 4 minutes, or until reduced by half, stirring occasionally.

In a small bowl, stir together the oats, brown sugar, flour, and nutmeg. Using a fork, stir in the oil, then the pecans. Sprinkle over the pears. Pour the sauce over all.

Bake for 20 minutes, or until the top is lightly browned and the sauce is bubbly. Let cool for 20 minutes before serving.

PER SERVING
calories 245
total fat 6.0 g
saturated 0.5 g
trans 0.0 g
polyunsaturated 1.5 g
monounsaturated 3.0 g
cholesterol 0 mg
sodium 11 mg
carbohydrates 47 g
fiber 4 g
sugars 36 g
protein 2 g
dietary exchanges
1 fruit
2 carbohydrate
1 fat

Apple Crisp

Replace the pears with canned apple slices, and replace the ginger with ⅛ teaspoon ground nutmeg. Use ¼ teaspoon ground cinnamon, not ground cloves.

PER SERVING

calories 238
total fat 6.0 g
  saturated 0.5 g
  trans 0.0 g
  polyunsaturated 1.5 g
  monounsaturated 3.0 g
cholesterol 0 mg
sodium 10 mg
carbohydrates 46 g
  fiber 4 g
  sugars 35 g
protein 2 g
dietary exchanges
  1 fruit
  2 carbohydrate
  1 fat

lemon mini tarts

SERVES 12 · 2 tarts per serving
PREPARATION TIME · 10 to 12 minutes
COOKING TIME · 3 to 5 minutes
COOLING TIME · 10 to 15 minutes

These creamy tarts will solve the problem of what to serve for dessert when you have company for dinner. Vary the yogurt and fruit combination to suit your family's preferences.

24 frozen mini phyllo shells

3 tablespoons light tub cream cheese

6 ounces fat-free lemon yogurt

1½ teaspoons lemon zest

2 tablespoons lemon juice

2 cups fat-free frozen whipped topping, thawed in refrigerator

24 fresh blueberries

Preheat the oven to 350°F.

Place the phyllo shells on a baking sheet.

Bake for 3 to 5 minutes, or until crisp. Transfer to a cooling rack. Let cool completely, 10 to 15 minutes.

In a medium mixing bowl, using an electric mixer on medium speed, beat the cream cheese, yogurt, lemon zest, and lemon juice until smooth.

Gently fold in the whipped topping until blended.

Spoon about 1½ tablespoons of the mixture into each cooled phyllo shell. Top each with a blueberry.

PER SERVING
calories 79
total fat 2.5 g
saturated 0.5 g
trans 0.0 g
polyunsaturated 0.0 g
monounsaturated 0.0 g
cholesterol 3 mg
sodium 59 mg
carbohydrates 11 g
fiber 0 g
sugars 4 g
protein 1 g
dietary exchanges
1 carbohydrate
½ fat

Lemon-Blueberry Parfaits

SERVES 6 · ½ cup pudding and 1 tablespoon blueberries per serving

Increase the blueberries to ¼ cup plus 2 tablespoons. Prepare the filling as directed, then spoon ¼ cup into each of 6 individual serving dishes. Top each with 1½ teaspoons blueberries. Repeat the layers.

bread pudding with peaches and bourbon sauce

SERVES 8 · 1/2 cup pudding and 1/4 cup sauce per serving
PREPARATION TIME · 15 minutes
COOKING TIME · 30 to 35 minutes

Grace your dinner table with this show-stopping dessert. It's the perfect end to a southern meal.

Butter-flavor cooking spray

PUDDING

2 tablespoons light tub margarine

8 1/2-inch slices baguette-style French bread (about 3 ounces)

1/2 teaspoon ground cinnamon

20 ounces frozen unsweetened sliced peaches, thawed, or peeled, sliced fresh peaches (about 3 medium)

2 tablespoons dried unsweetened cherries, raisins, or dried blueberries (optional)

1/2 cup egg substitute

1 cup fat-free milk

1/4 to 1/2 cup sugar (depending on sweetness of the peaches)

BOURBON SAUCE

1 cup fat-free milk

1/2 small package (4-serving size) fat-free, sugar-free vanilla cook-and-serve pudding mix (about 4 1/2 tablespoons)

1 tablespoon bourbon or rum or 1/4 teaspoon rum flavoring

Preheat the oven to 350°F. Lightly spray eight 6-ounce glass or porcelain custard cups or a 9-inch square metal baking pan with cooking spray. If using custard cups, set on a baking sheet.

Spread a thin layer of margarine on one side of each bread slice. Sprinkle with the cinnamon. Cut into 1/2-inch cubes. Put the cubes in the custard cups. Top with the peaches, then the cherries.

In a medium bowl, whisk together the egg substitute, 1 cup milk, and sugar. Pour into the custard cups. Leave the custard cups on the baking sheet.

PER SERVING	
calories 135	
total fat 1.5 g	
saturated 0.0 g	
trans 0.0 g	
polyunsaturated 0.5 g	
monounsaturated 1.0 g	
cholesterol 1 mg	
sodium 176 mg	
carbohydrates 24 g	
fiber 1 g	
sugars 16 g	
protein 5 g	
dietary exchanges	
1 1/2 carbohydrate	
1/2 lean meat	

Bake for 30 to 35 minutes, or until the center of the pudding is set. (Bake for the same amount of time if using the baking pan, but don't set it on the baking sheet.)

About 10 minutes before the pudding is done, make the sauce. Put the remaining 1 cup milk and pudding mix in a medium saucepan. Whisk together for 30 to 60 seconds, or until well blended. Bring to a boil over medium-high heat, 2 to 3 minutes, whisking occasionally.

Reduce the heat to medium low. Whisk in the bourbon. Cook for 1 to 2 minutes, or until almost the desired consistency. (The sauce will thicken more as it stands.) Keep the sauce warm over low heat until the pudding is done.

Spoon the sauce over the pudding. If you prefer, spoon the sauce onto dessert plates. Slide a small, thin spatula around the sides of the custard cups, remove the puddings with a spoon, and place them on the sauce.

ambrosia parfait

SERVES 6 · 1 cup per serving
PREPARATION TIME · 15 minutes

Here's a modern twist to a comforting favorite. It's perfect not only for dessert but also as a starter for a summer brunch.

1 11-ounce can mandarin oranges in water or light syrup, drained

1 cup cubed fresh or bottled mango

1 8-ounce can pineapple tidbits in their own juice, drained

1 medium banana, sliced

1/2 cup sliced strawberries

1 tablespoon shredded sweetened coconut

3 cups fat-free lemon yogurt

2 tablespoons dried sweetened cranberries (optional)

In a medium bowl, stir together the mandarin oranges, mango, pineapple, banana, strawberries, and coconut.

To assemble, spoon about 1/4 cup yogurt into each parfait glass or small bowl. Top each with 1/4 cup fruit mixture. Repeat. Sprinkle with the cranberries. Serve or cover and refrigerate for up to 4 hours.

PER SERVING

calories 188
total fat 0.5 g
  saturated 0.5 g
  trans 0.0 g
  polyunsaturated 0.0 g
  monounsaturated 0.0 g
cholesterol 2 mg
sodium 92 mg
carbohydrates 41 g
  fiber 2 g
  sugars 37 g
protein 7 g
dietary exchanges
  1 fruit
  1 fat-free milk
  1 carbohydrate

cranberry cinnamon baked apples

SERVES 4 · ½ apple per serving
PREPARATION TIME · 10 minutes
COOKING TIME · 35 to 40 minutes

As the apples bake, their juice combines with brown sugar and orange juice to create a light caramel sauce.

Cooking spray

2 baking apples, such as Rome Beauty, Winesap, or Stayman (about 8 ounces each), halved lengthwise and cored

½ cup dried sweetened cranberries

2 tablespoons finely chopped pecans

2 tablespoons dark brown sugar

3 tablespoons orange juice, unsweetened apple juice, or water

1 teaspoon ground cinnamon

1 teaspoon vanilla extract or vanilla, butter, and nut flavoring

Preheat the oven to 350°F. Lightly spray an 8-inch square metal baking pan with cooking spray.

Put the apples with the cut sides up in the pan. (If needed to keep the apples from rocking, cut a very thin slice off the bottom of each half.)

In a small bowl, stir together the remaining ingredients. Spoon onto each apple half.

Bake, covered, for 10 minutes. Bake, uncovered, for 25 to 30 minutes, or until the apples are easily pierced with a fork.

PER SERVING
calories 165
total fat 3.0 g
saturated 0.5 g
trans 0.0 g
polyunsaturated 1.0 g
monounsaturated 1.5 g
cholesterol 0 mg
sodium 3 mg
carbohydrates 36 g
fiber 4 g
sugars 31 g
protein 1 g
dietary exchanges
1 fruit
1½ carbohydrate
½ fat

two-way strawberry freeze

SERVES 8 · scant ¾ cup per serving
PREPARATION TIME · 5 minutes
FREEZING TIME (OPTIONAL) · 1 hour

Blend sweet strawberries with white grape juice and a bit of wine for a fruity drink or a refreshing ice.

16 ounces frozen unsweetened
   strawberries
2 cups white grape juice

1 cup dry white wine (regular or
   nonalcoholic) or diet ginger ale

In a food processor or blender, process the strawberries and grape juice until smooth.

Slowly add the wine, processing the strawberry mixture until well blended. Pour into glasses to serve as a beverage, or seal in a large airtight plastic bag and lay flat in the freezer for about 1 hour, or until semisoft, to serve as an ice.

WHITE WINE

PER SERVING

calories 79
total fat 0.0 g
  saturated 0.0 g
  trans 0.0 g
  polyunsaturated 0.0 g
  monounsaturated 0.0 g
cholesterol 0 mg
sodium 5 mg
carbohydrates 15 g
  fiber 1 g
  sugars 12 g
protein 1 g
dietary exchanges
  1 fruit

GINGER ALE

PER SERVING

calories 58
total fat 0.0 g
  saturated 0.0 g
  trans 0.0 g
  polyunsaturated 0.0 g
  monounsaturated 0.0 g
cholesterol 0 mg
sodium 12 mg
carbohydrates 15 g
  fiber 1 g
  sugars 12 g
protein 1 g
dietary exchanges
  1 fruit

Two-Way Mixed-Fruit Freeze

Substitute 2 cups pineapple-orange juice for the grape juice; 16 ounces frozen mixed melon or mixed fruit for the strawberries; and 1 cup diet lemon-lime soda, or $1/4$ cup lemon juice and 1 tablespoon sugar, for the wine. Blend as directed on page 322. Serve immediately or freeze until semisoft.

TIME-SAVER Laying a bag of liquid flat in the freezer helps speed up the freezing process.

PER SERVING

calories 54
total fat 0.0 g
  saturated 0.0 g
  trans 0.0 g
  polyunsaturated 0.0 g
  monounsaturated 0.0 g
cholesterol 0 mg
sodium 8 mg
carbohydrates 14 g
  fiber 2 g
  sugars 11 g
protein 1 g
dietary exchanges
  1 fruit

cheesecake-sauced fruit

SERVES 16 · ½ cup fruit and 2 tablespoons sauce per serving
PREPARATION TIME · 10 minutes

Turn a serving of your favorite fruit into a delectable dessert with an extra-easy sauce reminiscent of cheesecake.

1 8-ounce tub fat-free cream cheese

8 ounces fat-free vanilla yogurt

⅔ cup unsifted confectioners' sugar

¾ teaspoon vanilla extract

8 cups sliced or chopped fruit, such as mango and strawberries

In a food processor or blender, process all the ingredients except the fruit until completely smooth. Serve the sauce over the fruit or cover with plastic wrap and refrigerate until needed.

COOK'S TIP

You can easily cut this recipe in half, or refrigerate any leftover sauce for up to five days.

PER SERVING

calories 100
total fat 0.5 g
  saturated 0.0 g
  trans 0.0 g
  polyunsaturated 0.0 g
  monounsaturated 0.0 g
cholesterol 2 mg
sodium 97 mg
carbohydrates 22 g
  fiber 2 g
  sugars 20 g
protein 3 g
dietary exchanges
  1 fruit
  ½ carbohydrate

entrée recipe icon index

(continued)

325

(continued)

equivalents and substitutions

Ingredient Equivalents

INGREDIENT	MEASUREMENT
Almonds	1 ounce = 1/4 cup slivers
Apple	1 medium = 3/4 to 1 cup chopped; 1 cup sliced
Basil leaves, fresh	2/3 ounce = 1/2 cup, chopped
Bell pepper, any color	1 medium = 1 cup chopped or sliced
Carrot	1 medium = 1/3 to 1/2 cup chopped or sliced; 1/2 cup shredded
Celery	1 medium rib = 1/2 cup chopped or sliced
Cheese, hard, such as Parmesan	3 1/2 ounces = 1 cup shredded 4 ounces = 1 cup grated
Cheese, semihard, such as Cheddar, mozzarella, or Swiss	4 ounces = 1 cup grated
Cheese, soft, such as blue, feta, or goat	1 ounce crumbled = 1/4 cup
Cucumber	1 medium = 1 cup sliced
Lemon juice	1 medium = 2 to 3 tablespoons
Lemon zest	1 medium = 2 to 3 teaspoons
Lime juice	1 medium = 1 1/2 to 2 tablespoons
Lime zest	1 medium = 1 teaspoon
Mushrooms (button)	1 pound = 5 to 6 cups sliced; 6 cups chopped
Onions, green	8 to 9 medium = 1 cup sliced (green and white parts)

INGREDIENT	MEASUREMENT
Onions, white or yellow	1 large = 1 cup chopped 1 medium = $1/2$ to $2/3$ cup chopped 1 small = $1/3$ cup chopped
Orange juice	1 medium = $1/3$ to $1/2$ cup
Orange zest	1 medium = $1^1/2$ to 2 tablespoons
Strawberries	1 pint = 2 cups sliced or chopped
Tomatoes	2 large, 3 medium, or 4 small = $1^1/2$ to 2 cups chopped
Walnuts	1 ounce = $1/4$ cup chopped

Emergency Substitutions

When you see a recipe you'd like to prepare but don't have certain ingredients on hand, or you begin a recipe only to find you're out of something, try these in-a-pinch substitutions.

IF YOUR RECIPE CALLS FOR	USE
Allspice, 1 teaspoon	$1/2$ teaspoon ground cinnamon + 1 teaspoon ground cloves
Baking powder, 1 teaspoon	$1/4$ teaspoon baking soda + $3/4$ teaspoon cream of tartar
Brown sugar, 1 cup	1 cup granulated sugar + 2 tablespoons molasses
Buttermilk, 1 cup	1 tablespoon vinegar or lemon juice + enough fat-free milk to equal 1 cup; or 1 cup fat-free plain yogurt
Cake flour, 1 cup sifted	1 cup minus 2 tablespoons sifted all-purpose flour

(continued)

IF YOUR RECIPE CALLS FOR	USE
Confectioners' sugar, 1 cup	$1/2$ cup + 1 tablespoon granulated sugar
Cornstarch, 1 tablespoon	2 tablespoons all-purpose flour
Cracker crumbs, $3/4$ cup	$3/4$ to 1 cup dry bread crumbs
Flour for thickening, 2 tablespoons all-purpose	1 tablespoon cornstarch
Flour, whole-wheat, 1 cup (for baking)	$7/8$ cup all-purpose flour
Fresh herbs, 1 tablespoon	1 teaspoon dried herbs
Gingerroot, peeled and grated, 1 tablespoon	$1/8$ teaspoon ground ginger
Honey, 1 tablespoon	4 teaspoons granulated sugar + $1^1/2$ teaspoons water
Lemon juice, 1 teaspoon	$1/2$ teaspoon vinegar
Lemon zest, 1 teaspoon	$1/2$ teaspoon lemon extract
Lemongrass	Grated lemon zest moistened with lemon juice
Mustard, dry, 1 teaspoon	1 tablespoon yellow mustard
Onion, 1 small	1 teaspoon onion powder or 1 tablespoon minced dried onion
Ricotta cheese, $1/2$ cup fat-free	$1/2$ cup fat-free cottage cheese
Sherry, 2 tablespoons	1 to 2 teaspoons vanilla extract
Sour cream, 1 cup fat-free	1 cup fat-free plain yogurt
Tomato juice, 1 cup	$1/2$ cup tomato sauce + $1/2$ cup water
Tomato sauce, 2 cups	$3/4$ cup tomato paste + 1 cup water
Wine, red, $1/2$ cup	$1/2$ cup fat-free, no-salt-added beef broth
Wine, white, $1/2$ cup	$1/2$ cup fat-free, low-sodium chicken broth
Yeast, active dry, $1^1/4$-ounce package	$2^1/2$ teaspoons active dry or $2/3$ ounce cake yeast, crumbled

Adapting Existing Recipes

You don't need to throw away old family recipes just because you want to eat healthy. By making a few simple ingredient substitutions, you can rework almost any recipe to be high in flavor and lower in calories, saturated fat, trans fat, cholesterol, and sodium.

IF YOUR RECIPE CALLS FOR	USE
Regular broth or bouillon	Fat-free, low-sodium broths, either homemade or commercially prepared; salt-free or low-sodium bouillon granules or cubes, reconstituted according to package directions.
Butter or shortening	When possible, use fat-free spray margarine or light tub margarine. However, if the type of fat is critical to the recipe, especially in baked goods, you may need to use stick margarine. Choose the product that is lowest in saturated and trans fats.
Butter for sautéing	Vegetable oil, such as canola, corn, or olive; cooking spray; fat-free, low-sodium broth; wine; fruit or vegetable juice
Cream	Fat-free half-and-half; fat-free nondairy creamer; fat-free evaporated milk
Eggs	Cholesterol-free egg substitutes; 2 egg whites for 1 whole egg
Evaporated milk	Fat-free evaporated milk
Flavored salts, such as onion salt, garlic salt, and celery salt	Onion powder, garlic powder, celery seeds or flakes; or about one-fourth the amount of flavored salt indicated in the recipe
Ice cream	Fat-free, low-fat, or light ice cream; fat-free or low-fat frozen yogurt; sorbet; sherbet; gelato
Table salt	No-salt-added seasoning blends

(continued)

IF YOUR RECIPE CALLS FOR	USE
Tomato juice	No-salt-added tomato juice
Tomato sauce	No-salt-added tomato sauce; 6-ounce can of no-salt-added tomato paste diluted with 1 can of water
Unsweetened baking chocolate	3 tablespoons cocoa powder plus 1 tablespoon unsaturated oil or light tub margarine for every 1-ounce square of chocolate
Whipping cream for topping	Fat-free whipped topping; fat-free evaporated milk (thoroughly chilled before whipping)
Whole milk	Fat-free milk

index